NEVER BE AFRAID

2nd edition

A Belgian Jew in the French Resistance

Ken Wachsberger and Bernard Mednicki

Azenphony Press
Ann Arbor, MI

Published by
Azenphony Press
PO Box 130884
Ann Arbor, MI 48113-0884
U.S.A.
info@azenphonypress.com
www.azenphonypress.com
Telephone: (734) 635-0577

Never Be Afraid, 2nd edition
© January 2, 2015 by Ken Wachsberger and Bernard Mednicki
ISBN 978-0-945531-08-1 (pbk)
ISBN 978-0-945531-07-4 (ebook)

Cover and typesetting by Caligraphics

Image of Maquis ID card on cover courtesy of
Special Collections Research Center, Temple University Libraries,
Philadelphia, PA
Image was cropped from original

All rights reserved. Without limiting the rights under copyright reserved above, no part of this publication may be reproduced, stored in or introduced into a retrieval system, or transmitted, in any form, or by any means (electronic, mechanical, photocopying, recording, or otherwise) without the prior written permission of both the copyright owner and the above publisher of this book.

What others are saying about
NEVER BE AFRAID:

"Bernard Mednicki's story should be told for its own worth. It also represents a genre that reveals those Jews who, in the face of overwhelming odds, found a way of cheating Hitler and fighting back against their would-be murderers."—Philip Rosen, Director of Holocaust Awareness Museum, Gratz College, Philadelphia, in his Appendix to *Never Be Afraid*

"moving, profoundly moving"—Elie Wiesel

"engrossing … wonderful"—George Cohen, *Booklist*

DEDICATION

To Bernard, who joined his ancestors and his two beloved wives on January 2, 1995

NEVER BE AFRAID
2nd edition
A Belgian Jew in the French Resistance

TABLE OF CONTENTS

DEDICATION

ABOUT THE AUTHOR

ACKNOWLEDGMENTS

A WORD FROM THE AUTHOR

INTRODUCTION, by Ken Wachsberger

PART I: COMING INTO BELGIUM—THE PRE-WAR YEARS

Chapter 1 My Father Fights in the Kishinev Pogrom, Then Brings the Family to Belgium	1
Chapter 2 Mothballs, Losing My Bowels, and a Bucket of Mussels	7
Chapter 3 "Your Son Bernard Is Fighting with Everybody"	21
Chapter 4 "A Jew Must Have a Trade," and My Mother Dies	29
Chapter 5 I Marry Chana Laja and Join the Union, the Imperialists Lift Their Heads	35

PART II: FLIGHT FROM BELGIUM

Chapter 6 Hitler Invades Belgium, I'm Separated from My Family	45
Chapter 7 We Become Christians in Vichy, I'm Summoned to Saint-Liguaire	57
Chapter 8 I Risk My Neck to Make Ladies' Eight-Button Gloves in Saint-Liguaire	65
Chapter 9 "*Seig Heil*, I'm a Belgian and I'm Proud of You"	73
Chapter 10 Cadavers on Phone Wires, *Schleppers* on the Train, and I Arrive in Riom	79
Chapter 11 Family Reunion, Colored Water, and Eggs on the Cross	83

PART III: THE MOVE TO VOLVIC AND THE BEGINNING OF LIFE IN THE RESISTANCE

Chapter 12 Life Begins in Volvic	91
Chapter 13 The Eyes of the Bull	99
Chapter 14 "Do You Know How to Steal?"	107
Chapter 15 "I Am Jewish"	119
Chapter 16 Emory Powder and 1,001 Nights	129
Chapter 17 Vials of Diseases	141

PART IV: FROM MAQUIS TO AMERICA

Chapter 18 The Maquis	153
Chapter 19 Like Blood out of the Aorta of a Pig	171
Chapter 20 Return to Brussels	187
Chapter 21 Never Be Afraid	199
EPILOGUE (1996)	215
APPENDIX, by Dr. Philip Rosen	223
FINAL WORD TO READERS	235
OTHER BOOKS BY KEN WACHSBERGER	237

ABOUT THE AUTHOR

Ken Wachsberger, founder of Azenphony Press, is a long-time author, editor, educator, political organizer, and book consultant who has written, edited, and lectured widely on the Holocaust and Jewish resistance during World War II, the First Amendment, the Vietnam era, writing in the electronic age, copyright, teachers' rights, writers' rights, the I-Search paper, and writing for healing and self-discovery.

Ken is also a book contract adviser with the National Writers Union as well as a former national officer, creator of the NWU's electronic Authors Network, and advocate of independent publishing.

Never Be Afraid: A Belgian Jew in the French Resistance is also available as an ebook. Ken's first ebook, *Your Partner Has Breast Cancer: 21 Ways to Keep Sane as a Support Person on Your Journey from Victim to Survivor*, was released in 2013. His print books and ebooks may be found at www.azenphonypress.com and www.voicesfromtheunderground.com. Look for more of them to go electronic as he learns his way around the ebook universe.

For book offers, editing services, and speaking engagements, including booking a "Writing to Keep Sane" or "Transforming Lives through Writing" workshop, he may be reached at info@azenphonypress.com.

ACKNOWLEDGMENTS

Although it's been many years since the first print edition of this book came out, I was deeply grateful then to Dr. Philip Rosen, Director of the Holocaust Awareness Museum at Gratz College in Philadelphia, for contributing the Appendix to Bernard's story. I am deeply honored now to reprint it in this second print edition, as well as the first electronic edition.

Many thanks to the English Department at Eastern Michigan University, where I was teaching at the time, for giving me a grant that enabled me to pay to have my interview tapes with Bernard transcribed.

All my love to Emily, David, and Carrie for keeping me honest and strong, as always.

Finally, I'm grateful to Bernard for his patience in answering all of my questions and humbled by the trust he gave me to dig deeper into the hidden pockets of his story than he had ever ventured before.

A WORD FROM THE AUTHOR

In this second edition of *Never Be Afraid: A Belgian Jew in the French Resistance*, Bernard Mednicki's incredible Holocaust journey, which is also available as an ebook, I've changed the byline and subtitle slightly. Bernard would not have cared. His vision was to get his journey down on paper so he could pass it along to his family before he died. He succeeded. Some might call my role in helping him to succeed my *mitzvah*, my good deed, but to me it was my honor and my passion to help him realize that vision. Bernard's gift to me was the opportunity to share in his adventure and to help him to organize, expand, and shape his story into print, and now electronic, form.

The byline I changed only because in the e-world authors' books are brought together in display. I wanted to bring this book together with my other books so it could be more easily found. In the traditional print world where the first edition appeared, our byline read, "By Bernard Mednicki with Ken Wachsberger," which means it's his story but I wrote it. Here it is "By Ken Wachsberger and Bernard Mednicki." It's still his story; I still wrote it.

I also changed the subtitle. I had first been attracted to Bernard's story because I grew up in the fifties, the immediate postwar period, when Jews who survived the Holocaust were too close to the event to talk about it. Because Jews who had fought in the Resistance had been equally traumatized and were among those not talking, the mythology grew that there had been no resistance, and, in fact, that the Jews had gone to their gaseous fate "like lambs to the slaughter." I talk about this idea more in my introduction to Bernard's story. I mention it here only to explain that Bernard's role in the Maquis, the French Resistance, was to me a one-man refutation of that ugly myth and so I called attention to it in the subtitle: *A Jew in the Maquis*. Much to my dismay, I discovered too late that most potential readers had no idea what the Maquis was. Hence: *A Belgian Jew in the French Resistance*. Not as romantic, okay, but understandable. If you're a Maquis-ophile, have mercy on me in your reviews.

Most important, Bernard would not have cared.

INTRODUCTION

As a Jew growing up in the fifties and sixties, I was haunted by the "lambs to the slaughter" image attributed to my East European ancestors. According to that image, six million Jews in Nazi-controlled Europe, including many of my own blood relatives, willingly went to their slaughter during World War II without so much as a flexed muscle.

Why, I asked, didn't they at least fight? Certainly, I conceded, they were malnourished and impoverished, surrounded by hostile forces and poorly armed to defend themselves. Had they fought back, they would no doubt have been overwhelmed anyhow.

Nevertheless, I wondered, wouldn't it have been better if they had at least gone down fighting? Look at the legacy they left us. Embarrassment intruded on my grief and anger. And so did disbelief. Deep down, I couldn't believe that nobody had resisted, the Warsaw Ghetto exception notwithstanding.

Fortunately, I was right, as I began to learn while working on a research project for a Master's degree in Creative Writing at Michigan State University. In fact, I found, Jewish resistance had been substantial. Unfortunately, those who fought and died couldn't tell their stories; while those who fought and survived wouldn't tell their stories because the memories were too painful or the survivors were still trying to find the words to make sense out of what they had experienced. When I began my research for a course in "Literature of the Holocaust," my goal was to find out if there had been a Resistance. I found not only a Jewish Resistance but a growing body of literature about it.

Bernard Mednicki is part of that legacy.

Bernard Mednicki is a Belgian Jew who fled to France with his wife and two children when the Nazis invaded in 1940. In France, they assumed a Christian identity and settled in Volvic, a small town in the mountainous southern region. There, a chance encounter with a prominent Nazi collaborator named Duhin forced Bernard to confess his Jewish roots.

"The lives of my family are in your hands," Bernard pleaded to him.

"Did you kill somebody?" Duhin asked.

"It's worse. I'm a Jew." Bernard threw himself on the man's mercy. But the joke was on Bernard.

"I've been looking for a guy like you," Duhin smiled. And Duhin, who was secretly a Resistance leader in southern France, embraced Bernard. Through Duhin, Bernard became active in the Resistance and eventually joined the Maquis, an underground army that fought the German occupation forces and the French collaborationist regime of Marshal Philippe Petain in Vichy, France.

I met Bernard in March 1986 at a Holocaust Conference at Millersville University in Pennsylvania. The conference theme that year was the Resistance and I was there to deliver the paper I had written for my "Literature of the Holocaust" course. Bernard was a fellow speaker, but he didn't have to write anything. He just had to relive his experiences.

The afternoon before the conference began, Hillel, the Jewish student organization, hosted a luncheon for out-of-town visitors. There, we were able to meet the sponsors of the conference and other speakers. While the others mingled, paper plates in one hand, coffee cups in the other, exchanging the usual small talk that strangers offer at icebreakers, one old man sat alone against the wall. His heavyset frame covered the entire seat of the chair and he was leaning slightly forward, his arms resting comfortably on his legs. Between his legs, a walking cane supported his cupped hands, and the full weight of his upper body. He smiled knowingly through a bushy beard that could easily have been mistaken for Santa Claus' had we not been at a Holocaust Conference luncheon. He sat alone and I thought it was for that reason that I was drawn to him.

I didn't know he was a speaker. I thought perhaps he was the father of someone who was a speaker. I had no idea I was about to become mesmerized. But when he began telling me stories, through his thick, European Jewish dialect—about how he took his family out of Belgium to escape the Nazis and begin life anew in France posing as a Christian to avoid capture; and about the time he hiked to a Passover Seder in the woods with his young son, trekking through thick underbrush to avoid possible detection on the open road, so that his son would not forget his Jewish roots; and about the time he disobeyed a Nazi order to not kill animals for food by personally slaughtering a bull kosher style, so the animal would die silently and the villagers could eat; and about blowing up factories and dams and trains, and gathering information; and about scrounging for food to feed his family—I knew I was hearing, in a sense witnessing, a part of history that I had grown up believing didn't exist, with the well-known exception of the Warsaw Ghetto uprising.

The writer in me wanted to write down his every word, or at least jot down notes so I could reconstruct our conversation at a later time, but I saw myself as a peer at that moment—we were, after all, both speakers—and so the word "tacky" came to mind. Instead, I listened avidly until my mind was bulging like a full bladder after a pot of coffee. Unable to remember anymore key phrases than I already had brewing in my memory, I excused myself politely and hurried to the bathroom, where I pulled out the 3" x 5" notebook I always carry in my back pocket and relieved my mind. Then I rejoined Bernard. But when he began a new story that led to a Yiddish anecdote, my mind soon overflowed again, so I excused myself once more. When I found myself starting for the bathroom a third time, embarrassment finally forced me to reveal my motives.

Bernard was flattered and pleased, because he has a story that he is compelled to tell. He wants the world to know about the war, and the Resistance, and his experiences, and so he speaks with his whole body, his hands waving, his eyes dancing.

"You have a wife and family, no?" he asked me.

I said I had a wife and son.

"Next time you are through Philadelphia with your family, you stay with me and Minnie and I'll tell you everything you want to know."

Five months later, on a family trip from Lansing, where we were living then, to New York City, we stopped to spend a night with Bernard and his second wife, Minnie. The next morning, as we were finishing breakfast, he told me he wanted me to write his life story.

And so it was my turn to be flattered. But now, in the same way that he is compelled to tell his story, I felt compelled to write it. I'm not the first person to realize the historical value of Bernard's story. Articles have already appeared in newspapers and magazines all over the country wherever he has spoken.

This book was developed from a series of interviews I held with Bernard in Ann Arbor during the week of Yom Ha Shoah, 1988. Our timing was intentional. Yom Ha Shoah is the one day each year when Jews around the world formally commemorate the victims of the Holocaust. It was my belief that Bernard would be sought after as a public speaker during that time and I knew we'd need funds to pay for transcribing the interview tapes.

I was right. Bernard was much in demand during his brief stay in the Ann Arbor area. In the first few days alone, he sat for newspaper interviews and made radio and public appearances in Ypsilanti, Detroit, and Ann Arbor. Then we got down to book business.

Over the course of the next ten days, he sat with me for eighteen hours of interview time. Bernard was the ideal interview subject. Even yes or no questions elicited detailed anecdotes, sprinkled with Yiddish or French expressions. As a result, the interviewing consisted of two distinct phases. The first began by my asking, "Where does your story begin?" It ended nine hours later with Bernard saying, "And that's my story." Essentially he spoke the entire time. My role consisted of listening to him tell his story, nudging him at times when I thought clarification or elaboration were called for, and tape recording our conversations. For the most part, though, I listened, more often writing questions in my notebook to discuss later rather than asking them immediately and interrupting his flow of thoughts. Occasionally, I asked him to repeat or spell a name or foreign term that I didn't recognize, but even this method of clarification soon began to feel intrusive. Eventually, we worked out a silent signal, whereby I would point to his pen and he would write down the name or term without even breaking his flow.

Our second phase, which also lasted nine hours, was more structured, question-answer style. During that time, I asked for details he had omitted the first time through. That second phase not only recorded history but actually made history, as Bernard revealed secrets he had never told anyone before and even uncovered blocked memories that had haunted him during feverish nightmares but been forgotten by morning. A momentous conversation that followed his description of his second political killing began with my asking, "What did you do that night?" I believed the question was intelligent and insightful. At night, I reasoned, safe in the security of familiar surroundings and trusted comrades, away from the numbing stress of the occasion, his repressed natural feelings would emerge and he would respond not as the animal that he said his Resistance activities turned him into but as the warm Bernard whom I knew.

I was confused, and even shaken somewhat, by his abrupt response: "I don't remember." I waited momentarily, and was just returning to my standby list of questions when he exclaimed suddenly, "Oh yes, I remember!" And he broke down in relief and shame.

I realized that day, as I watched and listened, that Bernard's motivation in telling and retelling his story was not simply "so that others wouldn't forget," but to make inner peace with acts he had committed under stress years before that continued to haunt him until that cathartic moment.

Soon after that exchange was over, Bernard became impatient, for the first time since we had begun. Tape eleven was the only one that we shut off before the second side was finished. The next morning, Bernard slept in for the first time. Before that, he was without exception the first to arise every morning, even when no interviews were scheduled because I had classes to teach.

We completed the final tape of the second phase two days later, after a rest day. These two phases were then incorporated and expanded through subsequent follow-up correspondence and interviews.

To supplement Bernard's story and this introduction, Dr. Philip Rosen, an expert on the Holocaust as well as the director of the Holocaust Awareness Museum at Gratz College in Philadelphia, has written the appendix. In his appendix, Dr. Rosen places Bernard's story in its proper historical perspective by writing of, first, the Holocaust in France, then the Resistance in all of France, and finally the Resistance in southern France, where Bernard's own story takes place.

In addition to being an expert on the Holocaust, Dr. Rosen holds another special place in Bernard's story. It was Dr. Rosen who first encouraged Bernard to speak publicly by inviting him to appear in front of a group of teachers whom he was instructing about the Holocaust. Even twelve years later, when our series of interviews took place, Bernard still felt an indebtedness to Dr. Rosen. As he said, "Now I am volunteering less to speak because I don't have the physical strength. But for Dr. Rosen, I will never refuse to speak in front of one of his groups."

Bernard is a survivor and a fighter, a role model for anyone who has ever faced adversity. For me, and for other Jews of the generation who grew up believing our ancestors in Nazi-controlled Europe "went like lambs to the slaughter," his example is a glorious refutation of an ugly myth. Bernard's story by itself is fascinating. His delightful ability to combine historical incidents and Yiddish anecdotes in a jovial down-to-earth manner adds a further, and often humorous, dimension to his story.

—Ken Wachsberger
Ann Arbor, MI

PART I: COMING INTO BELGIUM—THE PRE-WAR YEARS

CHAPTER 1

MY FATHER FIGHTS IN THE KISHINEV POGROM, THEN BRINGS THE FAMILY TO BELGIUM

My mother, Zlata Lanzman, was born in the city of Uman in the Ukraine, about 250 kilometers north of Odessa. My father, Leon, was born in Kishinev in Moldavia, which was part of Bessarabia. I don't know how they met or when they got married but they lived in Kishinev.

The piece of land that was Bessarabia belonged alternately to Russia and Rumania. It was part of Russia under the tsar. Then, after World War I, it was given to Rumania. In 1940, when World War II was brewing, Russia, which was now Communist, took back parts of tsarist Russia, to serve as a buffer between itself and Nazi Germany. Moldavia was part of the territory they took back. A year later it was taken from them again, but they reclaimed it in 1944 and still have it today.

Around the turn of the century, from 1881 to 1903, Kishinev was subject to many pogroms, but the pogrom of 1903 was the one that made my father desert, with a couple other Jewish soldiers, from the Russian army. He heard of the impending pogrom through the grapevine while he was in Vladivostok, in the eastern part of Asian Russia, fighting against the Japanese over Manchuria. Evidently it took him a long time to come home to Kishinev because he arrived there just in time to fight the battle in the pogrom. Being of the "new" generation, and a strong man, he fought hard, and he saved the family, which included my mother; my two sisters Rosa and Sheva; his father, a pious Jew and a cap maker; his sisters Baila, Sosel, and Chaika; and his brother Boris. But many Jews died and much property was lost in Kishinev. That's all I know.

Then my father took my mother and two sisters and he ran away. Where does one run to? America. What was the only way to America? Through the port of Antwerp in Belgium.

It took him a year to reach Belgium because from Kishinev he had to cross Rumania, Hungary, Austria, and Germany. In those days, in Kishinev, Jews were mostly small craftsmen: furriers, cap makers, tailors, shoemakers, bakers. But being of the new generation, my father had learned a trade where he had to use his tremendous physical strength as well as his mechanical knowledge. He was a fine locksmith and a tool and die maker, and so he was always able to make a living.

In Austria he spent some time, and I have an anecdote to tell about this. When my parents left Kishinev they had no documents or passports, but while my parents were in Austria they gave away laundry to be washed and they received back from the store a receipt that had their names on it. It was an official looking paper—signatures, official rubber stamping—and my father kept that. Later on, when they came to Belgium, he was asked if he had any kind of a passport for his identity. At that time passports didn't really exist, so he showed the laundry paper with the rubber stamps and this was enough for him to show that they were Leon and Zlata Mednicki. In Russia it was pronounced Mednitski. In Belgium we started calling ourselves Mednicki.

Belgium was a small provincial country. By the time of World War II, it only had a population of about eight million. Roughly 60,000 were Jews, who lived mostly in Antwerp and Brussels, but also in Liège and Charleroi. Belgium had gained its freedom just a hundred years before, in 1830, and they still were balancing between miners, sailors, and farmers. Before the Jew came, the main industries were agriculture, steel, and coal.

The Jews who came in after the pogroms were painters, furriers, and glove makers. The Hollandish Jews were diamond cutters. We were bringing prosperity to the land. Belgium did not have pogroms because Belgium was a tolerant society. Of course, there was a certain amount of xenophobia, hating of other nationalities, but not, per se, of anti-Semitism like in Poland and Russia. So it was nice for a country like Belgium to be the port in Europe where Russian, Polish, or Rumanian Jews could come to America.

See, you have to understand that, in those days, America was the dream. America is the one country in the world where you could obtain citizenship. There is no country in the world like that. It's like heaven here. With all the problems, with all the struggle, it's still one of the best countries in the world. Nobody gives you anything, the streets aren't paved with gold, but you have an opportunity. If you want it and you have the breaks then you can take it, but you must have the breaks. Who gives you the breaks? I don't know. I'm not smart enough. I never had the breaks to become rich. Only when I became a man of seventy practically did I make a few thousand dollars. I didn't even make $100,000 but what I made was nice for my old age.

There were no Jewish ghettoes in Belgium except for the Jews who made their own because they wanted to live among themselves. Polish Jews, Russian Jews, Rumanian Jews, Bulgarian Jews—we all came together. Ethnicity was not a problem then, because the Jewish store was there and the synagogue was there. We never took a trolley car or a bus to go to the synagogue because we obeyed the Jewish laws that said you couldn't drive on the Sabbath. My family walked a mile and a half.

In Belgium, there were coal mines and iron pits, and industry in Liège that was like our Pittsburgh, Pennsylvania. Every industry was in the hands of the government: gas, electricity, telephone, even the weapons factories. The government owned whatever it could, and this relieved people from paying taxes. I don't ever remember my parents paying taxes.

But coming into Belgium around 1908, being that my father was a craftsman, he could find a job very easily and he went to Brussels. My father must have been in his early twenties, because he was born in 1886.

And my mother was the same age. In fact, she was one month older. My mother was a short, heavy lady. She was always very sick because in Rumania or in Austria or somewhere on their way to Belgium they had to cross swamps and she took the "sickness," malaria. In Belgium she aborted twins, or so I was told. Of course I wasn't born yet. And though she later had other children, she always remained ill.

My father installed us in a small apartment in Brussels in the borough of Anderlecht, where there was a nucleus of Jewish people and a Jewish store where you could speak the language. Of course my father was not a linguist but the Flemish language was very close to Yiddish. The more he spoke Flemish, the more he improved and he picked it up quite fast, and also French, another native tongue.

Being that he was a sober man—the Belgians were big beer drinkers but he wasn't a drinker—he quickly received a job at a spigot factory, where he earned, I was told, fifteen cents an hour, which was a good wage. My father struggled, made quick progress, and was able to make a good living. At that time, he and mother had two children, Rosa, who was born in 1905, and Sheva, who was born in 1907. Just a few years later, in 1909, mother gave birth to Natan.

Then my father's younger brother, Boris, joined him from Kishinev. Boris was an artist and a painter, and he stayed with the family in Brussels until 1914.

In 1910 I was born. November thirtieth. That day, by carelessness, there was a tremendous fire at the International Exposition of Brussels. For the first time they had brought elephants and lions and all kinds of animals from the

Belgian colonies to the Palais du Cinquantenaire, an immense park and show room built fifty years after independence. Palais du Cinquantenaire was outside of Brussels, so immense it was. And that fire, I was told, consumed most of the animals. I know this was a fact; the history of Belgium will speak of it.

Then my parents got married again. My parents were married in Kishinev according to the Jewish faith, under the *chupah*, the wedding canopy. That's what counted in Russia. But when they came to Belgium, because they didn't have a civil marriage they were living in sin. Belgium was a Catholic country. They didn't accept the Jewish way. Only in America.

You cannot understand what America is. In America if tomorrow I make a religion that says you kiss my kneecaps, and people accept it, it's a religion. In Belgium there was just the Catholic religion and the Protestant religion. And that's all. Period. And for every religion you had to go to City Hall first. After you married in City Hall, then you could make everything you want religious in your home.

So, I was told by my mother, when the mayor of Anderlecht said to her, "Are those your children?"—we were four children—she said "Yes." Then the mayor said to her, "It's about time you get married." And that's when they went to City Hall and got married, even though they were already married. When I was getting married to my first wife, Chana Laja, the mayor wore a Belgian ribbon draped over his abdomen and his shoulders, he wore a sword on his left side, and he wore a hat like Lord Nelson's because that's the way they had hats at that time. When I was married, two officers lifted their swords and we went through and we received marriage. After that when the wedding was done, we had rabbis give us the *ketubah*, the Jewish marriage license. And that's the way it also was with my parents.

When I was born, there were not enough acquaintances in the Jewish population for me to have a godfather and godmother, according to Jewish tradition, and a *sondig*. A *sondig* is the person who holds the baby when the circumciser operates on the baby. My father held me, so he was my *sondig*. My godfather was Dr. Finkelstein—I remember that name. Being that they had nobody else, my sister Rosa, who was only five years old, became my godmother. Dr. Finkelstein was one of the rare Jewish doctors who had come from Germany, and he took sympathy on my family. Not having relatives or friends in Belgium, they were lonesome and not financially well off. Dr. Finkelstein came to see me until I grew up.

Then mother had other babies—eight, nine, ten children; I don't know exactly how many because one didn't make it, then another died at a young age. Do you know what I mean? And this was not unusual for those times; many babies died.

I remember my brother Natan. There is an incident that I never will forget. I was playing with him and with my sister Sheva. Sheva was seven years old, I must have been three, and my brother Natan was four. We were playing dog and cat, running after each other, and as we were running by accident we hit a table on which a stove was standing. On the stove a pot of chicken was boiling, and my brother was burned to death. Before Natan died, Uncle Boris took a picture, and for the longest time we had pictures in the house of my brother swaddled in gauze, and just his face and his nose you could see. Then he passed away. It was a tragic moment. That was 1914, before the beginning of the war. I remember so clearly because with my parents there was great sadness, and I couldn't understand.

Another thing I remember is that my sister Rosa, who was the oldest, always took care of me, but my sister Sheva was like a devil. As a child she was really restless. We lived in a house with Polish Jews by the name of Dorn. Mr. Dorn was a *kohen*, from the high priest tribe of Israel, and he had a red beard. Madame Dorn was a very gentle woman; and they had many children. One of their children, a daughter named Sarah, was the age of Sheva. One day my sister found a pair of scissors, and she cut Sarah's long hair. Madame Dorn came in screaming and Sheva rolled herself underneath the bed, like she wasn't there. My mother turned over the house, but she couldn't find her. The incident passed. I don't remember what punishment Sheva received.

Then another time, my sister Sheva's face swelled up. They didn't know what was happening. Finally they had to take her to the doctor; she had pushed two beans up her nose.

I remember one more thing, and then I'll quit this subject. We were playing and Sheva opened the drawer in the kitchen, took out a knife, folded her tongue backwards, and with the knife sliced it in two. We called Dr. Finkelstein, but he said we could do nothing. She would have to wait until it healed, and that's the way it was. She was fed with a straw. At that time, there were no paper straws, so I remember my father bringing from a farm yellow straw that he would cut in pieces, to fit a cup, and that was my sister Sheva's way of nourishment.

Rosa was a neat one. You could put her on the balcony and she wouldn't move. I know because we had a balcony where we lived in Anderlecht.

At that time there were not many Jews from Bessarabia, or from Kishinev, or from Russia living in Brussels. Poland was the land that brought Jewish immigrants to Belgium, and they had their own customs that we didn't like. For instance, my mother would cook fish for Saturday, for Sabbath, with pepper and salt. The Polish put sugar in it, with carrots or raisins, habits that we didn't know. And we had a few Jewish families who came together. They all had many children, so Friday night when we would come together I would hear women telling how they would cook, and my mother would always be very credulous about cooking, because how could you cook fish with sugar and carrots? The Polish people had another way of preparing chicken also. My mother learned from them and they learned from my mother. We ate a lot of mameliga, which is a national dish from Rumania. Mameliga is made from cornmeal, and it's like a mush, but if you make it thick it's like a bread, and the Polish didn't know of that, so there was a little conflict and a little loving, and like this we grew up with children from Polish homes, and we became more cosmopolitan. We were used to everything already.

CHAPTER 2

MEATBALLS, LOSING MY BOWELS, AND A BUCKET OF MUSSELS

In Brussels there were many Jews from Holland. The borough where I was born, Anderlecht, was one of the centers of Judaism, but our cemeteries were all on the Hollandish border because the Hollandish Jews were more organized than we were. See, in Holland Judaism had already been there for three, four hundred years, from when the Jews ran away from the Inquisition. Belgium, after the Inquisition, was dominated by the Catholics. The country was occupied by Spain, France, and the Dutch. The Belgian people were overtaxed and unhappiness grew.

Like always, when things did not go well, the Jews were blamed and tortured and at times thrown out of the country, until 1830 when the Belgian people revolted and all the provinces decided to change the yolk of oppression and tyranny. In that year, Belgium declared its independence from the Dutch government, whose people were mostly Protestants. The next year, they adopted their own constitution, which guaranteed freedom of religion. After that, Protestants, Catholics, and Jews started living without animosity.

However, the Catholic church was always the main religion in Belgium. In fact, we had a country of the churches. We had cities like Brugge and Ghent that were unique in the world for their old, well-preserved cathedrals and churches that were seven, eight hundred years old. In Brussels we had cathedrals so marvelous that in the last world war even the Germans surrounded them with sand bags, so they wouldn't be hit.

Amongst the Jews, the Hollandish Jews are Sephardim; the Belgians, Ashkenazi. That means we believe in the rite of Ashkenaze. The Sephardim are the ones who came from Spain; they pray a different way. In Belgium, when you are three years old, you start kindergarten. My sisters, first Rosa and then Sheva, went to a Catholic school. At that school, they had a religious service for the children every day between 11 and 11:30, where you would spend half an hour learning religion. The Jewish children would learn the Jewish religion and the Catholic children would learn Catholicism.

But when I was three years old, my parents put me in a Jewish orphanage that was started after the first world war began. The orphanage was also a day school for children. My parents put me there because it was near the house and because it was Jewish. But it was held by the Hollandish Jews, so I learned the Sephardic rite, and with all the prayers in French. When I would come home, my mother would say, "What kind of an apostate are you? How dare you disturb the Hebraic letters." I'd say, "I'm learning this, Mom; what can I tell you?" So instead of *Shema Yisrael*, I would say *Ecoute Israel*, that means "Listen, Israel. The eternal your God is one." This is in English but in French it comes out, *Ecoute Israel l'eternel est notre Dieu, l'eternal est Un.*

Growing up, we dressed comfortably, but plain. For Passover we received a new pair of shoes and a suit. The rest of the year we ran barefooted or wore wooden shoes like the Hollanders wore, and we wore dungarees. That was the uniform of the Belgians. Typical period. Dungarees during the week to go to work and on Saturday—you worked Saturday, too. But on Sunday it was ironed clothes, with nice clean pants and a jacket of blue to wear to church, and that's it.

In Belgium it was stylish, in the summer, for little boys and girls to wear a long apron with sleeves, buttoned from the back, with no pants or underwear underneath, and we wore little wooden shoes, *sabots*. The orphanage where I went to school was in Place du Conseil, which is the center of Anderlecht, where City Hall is. The Place is very big, and that was where, for the first time in the history of Anderlecht, they mounted a balloon to fly in the air. The balloon was called Montgolfier, which comes from the name of the two brothers who invented it. They made the balloon go up and I, looking on from the yard, saw the balloon going up and became panicky, and I lost my bowels and it ran down my legs.

The teacher—of course, it wasn't roses—the teacher grabbed me by a shoulder and she ran me home. We didn't live far from the school. I'll never forget. I passed that place where other people were, and the balloon was floating, and I was terrorized. All the way my nose was running. I was filthy. I finally came home, and my mother walked in the room, and she said, "My poor baby, what did they do to you?" She grabbed me, put me in a basin of water, washed me up, and fed me. That was the first thing a Jewish mother did, feed you. And I was three years old.

After this we moved, and my father found a better position, as a foreman in a factory where they made all kinds of spigots and other bathroom fixtures.

My father had not been a beer drinker in Kishinev, but in Belgium he drank a lot of beer. In our home we drank tea in glasses and beer we drank in glasses also, and the color of tea and the color of Belgian beer is almost the same. My father invited a few fellows from the shop to the house one Sunday, and he served them hot tea in glasses. When tea is hot it doesn't steam, so one guy grabbed the glass and he burned his gizzard. There was almost a fight until my father explained to him.

I remember my Uncle Boris Mednick—he dropped the "i" in America. The day after the first world war started in Belgium, in August of 1914, he was leaving on one of the last trains out before the Germans occupied Brussels and I was crying, so he left me a mortar and pestle, a little pot with a mortar from the pharmacist, and he said, "I will see you later." Then he went away, and the train passed our house from the Gare du Midi, the south station. He was going to Paris, and from there to New York. I was heartbroken for years.

When I was four years old, I learned Aleph Bes, the Hebrew alphabet, from a rabbi who came to the house. When I was six years old, I started going to *Cheder* to learn davening, the Jewish method of praying. For *Cheder*, we sat in an old study, an old school, with a pinewood floor that had knots of wood missing. Our rabbi was a sadist who loved to hit us with his cane. One day, we took his cane and we shoved it in a hole. When he was in a rage he grabbed it, and he broke the cane. On Sabbath it is a blessing to have an extra meal in the synagogue so we would eat to close the Sabbath. We were fed herring and challah and onions and drank schnapps. The schnapps—it was pure grain alcohol—was always left in the synagogue. One day one of the boys found some pepper. So we took the rabbi's snuff box that he left on his desk and poured some alcohol and some pepper in his tobacco. When he sniffed, he almost lost his head. My father was called and also fathers of other children.

I had a private rabbi, an old man in his seventies. He was the oldest Jew in Brussels. His grandson was my best friend, and we would drive the poor devil crazy. We would sing *Shema Yisrael* to the melody of an army song, *La Madellon*, and he would say, "What is that? What kind of Jews are you?" *Vous far a iden zent hir.* But when you are seven, eight, nine years old, what do you know about that? And the books smelled from naphthalene mothballs that the rabbi used to keep the books clean from mice. *Oy gavolt*, I had it for the longest time in my nostril, those mothballs. There was always the smell of mothballs. You would come in and you would gasp.

But I learned to understand Yiddish. We learned to pray quick, turn the pages, and say, "Hey beedadabeedadabeedada...." Then you would shake yourself but you wouldn't understand anything because it was the *loshen kadish*, holy tongue.

After awhile, of course, I learned to understand and to write. Yiddish is my favorite tongue. It's the easiest. It's near my heart, the tongue of my people. In

Ken Wachsberger

America, you speak English; in France, French. But as Jews we all have a common language, Yiddish. Unfortunately, nobody speaks it perfectly anymore. I have tried to keep it distinct. When I speak French, it's French; when I speak Yiddish, it's Yiddish. In America, they bastardize the language and in France they do, too, and in Belgium. Everywhere you go, the people getting accustomed to the country nationalize Yiddish. We have Americanized Yiddish. It's on television. You have *chutzpah* and all kinds of other little words that I don't have to tell you. But being that I haven't written or read it for a long time, I have difficulties now. The reading I'm still all right, but the writing I'm completely lost in Yiddish. But I speak it perfectly; that's the way it is.

But Hebrew I didn't understand. I can pray in Hebrew very fast, but only now in America am I starting to understand it because prayer books in America have the words in Hebrew and in English. But God understands.

Listen, I have committed sins according to tradition like eating non-kosher, and I'll give you a little history. I had two friends from very religious families. We smoked a cigarette on Sabbath, and, I don't know how, it became known to our fathers and the rabbi. There was a *din Torah*, that means a religious court of law, and the rabbi called me. On the *din Torah* were six Jews, very old men. "What do you mean that the son of Albert had smoked a cigarette, and you, too?" Mea culpa. Shoot me. The rabbi said no. There was a box from the Jewish National Fund. "Whatever money you have in your pocket you put here." Luckily, I didn't have much.

My mother was a religious woman from a religious family. Her father was a *shoichet*, a ritual slaughterer. She believed a hundred percent of what was said in the Tanach, the Hebrew history. Because of her, we kept our home religiously kosher. When I was only about seven or eight, I couldn't sit down before washing my hands; couldn't eat without making a *motse*, a blessing over bread. I had to say my benediction after dinner, and all those other things that for the moment I took to be normal. But as I grew up I found this very cumbersome luggage. I had to go to school, I was an apprentice learning a trade, and I had to go to *Cheder*, Hebrew school. The boys were playing on the street, but I had no chance to go and play with them. If I went to play I was like wild because I had some freedom. And like this my pre-youth started. I was never young in my life. Never had any toys. Of course, they didn't exist, at least not in our family.

My father, of course, was also a Jew, but he was already what you call a red Jew. He was reading a social democrat paper, he believed a little in Marxism already, and he was a working man with liberal ideas. In Belgium, having already left the Pale and the ghettoes, he wanted to live with more freedom. There was a great wind of freedom after the Russian Revolution. Many Jews had read the words of Lenin saying that religion was opium. In the synagogue, my father and other parents and friends, liberal people, would argue politics, and the rabbi would become very angry and ask, "Why during the reading of the Torah do they discuss politics?"

I remember there was conflict between my mother and my father, because my mother insisted he shouldn't work on Sabbath, so every time he found a job he had to quit on Saturday and then he couldn't find another job. One day they went into the rabbi and the rabbi gave my father permission. "If it is necessary, you cannot help it, you have to work," he said. "But if you can, get out of it."

My father's father, my grandfather Zourech, died after the first world war. The letter didn't come to us in Brussels. It went first from Russia to Philadelphia to my Uncle Boris, who had immigrated to America before the war. Boris waited for the *shloyshim*, the thirty days of mourning, to pass, so my father wouldn't have to put down his hands and stop working for the *shivah*, the mourning period. But when the letter came, my mother said to my father, "No, I knew your father. He was a respectable, honorable Jew. You will sit seven days of mourning." My father fought with her—I mean fought in the sense of arguing—but nevertheless my mother had the last word. He didn't work for a week, and he left his job again. There was always a problem keeping a job.

Fortunately, my father was very ingenious, and he saw that he couldn't work anymore in a factory because of the Sabbath. As I said before, the Jews brought industries to Belgium: pocketbook making, fur making, shoemaking, leather clothes making, tailoring. So, when I was nine years old, my father found a way of latching on. We brought old rags and we dyed them in different colors. My father had bought an old washing machine with two cylinders of metal, which he engraved by hand for making *moyrer*, a material that, when you look, changes colors and shapes. The process was one of impressing a design in humid material inside a tube of cooking gas. We took a rag from the vat of color and we put it through the heated tube of gas. As the vat turned, the rag came out the other side a gorgeous piece of *moyrer*. And this was lining for pocketbooks. Today, seventy years later, it is used in high fashion.

Next, he bought himself a sciving machine. When they make pocketbooks, they cut the pattern of the pocketbook and then all around that you have to scive, or thin, the leather so it will come out nice and smooth. My father bought a sciving machine and he bought a heavy press, and he started making locks for pocketbooks. He bought old metal and sulfur acid. I remember we had a big vat of sawdust. After dipping the metal into the sulfur acid we would roll it in the sawdust and all the rust would be eaten up, and we would have nice, clean metal. Then, in a vat, using electricity, we would coat the metal with copper pieces. My father would make beautiful locks for pocketbooks. But he was competing with one of the great manufacturers in Brussels, a Mr. Albert, a

Jew who had succeeded because he had inventiveness. The king of Belgium had given him the right to become a Belgian citizen; that was a big honor. Unfortunately, my father lost. He didn't have the financial means to continue. Every year he had another child, and we were, like I said, nine children.

After that, when I was thirteen, my father started receiving work from people with pocketbook factories. They would send him the leather to be scived, because they didn't have a machine. We lived in a house where you had to go up steps to be on the first floor. Direct from the street you came into a room and in the second room from the front were steps going upstairs. In the room upstairs was my sisters' bedroom and in that bedroom we had installed a table. On that table my father had a pressing machine that was run by gas coming in from a duct. On it, he would take the raw pieces of leather and he would make gold imprints by having plates of nickel heated. Like this he made ugly leather beautiful. Or, he would take sheepskins and he made special dyes that would come out like the skin of a snake, or the skin of a crocodile, and this was to make pocketbooks. Then we would paint the designs with the colors.

At this time, it was stylish to have pictures of old Egyptian thrones and statues and Pharaohs, so my father engraved the dyes himself. First, he bought a calendar that was embossed so he could reproduce the relief imprint. On the embossing he smeared oil. Then, with a composition of plaster of Paris, he made a mold of the design, and he deepened the engraving with chisels. Next, he would melt brass, pour it in the mold, and throw the mold in water and petrol. When it came out cold, he would finally chisel the plaster out and then he had a Matrice, an impressing plate, to make engraving on leather or embossing. It was a marvelous process. Then we—the children and mother, may she rest in peace—would start painting. Everyone had his own color, one in red, one in blue, and my father would get so much money for it, I don't remember. But we lived well and paid our bills.

But I do remember one incident and it wasn't so marvelous. Like I said, all the children worked for my father. The sister putting the gold down would take white of egg and with a fine brush make a line. Then she would apply cut sheets of gold that a fly could take with her if it flew past. One gram of gold is twenty-four leaves. It's what the guilders use to write in gold on windows. They have a special system of varnish, but we used white of egg, albumen, for our gold, and I would work that. We had a gas lamp that was all copper. My father would unscrew it to polish it because copper had to be polished once a year at least. One day, two weeks before Passover the year I was thirteen, I was working upstairs and I had on a short sleeve shirt. My father had not closed well the gas meter that was downstairs in the front room near the street. Suddenly I noticed it smelled like gas. I ran down and jumped on the table. Then I struck a match so I could see and it blew up on me.

It threw me through the window my mother had left open. As I fell on the street I was burning. We always scrubbed the streets in Belgium, so a neighbor was able to throw a pail of water on me to put out the fire on the clothes I was wearing. After he did that, I made like it was nothing even though skin was hanging from my arm, my face, my neck, and my hand. He said, "You laugh now; it's nothing. Wait a half hour."

Well, in a half hour the pains started shooting up. They ran me to the pharmacist around the corner for first aid and he started giving me compresses made from all kinds of medication. Then, the ambulance came and they took me to the hospital. At that time there was no antibiotic, there was no penicillin, there was nothing. So what the doctors did was they soaked my arm and my hand in basins of salt water, then applied gauze dunked in ether and put it on my body and let it dry. When it dried they pulled it off so I shouldn't have any decayed flesh on me. My screaming was fierce.

It was just a week before Passover so we were lucky because Sheva, my sister, had taken the children to the city to buy clothes for Passover. So I was hurt, my mother and Rosa were hurt a little bit. I was in the hospital for three weeks with third degree burns swathed in gauze and cotton, and only my mouth and my nose could be seen, and one eye. I still have a scar along my whole arm. And do you know something else? At that time, I belonged to the *Histadrut hachomer hatzair*, an organization of young Zionists similar to Belgium Boy Scouts. My mother enlisted all the *chomrim*, the guardians, all twenty-four of them, to bring me food for Passover at the hospital, which was strictly goyish: you know, nothing kosher. That didn't exist. And they brought me food. My best food was matzos with eggs and potatoes and onions crushed together. I had just an opening in the gauze for my mouth, but I was fed the whole day. I could swear that that saved my life, because what they did to me was unbelievable. No morphine or tranquilizers. After three weeks in the hospital, they finally released me and I came home.

After awhile I started going to school again and I went back to work and it healed, but I felt very bad because I was deformed. I had a scar from the elbow all the way down and part of my hand was burned and the skin of my face was very irritated because it goes into your skin. But I'm telling a story of sixty-five years ago.

As I said before, the first world war began in 1914. During that war, I was going to school, to first grade, second grade, third grade. In Belgium at that time, the same teacher would follow you from the first grade until the sixth grade. My teacher, Mlle. Hirshbulaire, was the antithesis of the Jewish mother: She wore a little red lipstick, she smelled good, she was dressed very elegantly. Our mothers were harried; they had no time for all that stuff.

When the Germans occupied Belgium, we knew the king of Belgium, Albert I, was in England to avoid being a P.O.W. We would sing patriotic songs in defiance until the Germans forbade us. One day in 1916, going on an outing with our schoolteacher, we went to the racetrack, and going there we were singing patriotic songs. A group of German soldiers came around us but they didn't know what to do with us. We were six years old singing patriotic songs.

The next year, when I was seven years old, the Germans would bring the bread in trucks for the German army, and every loaf of bread whetted the tongue; it was black sour bread. The wheels of the truck were solid rubber; there was no way of cutting a tire, so we unscrewed the wheel. When the truck started moving, everything fell off and we opened the door, stole the bread, and started running like birds, from one side of the street to the other, and they couldn't arrest anybody. I came home with a half a loaf of sour bread. My father was so angry at me. "Why did you risk your life for a piece of bread?" I said, "It's not the bread, Pa. It's the *Boche*." *Boche*: it was a derogatory word for a German. They don't like to be called that. It was the *Boche*. I remember the Belgian underground sent us a newspaper called *Free Belgium—La Libre Belgigue*. They had told us to pin it on the clothes of everybody going through or give it to the people, so we gave it to the Belgians and the Germans were very angry at us.

But one time we were obliged to lodge Germans. It wasn't a war of anti-Semitism; it was an imperialistic war. Kaiser Wilhelm wanted colonies so he took colonies into Gabon. He took Africa. And he wanted land. He wanted a piece of Belgium; he wanted Alsace-Lorraine. He wanted. He wanted. Finally, his "requests" became too big, and then the Russian Revolution broke his back.

He was hoping the tsar was going to help him, but when the Revolution started the working men took a little bit more courage and started fighting for their own gratifications, for their own needs. You cannot help it. When you are a working man, you cannot be a capitalist. We had a dream Marxism would be the saviour of the world because we saw in it equality for everybody. For everybody when it's noon it's noon. And when the sun shines for you, it shines for me, too. Not that you would have very nice clothes and food and I'm hungry. I remember when I was about ten years old, in 1920, we were speaking of the Russian Revolution and of Marxism. My father's friends from the synagogue would come and I would listen to their conversations and discussions, and my father would tell me, "Bernard, when Russia will be Soviet it will come all over the world and everybody will make a living. There will be no anti-Semitism, and there will be no hatred between the races." And I was so happy because everybody was going to love everybody.

You know, there were coal mines in Belgium where the miners would go on strike, and at that time, Emile vanDervelde, who was the leader of the socialist party, was one of the big owners of the coal mines. He was the leader of the socialists and he was also the owner of the coal mines. He owned homes that he rented to the coal miners. He had grocery stores where you bought your food. And when it came time to pay you, you never received a franc. There was no money because you had spent everything already. The coal miners died from tuberculosis and they had all kinds of accidents. There was no protection for the working man.

Of course, Emile vanDervelde wasn't the man who built the mines. His ancestors built them, so he couldn't give them away. Big fortunes are not created, except in America. But he didn't change anything either. Listen, making money is one way, and being a socialist is another way. He was an intellectual socialist. The theory was nice but he never applied it.

During the war we were very hungry. We were not citizens of Belgium, so we had no acquaintances in the countryside. But we knew the lady next door—she collected our rations on Passover because the food was not kosher. Her family had been Christian Belgians for generations. She had brothers in the countryside, farmers, who always had enough to eat. And she had only one son; his name was Richard.

We had a yard with a wall about eight feet tall, and I'd jump the wall when his mother was at work. Richard enjoyed watching me eat because he was skimpy; when he took a bite it was enough. So he would prepare for me on the table a bucket of honey, a box of sugar. His mother was able to get all kinds of meats from the countryside and I looked up to see if God would punish me, strike me dead. I was eating *traife*, not kosher, and I was seven years old. I would swallow one into the other, the sugar, the milk, and the milk was concentrated milk, and oh my goodness. Then he would say, "Where did you put it?" I would say, "I don't know." And I would jump the wall over.

When I would sit down for supper that evening I would eat slow and my mother would say, "Are you not feeling well?" Because she was used to seeing me eating. I had good teeth and a solid stomach.

We lived in a house where there was only one spigot for cold water. We had a system with the rainwater. If you had to wash your head, you took rainwater and you warmed it up on the stove. We had a coal stove, and the bedrooms were never warm because there was no installation for the heat. We also had a tub made out of lead that you would bring in the house only once a week, on Thursday evening, to bathe the children before the Sabbath. You bathe three children in the same water—the small one, then the two sisters in one water. Then the boys would bathe two or three in one water, and then they would give the tub water to the parents, and whatever they did we don't know because we went to sleep. My parents would go to the communal bathhouse in the center of town. The bathhouse was a tub of water that was controlled by a city employee. You brought your own soap and towel and for a nominal fee you could soak for thirty minutes.

So that tub we carried in and out on the weekends. Our floor was made of red bricks. After we finished bathing with that water, my sister and I washed the red bricks. The barges coming down the canals to Antwerp and Brussels from the coal mines in Charleroi also brought ocean sand. You would buy a bucket of sand and spread it on the ground, and then, after you scrubbed with it for Sabbath, Saturday night after tending the light, with a broom you removed the sand, and the bricks were like shiny ruby, pieces of diamond, and they were smooth like satin. The tub was twisted and destroyed when that fire exploded before the Passover. The tub was standing outside in the yard, and the detonation crushed it.

When we washed laundry, we had a machine that was half a barrel of wood, and in that barrel of wood was a tripod with two handles on top. You put in the laundry and the sisters and I would throw the handles to beat the laundry. When it was finished, I would hold one side of a bed sheet and my sisters together would hold the other. Then I would turn it to wring it and we would hang it in the yard to dry up. It was pure linen, so it was very tough to dry. The rest of the laundry was washed by my sister, a little bit every day. But the bed sheets in that big tub I'll never forget, washing them and three people turning, two against me, just to wring them out.

The same barges that brought the sand would come from Holland with mussels, like oysters but with black shells, and they would sell them at twenty-five cents a bucket on the ship. You could go on board ship and give them twenty-five centime. But who had twenty-five centime? So five kids would go together and if you were lucky and you saved long enough you had twenty-five centime and could buy a bucket of mussels. I remember one day I saved twenty-five centime and we went to a marina.

One owner of barges had a habit of letting you eat until you had the first hiccup. When you got the first hiccup you stopped. I never hiccuped! I could eat three buckets of mussels and the guy would say, "Where do you put it?" You see, mussels you don't chew. You swallow like oysters. It wasn't kosher either, and I was always afraid that God shouldn't strike me dead, but he never touched me because he knew I was an honest fellow. A bucket I would say was three kilos, six pounds, and in six pounds of mussels you have maybe a pound and a half of meat, because the shell weighs a lot. And you would eat that with a hard roll and lemon juice. Bernard was known: "Come on, Bernard, show us how you eat." And I loved it. It was delicious.

At that time Gypsies roamed the cities in Belgium. They would come down from Czechoslovakia, Hungary, or Rumania, and there was traffic on the border, but there were no difficulties. Near the canals lived a gang of Gypsies with their little carriages, their homes. One hot Friday night, friends had come to sit with us outside the house, the Dorns and the Alberts and the Heimoviches, and there were about thirty children among the four of us. My mother had roasted peanuts that we would eat and then we would go in the house for a cup of tea. Everybody went into the house to drink, and there were maybe fifteen chairs outside on the sidewalk. But then we came back and there's not one chair. One of the neighbors said the Gypsies just went by. My father knew of the Gypsies from Rumania, so he said nothing.

The following morning, Saturday morning, before going to the synagogue, he said, "Come with me." We lived on Rue des Collecteur. I went with him to the street next to us, Rue d'es Constructeur. All the Gypsies were there in a big field. My father spoke the language of the Gypsies so he was speaking Voolechish, a Bohemian jargon. I heard some kind of conversation but I didn't understand it. My parents spoke Russian between themselves, but they never wanted us to learn. They wanted their tongue to be secret for themselves, which is why we never spoke Russian even though it was familiar to our ears. So my father speaks to this guy and I see them shake hands. We go to the synagogue, and when we come back from the synagogue all the chairs are in front of the house. I said to my father, "What happened?" He said, "I spoke their language and I explained to them who I was, and they understood that they made a big boo-boo by taking chairs from somebody from their own country." Oh my goodness, you know, it was an adventure.

Then the war ended. But before the Germans left Brussels and the armistice was signed, they mined all the trains in the stations. Belgium had a very modern railway system. From towns and hamlets throughout the country, the people were well provided with railroad tracks. There was a spur for the gigantic wholesale food markets and the huge slaughterhouse. We had a station for Luxembourg, we had the north station, we had a southern station, and then we had the stations near the slaughterhouse, where they would bring the cattle from the countryside. Belgium had one of the best-organized transportation systems in Europe. You didn't have to own a car, a bike, or any private transportation. You had public transportation everywhere. By trolley car you could go from the center of Brussels to one end of the country. Belgium being so small, today you cross Belgium, from Luxembourg to Putt on the Hollandish border, in two hours.

So just before the war ended the German occupants were blowing up trains while they were retreating and in our street everybody ran to the train station to see what they could get.

In our family, my father picked up bags of hobnails, cartons. My mother picked up an apron full of flour; she couldn't carry the bag because she was a sick lady. I saw a wooden barrel filled with marmalade. It was bigger than I was and heavier and I started rolling it on the ground and I rolled it until it split. When it split I almost dropped dead from anger and I put my hand in and started eating. My mother dropped the flour and she came with her apron and I dropped all the marmalade in her apron. Then we went home, took kegs and jars, and we saved the marmalade. But the flour, people stepped on it so we left it and went back to the station, and as we went back more explosions started.

They didn't mine that station, the station of Anderlecht. But they mined the station from the south going to Paris, the station from the Gare du Nord going to Germany, and the station going to Luxembourg. From our street we had a lot of killed and injured. Across the street the children were blinded and one lost his hand, one lost his fingers, and it was a tragedy. Oh, it was horrible. It was the last that the Germans did to us. Later on, of course, they paid damage for everything, but you can't replace hands and eyes. The Belgians instinctively had a tremendous dislike for the *Boche*. We had seen through history that the Germans always were the first ones to make a war.

On November 11, 1918, as the war finished, about 9:00 at night, the bells were ringing. An armistice had been signed with the Germans and the flags came out. The church bells rang and all the Belgians ran out. I was in my nightgown and I ran with everybody. We went around in the streets singing, going to the cafés, Jews, non-Jews, everybody. I had a nose for food so I sniffed in the air and smelled food in the direction of Chaussee du Mons, which was an avenue going from Paris to Brussels. I went there and saw thousands of people milling, and I spotted an English army kitchen on wheels coming with horse and wagon led by two English soldiers. The driver was riding a kitchen with pots twice the size of a washing machine, and the aroma was making me wild. I ran up to the guy and said to him in French, "Can you give me something to eat?" The guy looks down, he was an Englishman, and in the pot was cooking a hind piece of beef. He took it out and he gave it to me.

How can I take it; it's soaking from gravy? I took my nightgown and lifted it and ran with my everything naked. Then I sat in the corner of a doorway and I started chewing like a little animal. I had that meat and it was bigger than I was. My father told me he found me about 4:30 in the morning in the corner of the door, holding that meat like a tiger holds something precious. I didn't want to let it go, but in my mother's home it was very kosher. So what did he do? He threw a burlap over the meat and put me to bed with it.

In the morning I woke up with the meat in my mouth and the meat in my arms. I remember very vividly that that meat had a special flavor, and my mother said, "How do you dare eat non-kosher?" During the war we received the rations and we gave all the meat away to the *goyim*, to our neighbors. My mother would get rations from the kosher butcher. We would get the cheeks from a calf, or the lungs, or the liver, or the heart—all the organs and the intestines and the stomach from the cow, and a piece of udder. What delicious meals she could prepare with all these parts!

Udder we had to cook specially. See, udder you cannot cook in a pot because it's meat with milk inside, and you cannot mix milk with meat. So you take the udder and put it on lively coals until all the milk gets burned out. When it's finished and the meat is black, you throw it in boiling water. After it's finished boiling, then you cut away the outside, and you make very thin slices from the insides, like a calf's tongue. It was exquisite. Today we couldn't eat it: it's full of cholesterol.

After the war, in 1920, my mother, being asthmatic, was sent by my father to Badems, in Germany, for the waters and medicine, and to get some air. On the way back she would always bring a couple of friends she had made there. The couple were very elegant English people, so she would buy chicken for them even though we were very poor. We would look at that chicken, but she would tell us, "Don't you ever dare ask for any. And if I say to you, 'Do you want a piece of chicken?', you say no thank you you don't want any, because if you take a piece of chicken you won't get any dessert." We rarely had dessert in the house, but because those English came over mother made dessert. And those guests would take the skin off, and they would leave meat on the bone. I hated those English people then already, and I don't like them today, either, for all the trouble they have created in the world.

Anyway, I grew up with an appetite, a ferocious appetite, all my life. Imagine what the second world war did to me. Never to be able to eat full. But I always thought of my family first, and it's natural your wife and children come first. And it is a miracle I grew up. Period.

CHAPTER 3

"YOUR SON BERNARD IS FIGHTING WITH EVERYBODY"

And so we grew up slowly and none of us went to any high schools because for us they didn't exist. For those born in Belgium and their children, it was a very rich, capitalistic country, Belgium, and the capitalists would send their children to universities. The university for Brussels was called The Free University of Brussels—Universite *Libre d'Brussel*. Many French-speaking Belgians went there, and a lot of Flemish-speaking Belgians, and the students studied in different buildings and different sections that belonged to the same university.

There were also many poor people, and we were among the poor. I went to school until I was fourteen, and I worked all that time. You see, my father would wake me up at 5:00 in the morning to help him. I would work until a quarter of eight, make my prayers quickly, and at 8:00 go run up from the house because at 8:30 the bell would ring in school. At school, I would eat on the stairs a piece of bread when I was lucky enough to have it, because during the first world war in 1914-18 we didn't have any food, so we received rations from the Germans.

Only two Jewish families lived in our long street. I remember going with my two sisters with a basket to pick up our rations three times a week. The place we went was called a *cantine*. We would go there and they would measure exactly a half a pound or 250 grams or maybe eight ounces of bread a day per person, and you would get a lot of synthetics. They had honey made from coal, they had margarine made from coal, saccharine made from coal, all of it coming from Germany because the Germans were very brilliant, very smart, but we ate never to our full.

Only on Passover did we get enough. For four years, on Passover we had food, because America would send matzos over, and the next door neighbor would go and pick up everything that we would get from the Germans. My mother allowed her to keep all the items that were not kosher, but she always exchanged with her for something else that was. For Passover, that lady was entitled to keep just the bread meant for us until the end of Passover. For a whole week she would keep the bread, and when it came to the end of Passover we would turn over the basket and we would eat the old bread first and the fresh bread last. So we were very happy with Passover.

On Succoth, I would go into the swamps and bring home a lot of tall grasses with velvet-like black ends. In English and Flemish they're called cattails; in Hebrew they're called *srach*, or roof cover. You cover the roof of the *succah* with it, because the *succah* has to be built so you can see the stars through the roof. Then we garnished it with nuts and apples. I always had the habit of eating everything on the wall in the *succah*. At the time of Succoth, September or October, it already was winter and the beginning of school. So before my sisters would bring out the food, we thanked God when it rained because then we only went to the cold *succah* to make *kiddush* over the wine, and then we came into the warm house to eat. But on nice days we sat in the *succah*. We would sing all the old psalms, and the neighborhood gentiles would be very attentive because my father had a beautiful voice. He had sung in the choir with Chazen Serota, who had a fine reputation as a *chazen*, a cantor, in Odessa and Kishinev. All the children had good voices, too, and we would sing with my father. The week after Succoth we dismantled the *succah*, put away the wood and the roof, and life continued.

Of course, the week before Succoth was Rosh Hashanah, Yom Kippur, and naturally holidays were moments of rejoicing, family affairs. Being that we had nobody but our brothers and sisters, friends would come and visit with us, or we would go to friends, and we would go to synagogue with friends. On Yom Kippur you took food for the children below thirteen years old. I remember infringing upon the laws and snitching a bite away from the children, because who could pass the whole day when food was so important? We would come home starved and the tradition was when you came home from the synagogue, from all day fasting, you had a cup of tea and a small bite of leeker, or honeycake, and you made a *l'chaim*, a toast to life. Then the women prepared the table and we sat down. The whole evening long we tried to fill that cavity in our stomachs from not eating during the day. Being Jewish school children, we enjoyed double holidays, for Jews and for Christians, because if it was Rosh Hashanah and Yom Kippur, Jews didn't go to school, and when Christmas came nobody went to school.

And we had the minor holidays like Purim, Chanukah. We didn't have the habit of giving gifts. All the children received pennies, centimes, and those centimes we put into the saving bags for the Keren Kayemet Yisrael, the Jewish National Fund. So you received the gift and then you gave it away in *tzedakah*, charity. We also received small gifts but only at the beginning of the holiday. The Celebration of Lights, Chanukah, is eight days, in commemoration of the Maccabean victory over the Syrians, but we didn't have the American tradition of giving many large gifts. It was strictly European, and like this the holidays went by.

Our home was very observant because my mother was very observant and she inculcated that religion into us. Mother was the head of the family according to Jewish law. The woman always was the respected head of the family. It was not matriarchy. The father was the authority, but the mother was the rules and regulations. When she said, it went. I covered my head and wore a short *talis*, a prayer shawl, during the day, and observed all the kosher rules and regulations. If, God forbid, somebody would take a dairy knife and cut meat, that knife had to be stuck in the ground for three days to purify it, and it was serious. You had two sets of dishes, one for dairy, one for meat. You wouldn't mix one with the other. Of course, after I grew up, with my first wife, we became more liberal with our customs and we didn't observe *kaschris* a hundred percent. We didn't skip holidays, but we weren't afraid to take a trolley car or to light a match on Saturday. Little infringements.

But we had a tremendous amount of respect and love for our parents. There was never any contradiction. My father was very generous sometimes with rewarding the seat of your pants, but it was done with love. It was not like today with brutality of children. Oh no. We loved our parents tremendously. Among my brothers and sisters there was always a rivalry. That was natural. We had our disagreements like we had our tastes. One liked the top of the bread; the other one liked the inside of the bread. One didn't like rice; the other one didn't like noodles. My father hated boiled potatoes. He looked at potatoes and had a headache. So my mother would make noodles everyday for him, and he loved it. It was a loving family, very loving. In fact, because of that, in my family we don't have the habit of cursing. When somebody, sometime, comes out with a curse word, I am amazed. My worst curse in Yiddish was *Vaist dich the gitte your!*—"May the good times get you." That's all. Curses I could, of course, come out with, but it doesn't help. It makes no sense. Remember the old Jewish saying, "A curse and a blessing is not a bomb. It will never explode." So what's the use of speaking unnecessarily? And that's all. No, we had a good family.

At that time there was no gas or electricity in our home. We had petroleum lamps that you could lower from the ceiling to light. For Sabbath we would light candles and when they went out that's when we would go to sleep, because we were not allowed to touch them.

Ken Wachsberger

Food was a disease with me. My mother made *kischke*—that is, stuffed derma. And she made a type of Jewish stew, called a *choolent*. In a *choolent* you put all the cheap cuts of meat, and you add potatoes and barley and beans, all foods that stick to the ribs, and you cook it in a big, heavy pot for twenty-four hours, from Friday noon until Saturday noon, when you come back from the synagogue. I know that Saturday we ate to our hunger, but I would be woken up about three in the morning on Saturday with a big hunger. My nostril would swell with the aroma from the cooking because you cooked all night, so I would sneak down and very delicately lift the cover, because it was sealed with a piece of dough, and I would take a piece of bread, and the fat running on top of the stew. It was so good. No wonder I have cholesterol today!

In school, I had two Jewish friends, named Rosensweig and Hellman. They were timid boys. They came from Poland where oppression was big. Me? Where I grew up, like the non-Jewish boys, I wouldn't be afraid to go to school with an open shirt. I spoke the slang. I wasn't afraid to go into a fight. I knew my strength, but those two boys, Rosensweig and Hellman, they were skinny, pale, brought back to themselves. Very seldom did they speak. I would go to them and I would speak Yiddish because they were raised in Yiddish. I would tell them, "Why don't you play with us?" "We don't play with *chkoutsim*." *Chkoutsim* means non-Jewish people in Yiddish.

One day at recess, some kids from the school went against them, and they were fighting and pommeling and something came up in me, a rage. I was only a schoolboy like them, but even so they touched two Jewish boys and I jumped in the middle. I grabbed two, let myself go to the floor when I got them underneath me, sent two of them running and I threw them all off. From then on, I was the defender of all Jewish children in the school.

I grew up with a boy who was the son of the rabbi from our community. He was from Poland, a Warsaw rabbi. That means he was full of Torah and he wrote books, like holy books, *s'farim* it was called in Hebraic. I grew up with him, and he was like a little chicken next to me, and I was his rooster. Every time he had a problem he would come to me and say, "Bernard, this person did something to me," and I would pacify him, unless I would see a real injustice.

Whenever somebody had problems, he would come to Bernard. "Bernard, he insulted me." Then in Yiddish I would write a little note at school: "Don't worry. Don't look upon them." My father was called to the principal in the school maybe two hundred times a year, sometimes day after day. "Your son Bernard is fighting with everybody." And I would say, "Yes, if they do bad to this one and that one, and that one, and they are afraid, I am not afraid." Coming back from school one day, I was attacked by three boys, and they took my books and threw them in the river Senne. I came home with a black eye, but the three boys came back with split lips, because if I received it I gave it royally.

Finally, when I was thirteen, I was Bar Mitzvah'd. Of course, it had nothing to do with the American style, because here it's Hollywood. When we spoke of Bar Mitzvah it meant only coming to be called to the Torah, and then you made a little party in the house, and that was it. We had a little party in the house, long tables, invited a few close friends, and children, of course, and you invited all your relatives if you had any. But we had no one, so we had about forty-five friends, and my mother and sisters prepared the food. For my Bar Mitzvah, I studied for one year. Then I read from the Torah, and I recited the *parshe*, the speech. In fact, I still remember my speech, from sixty-five years ago. "Ladies and Gentlemen, according to my own intelligence, I'm going to try to explain to you the importance of my Bar Mitzvah." Then I told them the story of my Bar Mitzvah and the importance of being Jewish and I made a promise that I would always wear the *talis katan*; that means the short prayer shawl that you wear to the knee. And I received a fountain pen, ha! And that was my Bar Mitzvah.

Then I had an obligation between age thirteen and my mother's death when I was seventeen. I was a very observant Jew and every morning I put on *t'filin* and I wore the *tsetse comfas*, you know, a short prayer shawl with fringes on the corners, and I obeyed *kaschris* because I was afraid that God would get me around the corner. See, we were afraid of God because mother was so religious, mind you, that on Rosh Hodesh, the beginning of the month, she would never take a needle to sew because Rosh Hodesh should be a woman's holiday, and when it's a woman's holiday you don't sew. Tradition. Now remember also, every group of Jews from different countries had different traditions and different habits. Some Jews for Passover will not use rice or beans. The Sephardics from Morocco and Algeria, they use it. When we made a Seder, we sat and read from the Hagudah. Of course, today it's more complicated because we are accepting the plight that we went through, the Holocaust, and we speak of the Russian Jews and the loss of freedom in Russia, and we speak of the miseries of America. But in the olden days the Seder was something that my father never would sit down to before midnight, according to the tradition of his village.

The Seder began at midnight. We would be ready to eat about 2:00 in the morning. The children would collapse from tiredness, so one would give a *zetz* on the other one, "Wake up, Papa is saying the Hagudah." And you had to say every word. Finally the food came and nobody wanted to eat because they were exhausted, and there were people who said the Hagudah standing up around the table walking with a small bundle on their shoulders in remembrance of when the Jews had to leave Egypt.

Ken Wachsberger

I remember the morning before Passover my sisters and I would go to the early market where the storekeepers would buy wholesale for their shops, and I would buy a hundred kilos of potatoes for the week of Passover. Fifty kilos of onions, fifty kilos of carrots, and twenty-five kilos of parsnips. I was strong. I could carry a hundred kilos—that's 200 pounds—on my back then, and we would take the trolley car. We lived on a street where the trolley car made a bend, and then the driver would stop in the middle of the next block. So I would ask the driver of the trolley car, "Please stop for a second on that bend so I can throw down the stuff; my street is just there." He would be obliging and then we would *schlep* it into the house.

On the day of Passover until 9:00 in the morning, you were allowed to have *chomitz* of bread, bread that wasn't kosher for Passover. After this, no more. So we took the big bucket of potatoes and hard-boiled eggs and onions and mixed it with a drop of oil. Whew! That was some Jewish treat!

In the meantime, after my Bar Mitzvah, I received a brand new pair of shoes. I wore those shoes all around the house. I was proud of those shoes. At that time I was reading books about fortunes in Spain, castles in Spain, and I had two non-Jewish friends. Their mother was the owner of the tobacco cigarette store and their father was a fireman. We still lived in Rue de Collecteur near Chaussee de Mons.

Chaussee de Mons is a road going from Brussels to Paris, direct; if you follow that road you can't get lost. So one day we decided that tomorrow we would go to Spain. Usually I came home for lunch. After lunch, I took a snack from home. The snack was a pound loaf of bread cut in two, and cheese and honey cake and butter and everything was put in between. It was a meal that we ate at 4:00, but for me it was a snack.

I took two of them and my mother, may she rest in peace, said, "Why do you take such a big snack?" I said, "Ma, I was so hungry yesterday." I knew that I was going away, but she didn't know. And my two friends and I, I waited for them, they waited for me. I had change left over from the money my father gave me to buy paint to paint the leather, and my friends had received money from their mother to go to the post office to buy stamps for the store. We came together and that's it—we left. Chaussee de Mons went all the way out to the town of Ninove, and in Ninove there was a way to go to the French border, so we went there and waited for trucks.

At that time there were trucks with horses and beer barrels. They had four horses up front, *schlepping* those big trucks with the beer barrels hanging on chains. We jumped on the barrels in the back and we went to France. The day went by and we were in Peruwee, a farmland on the French border. It was evening, it was getting dark, and we already had finished our food. We decided that I was going to be the captain, the treasurer, and keep the money. So I took their money with my money. I said, "Instead of buying food, let's stop at the farmer's door and see if we can get hospitality."

In the meantime, unknown to us because we were children and dumb, our parents went to the police and the police had sent out signals all over Belgium. So when we came to that farm the man knew who we were and accepted us. He was very nice. He said, "Come in, sit down and eat," because we had told him we were on our way to Spain, and we were going to work and we told him our dreams and ambitions. The Belgian was so hospitable. After we finished eating he gave us blankets and he let us go into a shack to sleep for the night. "In the morning," he said, "you come in, we have breakfast, and then you go on your way to Paris."

In the morning we went in for breakfast and found two gendarmes. Gendarmes are national police. "Bernard Mednicki?" I said yes. "Pierre and Juliss Neys?" They said yes. "Okay," he said. "We have received orders from Brussels. We're going to put you on the train. When you come to Brussels your parents will go and pay the train station and you will present yourself to the commissar of police."

When we heard that our hearts sunk. It was the end of the dream. I gave them back the money, we went back to Brussels on the train station, and directly we went to the police as we had been ordered.

We came in and the commissar of police knew us from being children because at that time police walked the street with a walking cane. They knew every child in every neighborhood. And, for instance, if my window was closed, the police would say, "Hey, you on the second floor, open your window please." I would open my window. Or, "You didn't wash your street today." I would wash my street. It was like a family affair. We didn't see the authoritarianism. We were too small to understand that. Today it wouldn't go. We thought it was part of being neighborly.

The chief of police said, "Well, Bernard, we've got you. What are we going to do with you? Are we going to send you away until twenty-one with hard labor?" Oy, just thinking about it, we aged. He said, "What are you going to do? You want to go home? And after speaking to your parents, tomorrow you bring your father or your mother here." Then he said, "You are going to walk straight now."

Well, that admonition made us turn green. We had no one to blame but ourselves. We were going home; we weren't too far from the house. They lived on one street, I lived on another street. So I said to them, "You know what? I'll go home with you and I'll look how your mother receives you." They had a store and underneath the store was a cellar where they lived. There were grills in the sidewalk, so I laid down on my belly to look into the cellar. They open the door of the store, they holler, *"C'est moi"*—'It's me," and they go into the house and downstairs. As they come downstairs, the mother takes the coal stoker and she knocks them over their shoulders. "What did you do with my money?" They gave her the money. Calmed her a little bit. And she called them everything in the book.

Oy! When I heard that, I wondered what's going to be with me? I felt like a fox caught by the tail. I went home very slowly and I came to the door of the house. The door was directly in front of the family room, and I heard moaning and crying, "My son, my baby." I opened the door and I went in and said, "Ma, I'm back." My mother was a sick lady and she was sitting in the chair. Around her were a lot of her friends, Jewish women. Any sympathy for her son who ran away and God knows what's going to be of him? Jewish boy?

"Come to me," my mother said. I went to her. She grabbed me, kissed me. My sister Rosa came to me, gave me a *zetz* in my face. For my sister Rosa I have the greatest, biggest respect. She was my godmother, like I already explained. So when she hit me, I said, "Rosa, why?" "Because you made mother cry."

In the commotion, my father came in from the kitchen laughing. "You must be starved," he said. I said yes. He said, "Come on into the kitchen." And he didn't say anything. I sat down and I ate like it could be going out of style. We had three bedrooms upstairs, one room for the girls, one room for the boys, and one room for the parents. Then there was an attic, and in the attic were tiles, and the wind would blow through the tiles: "Oooooooh." When you are twelve or thirteen this is ghosts running around.

When I was done eating, my father said, "For the next two weeks you sleep in the attic. Go, get yourself a bunch of straw." At the end of the street was a guy selling straw, so I bought a bunch of straw, took it to the attic, and I slept in the attic for maybe three weeks and every night I was frightened to death.

I enjoyed reading a lot, but I had no light there. Usually we had coal lamps because there was no gas or electricity. Gas just came in then. So I took candles to the attic because I was afraid. Then, after the three weeks, I was treated like a man with a rare disease. Nobody spoke to me, and my sister was snickering at me. Only my mother had pity on me. "Why did you do that, my son?" I said, "Ma, I wanted to make you rich." She said, "You want to make me rich? Go to work. Learn to be a good man."

CHAPTER 4

"A JEW MUST HAVE A TRADE," AND MY MOTHER DIES

That year I became an apprentice at a tannery. There I learned to make gloves, leather jackets, all kinds of leather goods. Later on, I graduated to pocket books, and finally I learned the whole profession of orthopedics. That was my trade, but I had to learn from the beginning. It took me eleven years to become a craftsman.

I became an apprentice in leather work because that was my father's choice. My father had said, "You can be anything you want to, because you were born in Belgium—a policeman, a bank administrator, a postman." But he also said, "A Jew must have a trade, because wherever they throw you, you should make a living."

It was a fact. Wherever in the world I went, although I might not know the language, I could make a living. Even in America, in 1951, I went into Sauer's Orthopedic Shop, I oriented myself very well even with my limited English tongue, and I had a job in my trade which I did for twenty-six years. The same place. So I think my father had a good point, forcing me to have a trade. Unfortunately my other brothers didn't become craftsmen because they were too young and later things were different. They were more inclined to have non-Jewish occupations, because the Jews went for apprenticeship and non-Jews were already assistant truck drivers, or working on the flea mart, jobs like that. My brother Maurice was on the flea mart, and he made a good living. That doesn't mean that he did not know how to hold a hammer and nails in his hand. He was very apt to work. He had talent. Yet he never had a specific trade like I had.

I started in tannery because when you learned the trade you learned fundamentally, from the beginning. The trade was leatherwork. You had to know what the leather was made from, because you manipulated the leather. It was mostly very refined hides. In the trade we used dog hide to make all kinds of trusses, and pads for the support of abdomens and backs. We used dog hides but there was no slaughterhouse for dogs so we would catch dogs from the street. Some of them we would kill and just keep the hide. Or we would buy skins of whatever dogs the society for the prevention of cruelty to animals, the ASPCA, had that they would be disposing of by mercy killing.

I started when I was nine, actually. At that time there were no chemicals. We used human waste to put ammonia into the skins and make them soft. You would stand in buckets filled with waste up to your knees, stamping all day to masticate the skin. There were no laws then to protect children at work, so it would be tough for a child. Of course, I was kept by my parents and they paid attention to my health, but there were a lot of parents who didn't pay attention. The non-Jewish people were hard working, but the unhealthy working conditions affected them, so there was a lot of tuberculosis. Then laws came in to protect children, and laws against alcoholism and laws to regulate working conditions. But this is modern times. I'm speaking of sixty-five years ago and that's an eternity of difference.

For two years I was entitled to watch, my hands behind my back, and not slump and not rest. Watch! After two years I was entitled to help him. I would do all the errands, of course. I would bring back the water, and carry the bundles of skins and leather, and I would go to the store and so on and so forth. But I wasn't entitled to touch a pair of shears until I was fourteen years old.

So I watched, and when I started learning I really had to concentrate. There were no eight-hour days there. If at 9:00 at night there was the need for you to stay, you stayed. If you were a serious apprentice you had to learn on your own. Nobody would give you the opportunity unless you took it. You had to be like a volunteer. "I want to do it." And that's the way I turned out to be.

I had three employers as an apprentice; the last one was a non-Jewish firm, and that is where I really learned the finesse of the trade. The fundamentals I learned with Jewish fellows from Poland. Of course, as in every trade, you can do it one way and another can do it another way. It all depended on where you learned your job. A prosthesis may fit perfectly well on the body, but if the boss is a maniac and he cannot accept how you did it, it's no good. And that's how it was when I was young.

I became a complete apprentice when I was fourteen years old. When I was fifteen, I was working in the home of a Jew by the name of Mr. Weinberg. We used humid, warm towels, special drapes, to roll skins out and straighten out the wrinkling. One day he says to me, "Go downstairs and ask the ladies on the second floor to give you a pail of warm water."

I went downstairs and knocked on the door and they said come in. I went in and saw two young women, stark naked. They were prostitutes and their mother was there. She was crippled with rheumatism, and her hands were completely shrunk. I went in and I looked at those women, and I couldn't remove my eyes from looking at their naked bodies. I had never seen this in my life, and suddenly my face became illuminated and burning from shame. I saw the elderly woman and I asked for a pail of warm water, but I couldn't move my eyes. One girl said, "Why, you never saw a lady before?" The mother gave me the pail of water.

I went upstairs and told my employer and he started laughing. He knew they were prostitutes but he had sent me anyway. When I came home, I took my father aside and I told him the story. He was so angry. But in Belgium prostitution was legal and every day the ladies would go for a medical checkup.

A prostitute lived on our street. She had four children and her husband was a coal miner who would leave Monday and come back Friday or Saturday night. During the whole week she would go do her job and nobody would have any bad ideas or speak ill about her. She was a very heavy person and she was well made up. We children played with hers on the street, but we tried to avoid staring at her because we had been told to stay away from her. One day, when I was fifteen or sixteen, my father said to me, "Bernard, remember, you should never go to prostitutes because if you go to them you will get a disease, you will have to be operated on, or you will dry out and you'll have nothing to get married with."

This fear he put into me was very strong because we were very inexperienced. We had no sexual awareness until maybe age seventeen or eighteen. We knew that beautiful women had an anatomy. We knew about erections and wet dreams. We knew a baby came from the belly. But the phenomenon of birth we didn't know. Today, children three years old know Mommy has a baby in her belly. We thought the baby came in a suitcase. The midwife came to the house with a little dark suitcase and later there was the baby.

Mme. Vase was the name of the local midwife. She had a son by the name of Roger who was born the same time as I. We grew up together and went to school together. Mme. Vase was maybe four and a half feet tall, five feet maybe, and she had a black suitcase that she never wanted us to look inside of.

Usually, it seemed, she came on a Thursday afternoon, and we only went to school until noon on Thursday and Friday. Those afternoons were for the children to rest or play. Every time Mme. Vase came, she would send my brothers and sisters to the movies, and when we'd come back Mother was in bed. We would find her eating a piece of black bread and a piece of salty herring, holding the baby in her arms. Later, she would feed the baby and we would be amazed.

Mother breast-fed her babies. She had one of those suck glasses with a nipple, so when she had too much milk she would suck the milk out from her breast and put it in a glass. Then, when she would be sleeping, we had to pour it in a bottle and give it to the baby. One day I saw the cream on top, and I swallowed half of the glass. It was sweet as sugar. Mother was very angry. But we were only small, and we would say, "Why does he get everything that is so good?" because we had tasted it. So Mother took and squeezed the milk, and she said, "This belongs only to children who are babies. Once you are one year and a half you cannot get it anymore." That was all.

Religious Jews believe that whatever number of children you get you take. Like any other faith, you can see that religious Jews, the Orthodox and the Hasidim, have a lot of children. Only modern Jews control the birth of their children. We had a large family compared to now, but compared to then it wasn't so large. I remember large families, with fifteen and eighteen children. It was a misery. How were you supposed to support all of them and feed all of them? Growing up was nothing because one child helped the next one to grow up. My sister helped us; then I helped because even when I was three I was already the product of my older brothers and sisters. My parents just knew that they had to bring food and keep a roof over our heads, and clothes, and that was it. It was interesting, but it's not today.

And that's one reason why my wife and I now have a lot of patience with our family when we come together. When we come together for holidays we are at times forty. Children keep moving away: One is in Arizona, one is in Washington, one is in upstate Massachusetts. The children try to come together for holidays, but it's not always possible. Therefore, when we come together and Minnie and I cook for the forty children, it is tiresome but we feel the joy of being a family. When you sit at that table, you see those shiny faces, the candlesticks burning, and the holiday atmosphere in the house. Let it be a Rosh Hashanah or Passover or whatever holiday it could be, this is something we took with us as a gift from our parents, and my parents evidently must have gotten that from their parents. We carried with us all those traditions and we tried to give them to our children. Now I know that my children stopped observing many of these traditions. They are more liberal, more skeptical. They are reformed Jews, and so it is. I don't have one Orthodox Jew in my family.

When I was sixteen I became a Belgian citizen. My father had lost his nationality when he came to Belgium, of course, but right after the first world war, for all those who ran away from Russia or from any other country, thanks to Count Fridtjof Nansen of Norway, they made the Nansen Passport. The Nansen Passport was an identification paper that enabled my father to stay in Belgium but not as a citizen. Later, when he wanted to come to America he couldn't get a passport because he never did get citizenship. Even when Russia created the Soviet Union and then offered citizenship to all those who were of Russian descent, my father was never very keen about getting it. He remained without a country. It didn't bother him, and this existed all his life.

But amongst us children, my brothers and my sisters—except for Rosa and Sheva—and me, all of us born in Belgium, we became Belgian citizens because my father requested the right for his children born in the land to become Belgian, and it was accorded. At that time, being that Belgium had so few people throughout the whole country, the government was looking for people. In fact, later on they started paying a premium for every birth. If you had children, they paid so much a month for every child to the mother so she could give her children the same things as other children whose fathers made more. And it was not too bad. In fact, Belgium was a good country to live in.

But about my apprenticeship: Being an apprentice was a very, very good thing. When I was fifteen years old, my father paid one thousand francs for my training, and it was a lot of money. When I started earning, I made five francs a week to begin with. But later on I made a good living. When I was eighteen I joined the union of craftsmen. I became a full-fledged craftsman at age twenty. The apprenticeship was interesting. Unfortunately, nobody wants to learn a trade anymore because everything is mechanized.

My mother passed away at home after a long sickness when I was seventeen. We were then four young brothers: Maurice, Charles, Zourech, and I. I was still an apprentice but I stayed home that day. Everybody stayed home. People were milling in and out, and the doctor came, and then he said she's finished. That's it. So they put her on the ground, on straw. On her eyes they put broken pieces of ceramic; in old Yiddish it's called *charben*, for "fragment of porcelain." On her abdomen they put a crust of bread. Maybe it was a tradition from the village, I don't know. Then for the night came very pious Jews and two women and they sat the whole night saying the psalms, and in the morning was the funeral.

She passed away a few days into Chanukah, the sixth candle, near Christmas 1927, so there was a lot of snow. We walked a long distance behind the hearse to go to the cemetery. I remember I jumped in the grave on top of her casket. Yes, I jumped in the grave on top of her casket. I didn't want her to go. And I was seventeen then. They pulled me out and with sadness we walked home. We walked a long way. Then for one year I would go say *kaddish*, the mourners' prayer, with my two brothers; the little one was too young. We would go and say *kaddish* twice a day, morning and night. And we observed. I remember sleeping with objects belonging to my mother, just for the comfort.

Then my brother, Charles, drowned maybe a year after that, in 1928. We missed him, we couldn't find him, and then we were called by the police. They found his body in the canal. It was a tragedy. We went to the morgue—my father, my sister Rosa, and I—to identify our Charles. He was buried in a mausoleum because ground was expensive, and those who didn't have the means went into the mausoleum like going into a drawer in a closet. He was buried near to my brother Natan.

It was a very sad period. My father could not take anything in his hand to work for thirteen years because he was depressed and lost his ambition to live. For thirteen years I worked, my sisters worked, and we kept the family going. I was involved in working eighty to ninety hours a week. Not only did I work in the shop, but I had an opportunity to make more because of piecework. So I would come home at night, have a bite, and then work at my bench until 1 or 2 o'clock in the morning. Then I would get up at 5:30 in the morning to go to work. I didn't have a chance or time for vacations or relaxation or anything. I had to make money. When I was twenty-one I got married, but I told my family, "I won't let you go; I won't fail. I will give you half of my pay." And I divided my pay in two. Then, to compensate, I took a second job at night at home, and like this we were able to manage.

But as a result of all that happened, I started to believe less and less in God. Because if he took away the mother of eight children, then where was his image as a father? Of course, being young, I believed word for word about godliness, but getting older I understand it's a philosophy. God is not at my beck and call. He exists or he doesn't exist, that's a point of view. There is something up over us, but he is not there to say, "I'm gonna make it good or bad for you." I think everybody takes care of his own. Period. That's all.

By a miracle, in 1938, my father came back to himself. In that year, we lived in Brussels and he met a young woman from Poland. Her father was a rabbi near a city, but I don't remember the city, and my father went to see the father of that young woman in Poland.

She was a lot younger than my father, maybe twenty years younger. And they had a baby boy who was my little brother, Jacob. When the war started he was not yet two years old, so he was born in 1939. And so my father started life again. We led our own lives. We lived nicely before the war but we lived separately in different parts of the city.

CHAPTER 5

I MARRY CHANA LAJA AND JOIN THE UNION, THE IMPERIALISTS LIFT THEIR HEADS

When I was seventeen, a girl fell in love with me, but that was inconsequential. After mother passed away, we started having little conflicts in the house, and I decided to get away from my job. I wanted to become rich, so I became a salesman for a jewelry factory. While I was *schlepping* suitcases from store to store, trying to sell necklaces and all kinds of imitation jewelry, I met a young girl, Esther Silberberg, whose father had a factory once, and was very wealthy. She was of Polish nationality, but she would have loved to marry me just to become Belgian. So with her I spent some time. She would play piano. I had a good voice and I would sing very romantic songs. I'll never forget. Then her mother would invite us to eat. When food was there, ooh, that was the best. I loved the food and I enjoyed the girl, too. But we were naïve and young. To give a kiss you asked permission, and before you kissed, you blushed. You never kissed on the lips; you always kissed on the cheek. Only in America do you kiss the lips. Later on she married, I married, and we were good friends.

I was fortunate, in 1931, to meet a young lady named Chana Laja Sztroch, who came the year before also from Poland—from Warsaw. In Warsaw there was a lot of anti-Semitism, so she was smuggled in illegally by three of her sisters, who were already living in Brussels. She was working in a small factory in a mill for a manufacturer of fine underwear. Because she was in the country illegally, she couldn't walk the streets, so she had to sleep on a hard table in the plant, which was a primitive way of exploiting people. When I found out—I wasn't accustomed to the idea of people exploiting others like that—I said to my father, "This is inhuman." He said, "But she is illegal. If the government finds out they'll send her out of the country." I said nothing, but I knew that if I married her she would gain Belgian citizenship.

My father was a moderate Jew, taking care of all the obligations, but nothing sensational. When my mother was still alive he became active in the synagogue to please her, because she was the religious one. Later, he was president of the Lina Atsedek, a Jewish health relief society that helped sick people find doctors. My parents had a narrow circle of friends because there were very few Russian and Rumanian Jews then in Belgium; most were Polish, and to be friends with Polish Jews was a discredit because my father was a nationalist. To marry from another nationality was considered a misalliance. So when I told my father that I was going with a girl from Warsaw, my father almost disinherited me. "What do you mean you take out Polish girl, who's not from your descendants, from Russia, from Rumania? A Polish girl who makes fish with carrots and sugar?" Her Judaism was not in question. Jews didn't intermarry. But to marry a Polish girl? Whee, terrible. Well, my sister Rosa was married already, and she said, "Stick to your guns. If you love that girl, don't let father tell you what to do."

While I was courting her, I learned, from the man who owned the factory, and who knew her parents, that her parents in Poland found a very rich man from Cuba to marry her in exchange for a lot of money. Well, when I heard they were going to sell her, I said to my father, "I'm going to marry her and I don't care what you say." "All right," he said, even though it was hard for him. My brothers and sisters all took to her right away, but my father didn't accept her completely until the next year, when our son was born.

Her three sisters, who also had run away, through a lot of machinations, were able to get papers made by lawyers, and so on, because they worked for lawyers.

And so we were married in 1932. Oo la la. My wedding, it was beautiful. I worked until 10:00 in the morning on a Tuesday. My hands were discolored from the color of the hides, and I could not wash them clean. I put on my coat, underneath I had my apron, and I went to City Hall to get married. My father was there. And my sisters came, and the lady where Chana Laja was working, Mrs. Kligsberg.

At City Hall, we stood underneath the swords, and the mayor asked me if I accept that lady as my wife. I said yes. He asked her and she said yes. It took maybe an hour. Then she went back to her work and I went back to mine.

On Saturday night, Purim, we were married under the *chupah*, according to Jewish tradition. The *chupah* was at the home of her aunt and uncle who had come to Belgium many years before. They were respectable people. He was a pocketbook maker; the aunt made the wedding. We had three rabbis because she came from a family of Hasidim from Poland. For seven nights after that, I came for dinner for the seven *bruchas*, the seven blessings.

Chana Laja had a lot of relatives on her side: uncles and aunts, her sisters. Her sisters were married and they had children already, so from her side we had a family. They liked me because I was a likable chap. I was a Belgian citizen and that was very important because she was illegal, and by marrying me she gained legality. And I was young and acceptable. I was not wealthy, but money was of no consequence. Consequence was can you read, can you hold on a discussion, do you believe in progressive life, are you obscured with fanaticism? All those things counted.

Chana Laja had a brother-in-law, Maurice, a cobbler and the husband of her older sister, Topje. In Russia at that time, the Soviet government wanted the Jews to have a country, and so they gave them a piece of land in Russia called Byrobidjan. It was full of mosquitos and swamps and everything else. About 40,000 Jews worked there and died there. They created it and built it, and it exists today. My brother-in-law was part of that movement. I couldn't see it, but I went along because it was something to liberate my people. Zionism was not. Although I wasn't a member of the left-wing organization Histadrut hachomer hatzair—after my mother died, I ceased to belong to any organizations—I accepted the idea that not only Israel was for the Jews, but wherever there was a place for us.

But Chana Laja had a very liberal family. They had political ideas that were not to be tolerated by an alien living in Belgium. If you were a stranger in a land, you had no right, unfortunately, to take an opposite point of view from the government regulating you. And, being that Belgium was a royalist democratic government, they didn't accept aliens being involved with liberalism, even though they had political parties representing all positions, from extreme right to extreme left, and from capitalism to communism. In fact, Maurice was expelled out of Belgium by the government and he went to France and he remained there and became a Frenchman and everything. During the second world war, he became a prisoner of war for five years. His son David, my nephew, fought in the Resistance.

Chana Laja had a peach complexion and beautiful black eyes. She was very elegant, with a gentle nature. She was well read, educated, and of liberal mind because of her background. When we married and after all the religious ceremonies were done, we decided that we were not going to bother having all the paraphernalia of double dishes in the house, *kaschris*, and so forth. We wanted a liberal life. We observed holidays only because we had to go to relatives. How odd it was, to go from being very religious to being not just agnostics but unbelievers totally. And now in America we are in the mainstream of Jewish life. We go to the synagogue sometimes, for Rosh Hashanah and Yom Kippur. We keep our holidays. I don't know if it is decadence or getting old, I cannot answer you, or is it that you don't want to have any conflicts with anybody?

Ken Wachsberger

Being a Belgian, I could easily find a place to rent, so after we got married I rented a furnished room for us in Brussels, not far from where I worked. In the room we had a bed, a table and chairs, my workbench, a stove and a gas range, and a big armoire for our clothes. Period. That's it. We didn't need any more.

Then, within one year, Chana Laja became pregnant and we had a baby boy. We named him Avram, after the father of Chana Laja. After that, we moved out to an apartment. At that time you still bought a pail of coal or a bag of coal to keep warm, and we lived on top of a coal merchant. We lived a good life. For entertainment we would go sometimes to the Jewish theatre, or we would catch a movie. We were not, as working people, prone to spend too much time on entertainment. We worked sometimes seventy or eighty hours a week, so we didn't have time to futzel around. Socializing was with the family, my sisters-in-law, and their friends.

The war turned everything upside down. When I came to America and I saw the racism, I was so angry I wanted to go back to Belgium. There were Jews who would speak of the black with a lot of contempt. I couldn't see it. Here we had just come back from being destroyed. According to Hitler, the Jew and the black were below the monkey. And in America the Jew thinks he has the right to just forget about the black? Oh, I fought very much, and my family called me the black lover. But I didn't love the black more than the white because to me a *mensch* is a *mensch*. And that's all there was to me. I couldn't see color and I couldn't see race, because my people had been pulled through the fire of anti-Semitism for centuries, in the Inquisition and before that the Egyptians. Did I, a Jew, now have the right to discriminate because one had slanted eyes, or one's skin is yellow or black? Hey, where is a little bit of sense?

But with Chana Laja I had a marvelous life. Life was understanding because she was very calm when I was ebullient. I was always go-go-go, and she was always "Take it easy, take it easy." Thanks to her, I think I'm gonna live a little longer. She was a beautiful person. There is an old expression, a Jewish one, "to live like God in Odessa." Odessa was a very Jewish city. When there was peace, they lived well. With Chana Laja, I lived like God in Odessa. We had a job, we had friends, we had our family, then we had our children. The government was a democratic government. There was no racism that we knew, because in the same house on the bottom floor lived French-speaking people from Wallonia; on the second floor lived Flemish-speaking people from the Flanders; on the third floor were blacks from Belgian Congo; and on the fifth floor lived a Jew. And we lived like a whole family together. We never had any racism.

In fact, when the Belgian went to live and work in the colonies of the Belgian Congo, he was entitled to take a black woman. But he could not bring the woman back, only the children. So he would bring the children to Belgium to give them an education. We had many beautiful black people, of course Catholic, and we didn't know the difference. To us it was an honor to be friends to blacks, to Congolese, when I was a young man, you know. Until 1940.

During my early years with Chana Laja I became involved in the trade union. Syndicat it was called. We had a beautiful system throughout Belgium. We had syndicats, and we had guilds. Guilds were groups of people who were not numerous. Still we worked for syndicats because they were part of a large group: bottle makers, glove cutters, furriers, they all belonged to different guilds. The guild comes from a long tradition going back to the 1600s in Belgium where they started the movement of every trade coming together to defend each other against exploitation. Our syndicat was part of another big syndicat, and we were accepted like the Amalgamated in America: shoemakers, tailors, furriers. Our branch was a guild of the leather workers.

The syndicat gave us fantastic benefits. First of all, we paid, every month, a certain part of our salary. For this we had bakeries. The baker would come around every day with a truck, he would blow the whistle, and we would know he was there. Then we would go out and buy our bread. Because we belonged to the union we received special stamps. We had stores, immense cooperatives built by the government for the poor working man, for when we would buy from the union, clothing stores, grocery stores; and they would give us back a percentage at the end of the year. Before my children were born, my wife received the last few weeks of her pregnancy money for a rest in a vacation spot. Then, when the baby was born, I received money to buy a crib, the necessary outfits, blankets, and the maternity was paid a hundred percent. If she was a working lady, she was paid the first three months eighty percent of her wages through the union. Then she was entitled to receive food. Coal we would buy from them: they would bring a truck with coal and put it in the cellar; for the whole winter you would buy a ton. And that was the profit we got from belonging to the union. Once a week we had meetings. The meetings were held on Sunday morning or Saturday night because during the week we had to work. Usually a couple hundred members attended, but everybody was able to participate and you were able to criticize. Protests were organized when they were necessary.

The first of May was, of course, the working man's day. Huge parades of all unions and organizations took place in every province. We would reunite in Brussels and manifest our desire to fight or strike to gain support for our requests. We had big manifestations and bitter strikes. We turned over trolley cars, fought the police. When we had a general strike, everything was cut off. The whole country was paralyzed, from one end to the other.

But during a general strike, one helped the other. I give you for your child; you give me for my child. If you go to the country, you bring back some for me, too. We would share, and the strike would go on, and the country couldn't live with that because there was no income, so sometimes the employers gave in, or we made agreements, and that was the political life of Belgium.

I recall three serious general strikes, but there were more than that because the Belgians were very hot underneath the collar. America is very passive. The American working man has a strong potential for being very flaccid. We don't have backbone, because if there is a general strike here, it's only in Ohio, or only in Philadelphia, not in the whole country. No, you cannot compare America to any country in the world because all of Europe combined is like America. When there is a general strike in Belgium, it's in all of Belgium. And that's about nine million people. But in America there are 230 million people. You can't do it because we have too much opposition. We don't like each other here because we are not tolerant, and if we act tolerant it's because we figure it demands less effort. We in America are very cautious because a lot of money is involved. Is there any reason why only the Europeans have such a fantastic rail system? What's wrong with us? Then again, we are two hundred years old. You cannot demand in two hundred years what has taken a thousand years in other countries.

In the thirties in Belgium, we had Liberals, we had Catholics, we had socialist unions, and all those unions would also work together. But if you were a Catholic, you didn't want to belong to the Liberal union, you wanted to belong to the Catholic union because, being a Catholic, you would go to church and be blessed by the pope. If you didn't want to meet even the pope, you went to the Socialists. But when it came to business, they all came together in the struggle for life and freedom and redistribution of the wealth.

The Socialist Party, to which I belonged, was very strong. The Socialist Party was like the Democratic Party in America. There was a Communist Party, also, but the Communist Party had nothing to do with the Soviet Union because it was strictly a Belgian organization in the sense that every Communist would go to church on Sunday and would still listen to the Vatican. Well, you know very well that communism doesn't allow religion. You see, Belgium was a capitalistic country. With inheritances, for instance, a house could go six hundred years in the same family, from child to child, from cousin to nephew, but the house would never go out of the family. There are cities in Belgium where there are no realtors; they could never sell a house. The notary has the house in his hands. He knows that when you are ready to pass on sixty years from now, your son is going to get the house, and after your son, your grandson. We had houses that were four or five hundred years old in Brussels, made from white marble, never sold.

Of course, there was antagonism between the Socialists and the Communists. The Communist Party followed the Marxist-Leninist line, and the Social Democrats followed the leaders of the Socialist Party, the Internationale from France and England and Germany. But their goals were the same. Everybody wanted a better life for the working man. At one time the Communist Party had a relation to the Soviet Union; they belonged to the International Communist Party. Then there was a scandal and they moved away from the International and became the Belgian Communist Party. Our Communist senator and *deputee*, our congressman, would be received by the king, in audiences, to discuss the matters of the country and the working man. So our communism in Belgium was more like democratic socialism. Members might believe in the priests, but they had the spirit of communism. They wanted to share. They wanted the good things that come in this world. Nobody should be hungry. Everybody should make a living. Everybody according to his needs. But it was only a dream. It's a pity.

We were part of the International Socialist Organization, which was a bond between the French, the Netherlands, Belgium, Luxembourg, Italy before Mussolini brought fascism, Spain before Franco, Germany before Hitler. At International meetings, our leaders wrote the standards for working men. They were responsible for limiting our work week to 48 hours. Before that, you worked whatever the employer wanted. They also regulated child labor.

And it was good. There was no racketeering. It was hard not to belong to the union because of the advantages and the unity that it demanded. We knew that a working man belongs, must belong, because alone he is nothing, and we had good conditions. Our leaders were good. We never gave them a chance to become big, because every year or every two years we changed them. Every profession had a president who was elected from among the working men in the shop. They never became rich because they had the same wages as the other men. When his being president was finished he went back to his job. There was a gentleman's agreement between employer and employee that his job was reserved. While he was gone, we all pitched in to take his place. Each president belonged to a group of presidents from different unions referring to a central committee, and that committee from the city of Brussels was in communication with Antwerp and every other city of Belgium. We had nine provinces in our nationwide union. It worked pretty well.

However, during that time we reached slowly the years 1936-37 when fascism became very strong in Germany and the Belgium imperialists also lifted their heads.

PART II: FLIGHT FROM BELGIUM

CHAPTER 6

HITLER INVADES BELGIUM, I'M SEPARATED FROM MY FAMILY

In the years leading up to World War II, I was married, I moved, and then I moved again. I worked for the same Jewish employer for many long years, a man named Henri Strauss. Mr. Strauss had nine children, five sons and four daughters, because Belgium was a country of many large families. Working there, I grew up with his children. My parents went to the birth of their children, they came to the birth of my parents' children, and this was part of a very liberal interaction between all the Jewish families there. So one was a little richer, one was a little poorer, but one way and the other we managed, and we all grew up together like brothers and sisters. I don't think any of them are still living. I also had many non-Jewish friends.

On the job, I worked with six other fellows in a very democratic environment, where we all knew our jobs. The store was organized into two divisions, one for export and one for domestic. We worked from 7 a.m. to 7 p.m. making fashion gloves, corrective gloves, and orthopedic devices. Our work took hard concentration so I did not cultivate friendships, but our employer was a good person and we made a comfortable living.

Unfortunately, good times became bad times and the depression forced us to look for other jobs. In 1937, I went to work in a rubber plant making implements for the government. I worked hard on the night shift for minimum wage. The smell of chemicals and rubber made me sick, but I needed the money. Then work became slow and I was laid off again, after less than six months.

Then I began working again as a glove maker. The best glove makers were the Polish Jews who had taught me my trade. The Belgian glove makers, the

Christians, were perfectionists, but we were meticulous because we were hungry. We came from poverty and every nickel we could make, we did make.

When the employers measured the skin, they would tell you that you had to make five gloves from that skin. However, because of the holes in the skin and the scratches in the skin, they would allow you a waste of four or five gloves per pile of skins. By combining and by measuring out where to place those holes and scratches, I could make two gloves more per skin than the employer estimated. When I was finished with my job, I would give my employer his gloves and I could have five skins, eight skins, twelve skins left for my own use. I sometimes had two dozen skins, and a dozen skins were worth more to me than the whole package of work I did for my employer. We concentrated more on the amount of gloves than on how perfect the gloves were.

The Belgian employers didn't accept any Polish Jews, but being that I was a Belgian I could get a job, and that's the reason I was able to go in and get work. I was hungry and I was naked, so I worked twenty-two hours a day on my bench and then I would catch two hours sleep. I would eat at my bench while I worked.

Oo la la, I ate like a giant! My goodness. Belgium imported grapes from Czechoslovakia. I remember buying a thirty-six-pound case of grapes, and during the week I finished it. I couldn't hold the grapes in my hand because the juice would leave marks on the leather, so I took a string, and I attached it with a large thumbtack to the wall so I would be feeding from the wall without my hands even touching them, and it was a way of life. At 4 in the morning I could eat six rolls, two cans of sardines, a half a pound of butter, and a pot of coffee. That was 4 in the morning! Avram, my son, then was one year old. His mother would get up about 7:30 and go to the grocery store, and at 8:00 I would have breakfast. I had pickled herring, six bagels, and half a pumpernickel. I ate well. I ate five times a day and every meal was consistent. One day Chana Laja was sick and tired of cooking, so she said, "You know what? I'm going to buy a piece of veal, a roast of five kilos, a big roast. Let me cook for two, three days." I said fine. I finished it in two sittings. She said, "Where did it go?" I said, "I don't know," because I never sat down to eat. I would be working and eating. It was one of the habits I had. I always had food in my pockets. I was always afraid I would go hungry. The first world war taught me that.

Sometimes I would start on a Saturday night after Sabbath, and I would work the night of Saturday, the day of Sunday, the night of Sunday, the day of Monday, the day of Tuesday, the day of Wednesday, and then Thursday morning I would deliver my work and get paid right away. I did a week's worth of work in four days, but those four days were compressed. My son would always sit on the bench and watch me while I worked. I was young. I was full of strength and energy. Oo, I was a hard worker.

Glove making was a very delicate profession. In Belgium, it was like being a surgeon. Physician, pharmacist, and glove maker: those were the professions of respect, honor. "Your son is a glove maker? Oo! Bernard is a glove maker." I could have married rich. I married a poor woman, but she was a young woman, and very beautiful. We fell in love. We didn't have very much and we didn't know a lot. She had to make me my first underwear. I never wore underwear until I was twenty because it was not stylish. Not only stylish—we were too poor to understand you have to wear underwear. Since then I always wear underwear, thank goodness.

These were the years when fascism in Germany was getting stronger. We were aware of the advent of Hitler, but we were pacified by Belgium's neutrality into believing that we were not in danger. We could not believe he would be able to hypnotize the world the way he did.

I didn't know the full extent of what the Germans were doing, but I knew they were confiscating businesses because the first German refugees began coming, from Leipzig, from Berlin, from Cologne, in 1937 and 1938. Those Jews didn't come destitute. They came with lots of money, because at that time, before Kristalnacht, they still could sell their businesses. They came to Belgium waiting for permits to go to America, to South America, or to neutral countries, like Switzerland and Spain and Portugal.

And we gave them hospitality. We helped couples sent to us by friends who had more people asking for help than they could help. The union also sent us refugees.

See, the unions believed that we all had our responsibility, so they would ask, "How many do you want to feed tomorrow?" And you said you want to feed four or five. One time we took in a husband and a wife. We put a mattress on the floor and they slept there a few days, ate with us, and then moved on toward England. We never heard from them.

We were squeezing our belt just to meet the ends but my wife was compassionate, my son Avram was two years old, three years old, and could not care less, and we never thought of getting a financial reward from them. I always did what I thought I had to do. I had learned charity from home. *Tsedakah* is the expression: "Give a hand to somebody who needs it." Somebody I gave a hand to might have been wealthier than I was but at the time we didn't have it in mind to say, "The dinner will cost you three and a half francs." I would buy second-day bread, a bag of fruit and vegetables that were a little too ripe. We would cook big batches of food. And we managed. We put it into our budget. You don't always have to have steaks. We had good food, healthy food, plenty of bread, and that's it.

During these years in Belgium, Leon Degrelle was becoming a powerful force for fascism. Degrelle was a Catholic from an upper-middle-class family. He was a lawyer and a publisher at a house called Christus Rex—"Christ the King."

He was another McCarthy, a hateful person. He already had anti-Semitism in his heart. He already had racism in his heart. He already hated the black in the Belgian Congo. And he was a lunatic who, like Hitler, was looking for a new regime.

In 1935, Degrelle founded the Rexist movement and became its main spokesman. The next year, members of his party won twenty-one seats in the Lower House and eight in the Senate, which was almost ten percent of all the seats and half as many as the Socialists, the largest party, who had seventy. In 1939, Degrelle won a seat for himself. Although only three other Rexists sat with him, in that brief time he woke up the anti-Semitic instinct in the nation. You know, the Belgian government was not racist or anti-Semitic officially between 1934 and 1940, but there was always a lot of quiet anti-Semitism. There were always disgruntled followers of anti-Semitism who believed the Jew was guilty of all the trouble, and he woke them up like Hitler did in Germany. But Degrelle hated not only the Jews. He was a xenophobe. He hated whoever was an alien in his country.

In 1938, I volunteered for the Home Guard, which had been organized a year or so before by the local government in each borough. The Home Guard was formed to be able to control the public and see that they did not get panicky. So the leaders picked people who were reasonable, who were solid citizens of the neighborhood, who were known for their civil behavior. All those who were old enough to bear weapons could volunteer. We would have patrols going around day and night. Each volunteer would work so many times a week and so many hours a night. I did it two hours every evening for five days a week from the middle of 1938 until the invasion in May 1940. Because only descendants of Belgian citizens could serve as volunteers and most of the Jews of volunteer age were born of parents of Polish or Rumanian nationality, I was one of the few Jews in the Home Guard. We patrolled our direct streets, two men at a time. We checked public utilities and would report suspicious activity or disturbances of any nature. Our role was to see that when the sirens blew, all the windows would be sealed with black drapes, so there would be no light on the street, and no people running around. A certain group would watch the wells and the reservoir, the electricity converters, the gas stations, the telephone, to prevent sabotage. Every block of houses had watchmen who would watch for German spies who might try to come into Brussels from the sky on gliders, planes without motors, so they could bring in the Fifth Columnists with no noise.

The Fifth Columnists became very famous in the Spanish revolution of 1936, but they also were strong in Belgium, where Degrelle was their leader. They were made up of Germans and also the traitors of the land—the Rexists—and whoever was attached from Holland to the Nazi Party. There was a tremendous amount of sympathy to Hitler in Belgium, mostly among the Flemish, from Flanders, who supported Hitler because they felt oppressed by the Walloons. Degrelle was a Walloon. He supported Hitler because he was a fascist.

In 1940, Degrelle opened the gates of Belgium for Hitler by being in the Fifth Column. He prepared his German friends for their attack by simplifying the crossing into Belgium at certain spots. When the Nazis attacked, the Rexists right away became quislings and joined the *gendarmarie*. Degrelle also fought the Russians on their front. He was wounded in battle and was celebrated as a hero by the Nazis. Hitler said he would have liked to have Degrelle as a son.

After the war, Degrelle changed his nationality and became a Spaniard under General Franco. He is an old man now and living very well in Spain as a citizen. He was condemned to death in absentia in Belgium, but being that what he did happened some fifty years ago, he has now received clemency. That means it's of no value. However, his life is always guarded because many Belgians would love to kill him, even now.

But where I lived before the war, the Walloons and Flemish lived in peace. In Brussels, the school children spoke four hours of French in the morning, two hours of Flemish and two hours of German in the afternoon. The Antwerpers spoke four hours of Flemish, two of French, and two of German. And the people from Eupen-Malmedy would speak four hours of German, two of French, and two of Flemish. The result was we spoke three languages, but we didn't see the difference. If I was in the Flanders, I spoke Flemish; if I was in Liège or Namur, I spoke French; if I was in Brussels, I spoke everything.

We couldn't believe that Hitler would wage a war because we were sure that the Maginot Line would protect us, and with the English on our side we would have nothing to worry about. However, when the newspaper reports became very tragic after Hitler occupied Poland, we began to worry. Belgium had declared neutrality, like Holland and Switzerland in the first world war. We thought that would protect us. We wanted to be neutral. But Hitler had decided differently. The king of Belgium said, "No, I will not allow you to cross the land." But Hitler came anyway.

Passover of 1940 fell in the middle of April. I had always celebrated Passover with my father and my brothers and my sisters in my father's home. Now, having a family of my own, and Avram was already six years old, I had said to my father that I thought it was time I became my own master and made my own Seder. My father listened to me, and then he said, "You know, my son, with the grumbling going on in the world, God knows what will be later on, if we will even have another Seder. Who knows where next year we may be? Let's be together this year."

After more than a decade of being a widower, he had just remarried the year before. Now already he and his wife, Sabin, had a new son, Jacob. Jacob's face was nice and round with a gold-brown color, like he could be from the Mediterranean. He had white, milk-colored teeth and black eyes with black, curly hair. We did not dwell upon the fact that my father was an old man with a young child. I had a little brother and he was the uncle of my children, and my father loved him and Sabin also. His life was falling into place, and so I spoke to my wife and she said, "You know, your father may be right." And so I accepted his proposal of a Seder together.

My sister Sheva wasn't there. She already had moved out from Brussels with her three children, Cecile and Annie and Charles, and her husband Adolph to another borough far away. But my sister Rosa, her two children, Israel and Liliane, and her husband Maurice were there. So were my sister Rebecca, my brother Zourech, whom we called Zulu, my brother Maurice, and my family.

Usually our Sidurim were pleasant. They always started at midnight, according to tradition. At that time my father never skipped any of the Seder. We sang joyful songs and it usually took two and a half to three hours. That Seder was particularly sad because we hoped to be together again for the next Seder but our hearts were not in it. It was not the truth. We were speaking lies to console ourselves.

My father reminded us that, even though we were no longer slaves in Egypt, we did not now feel safe in Belgium. He said that we were together this time, but God knew if next year we would be together. And he said he hoped we would keep up the tradition and remember that we came from a family who believed in following our history and the memories of our people, and we made a promise never to have a Passover without a Seder.

After the Seder, we separated with heavy hearts and returned to our homes with hopes that next year we would see each other again. Unfortunately, it never happened. This was the last Seder I shared with my entire family.

That May first, for the first time in the history of the unions, there was no manifestation because the situation in Belgium and in the world was very tense. We didn't expect to be attacked by the Nazis, but we did not want to provoke them. We were afraid of any kind of manifestation because we knew that in any counter-manifestation we would have to deal with the Rexists and we didn't want that.

The year before, in 1939, we had had parades with red flags and speeches and music playing. We threw bricks; the Rexists threw them back. They had night sticks; we had our belts. I participated. I didn't serve in the International Socialist Organization. I was never in the executive branch of my local. No, I had no leadership role. But I was an activist Socialist Jew. I fought with my belt and my fists. These situations were part of life, and we did not accept events passively. The police were not on the side of the working man then; they already were going to the right, and that was very dangerous.

So on May 1, 1940, instead of a manifestation, we stayed quietly at home. We didn't want to irritate anyone. We didn't want anyone to have an excuse to say, "We had to."

After Mayday was over, I went back to work. As the days passed, we only knew what we read in the papers. The papers said there was grumbling and unhappiness. The Poles were unhappy. Chamberlain had just announced that he was satisfied that Hitler would do nothing and that our neutrality was guaranteed. I was still working with the gloves. I worked until the last moment.

Four weeks after the Seder, on May tenth, the Nazis bombed the airport in Brussels. My daughter Eliane was just one year old then. Her mother had weaned her that night. I had finished my Home Guard duty by 10:00 and I was at home. At 3:30 in the morning, Eliane was in my arms, and I was going around with her trying to give her a bottle.

The day was getting light already. We lived on the high point of Brussels. Suddenly I heard a sound like firecrackers from far away, "Poof, poof." I looked outside our veranda, sticking up from the house, and I could see little silver "flies" far away, like shrapnel from the sun. I couldn't understand. Nobody expected that invasion. So I put on the radio and I learned my country was being attacked by Hitler's army, the Nazis.

I woke up my wife immediately and I explained to her what was happening. Right away, we became extremely disturbed. We didn't know what we should do. I said, "Let's make a valise." In the suitcase, we threw diapers and clothes for the children, a little underwear, a couple of shirts, and a warm jacket. Avram, my son, wasn't at home. When we went swimming one day the summer before, the sun burned one of his lungs and he had a spot on it, a decalcification. Being that Belgium was very conscious of lung diseases, because Queen Elizabeth was a tubercular woman, the health board of the school had sent him right away to a sanitorium far away from Brussels.

In Brussels, we always traveled by trolley car. The sanitorium was only maybe a hundred kilometers from the house, but to get there I had to take four trolley cars. The ride sometimes took two and a half or three hours. In normal times it's a nice ride, but when it's war time and the trolley cars are packed, you don't know when they go and come, so I had to leave immediately.

First I took Eliane to Strauss, my employer. Before the war we had received instructions to prepare our homes against bombarding. I lived in an apartment, in a big house that had not been fortified, but Mr. Strauss lived in a big three hundred-year old house. He had fortified his basement with iron girders to support the ceiling so I figured I'd take Eliane over there.

Chana Laja remained in our house because we were afraid to leave anything alone, while I took Eliane in her crib. Running on the street, I saw a stukka plane flying low and dropping anti-personnel bombs, little bombs that would explode and make a lot of shrapnel, so I would jump from doorway to doorway. By the time I arrived at Strauss' house, many neighbors, terrorized by these events, had begun to gather there. I saw a sadness in the look of the adults. One of them was singing, trying to divert the attention of the children.

I left the little one at the shelter and came back home because it was maybe three minutes from the house. To Chana Laja I said, "It's a good idea. Come, let's go there," and I put her also at the shelter.

In the meantime, the radio was saying that we had received a lot of Fifth Columnists. They came in by train with explosives. We could not have watched everybody coming into the land because the border is long and they snuck in by gliders also. They would fly silently in the air, and land on the roofs dressed as different tradesmen, even as priests. Then they would make sabotage, cut wires, create panic in the land.

Many of the Fifth Columnists were arrested and executed because they were spies in our country and Belgians are tremendous patriots. The people were angry. They didn't even wait for justice. They summarily killed many of the Fifth Columnists, just like that.

When I went to pick up my son in the sanitorium I saw columns of people coming from Luxembourg. One man was pushing a carriage with a dead child that he didn't want to give up because he was hoping the child was asleep. He had walked all the way from Luxembourg to Brussels, maybe 120 kilometers, and columns of refugees were coming into Brussels already. It was terrible. Never since the hordes of Genghis Khan had we hoped to see this.

Later that day, after I had brought Avram back to his mother, I went alone to see my sister Rosa, who lived on the other side of the city with her two children and her husband. Rosa said, "Take care of your family. We all will take care of our families." It was each for himself at that time, and that's it. I never saw her again.

In my family, we did what we could to avoid trouble. We didn't participate in protests. I tried to be anonymous completely. We crouched in doors and slept nights in the basements, and that's all. We had to think fast. Fortunately, we had enough food and we had no personal encounters with Nazis.

Finally, on May 12, I said to Chana Laja, "Do you think we should go?" because I knew they would be coming after me. They didn't come after me because I was a leader, because I wasn't. But I was an activist Jew who belonged to the Socialist Party. I was an orator and a member of the strike action committee; I spoke at meetings as a delegate and I was not afraid. For instance, one year, around 1935 or '36, the government had cut the worker pensions and had cut off the money we usually received to buy milk for our children. I was one of three representatives the workers chose to go see the mayor. The rest of the workers stayed in front of the communal place while I explained to him that we thought it was outrageous that they had cut strike benefits for the working man, and that the milk our children had to drink was like weak, blue, skim milk. I was carrying a bottle of that milk in my bag, and he had a pencil holder on his desk. I pulled it closer to me and poured some milk into it. Then I said, "Would you give this to one of your grandchildren?"

The mayor was an elderly man who knew me as a child, because how many Belgian Jews did you have who would open their mouths? He wasn't Jewish. To them it was *chutzpah*, and right away they knew. So I would defend the working man and the mayor would make promises and then the committee would follow through to see that conditions were improving, and so I had the image of being a speaker for the working man.

In manifestations, I took an active part. I fought against Degrelle's men as a working man, as a Socialist, and as a member of the union. This was 1937, 1938, 1939. So when Hitler attacked us in 1940, I was on Degrelle's blacklist. At home, when someone rang the doorbell we would look through the window to see who it was. We were already scared, and that fear was not allowing us to speak very comfortably even with friends. When we walked on the streets we always looked back to see if anyone was following. We were already suspicious because we had done things that according to the government were now illegal. We showed our dislike, but they like a passive population, people who don't move. I'm sure I was on the blacklist already by 1938, when Degrelle came to power.

Chana Laja said, "Yes, we should go," because she had already seen all the German Jews coming to us and she knew of anti-Semitism, having run away from Poland. We decided together. I was not the type of man who would impose orders. We discussed it, and we both agreed, even though we had no detailed escape plan.

That evening, I took my family to the train station in Brussels so they could escape to Paris, where the authorities had decided all Belgian refugees should go. We functioned without thinking in order not to lose our minds. I had no definite plans for reuniting with my family. First I had to get them to safety. We would see later how to find each other.

The train station was chaos, mayhem. A train car that would take 350 people was packed with seven hundred. At the end of the train was a bathroom for human beings to do their needs, and that bathroom was piled to the ceiling with luggage. People were hanging out the windows and through the doors and doing their needs on the road. If you had a thin body, you snuck in through the window, because on the steps there was no room. I pushed in my children through the windows and told Avram to lay down across three seats so that my wife and Eliane should be able to have seats.

I waited until the train left, and then I went home. Our parting was very sad because we never had been separated until then. Avram started screaming, "Papa!" and I said, "Avram, go with Mama and your sister. You are the man of the family." He said, "But, Papa, you must come with me. The war is going to be there and you are not with us." I didn't go that day because I had to remain in case I had to go to the Belgian army. We had barracks in Brussels. I said, "Don't be afraid. Don't cry. You be the man. You take care of your mother and your sister." And he was six years old.

On the way back home, I stopped to see my employer, Strauss. One of his daughters-in-law, Regina, was expecting a baby. Her husband, Sam, said to me, "Bernard, you cannot remain here because Chana and the children are already gone and you were too active politically and we know what is happening already in Germany."

The next day, May 13, the Belgian army gave orders by radio for all soldiers to go by their own means to the French city of Montpelier, by the French-Italian border, because there they would assemble the army and help the French to fight the Nazis. I went as a Belgian soldier, not as a Jew, because for the Belgian government that did not exist, a Jew. There was never a distinction between Jews and non-Jews in Belgian.

I took the last train out of Brussels. Being that I had to leave, Sam Strauss had asked me, "Please take Regina with you and drop her in Paris. She has uncles there." So I took her with me.

When I left, the city was on alert for airplanes, so I returned to the apartment and in the commotion I grabbed twelve little silver glasses from my Bar Mitzvah, and an alarm clock, my winter coat and hat, three celluloid collars, and a suit, and with this I left. Nothing else. I locked the door and gave the key to a neighbor on the same floor, a non-Jewish person. Then I went to the train station. Later on, after the war, I was told that as soon as I left the neighbors came down and tore my door apart and stole everything. A few hours later, the Belgian Gestapo came looking for me.

At the train station, families were saying their goodbyes; people were crying from sadness and from anxiety.

To get into the train, I had to push that young lady with a heavy abdomen through the window, and I was wondering, I hope she doesn't have the baby. Finally, I placed her in a corner. It was very touching. And the train took off. The weather was balmy when we left, at 10:00 in the morning. I don't know how many cars were attached to the engine, but they were all full.

I was the only member of my family to flee Belgium in the first week of the war. The others remained in place. Six weeks later, my sister Sheva and her family also went to France, but they were sent back to Belgium by the French authorities, who were no longer taking refugees. My father stayed behind because, he said, "What God is going to do with all the Jews, he'll do with us, and you, my son, do what you think you have to do. It's your family." I never saw them again. They were all taken by the Nazis and destroyed.

CHAPTER 7

WE BECOME CHRISTIANS IN VICHY, I'M SUMMONED TO SAINT-LIGUAIRE

Soon after we started riding, the train was detoured because of sabotage. Instead of going directly to the French border, the train had to cross and come back and so on and so forth, and a two-hour trip from Brussels to the French border took eight hours. I shared a cabin with about twenty others, one on top of the other. Children sat in the luggage rack. During most of the trip we huddled together but we remained quiet. Nobody conversed with their neighbor. We were all minding our business because we worried about having spies in our midst. We thought only of saving our lives, of not falling into the hands of any Rexists or anti-Semites.

For food, we all had some bread with us and on unforeseen stops the Belgian Red Cross had set up refreshment stations where we received bread, coffee, milk, and water, and like that we had enough to keep going. The weather for most of the trip was gorgeous, like out of spite, because usually in Belgium in May when we are not in a train all day it rains a lot.

We came to the Belgian-French border at 7 p.m. There, Regina was met by her mother-in-law and her children, who took her to Paris. I was told I could not go to Paris because they were turning away refugees, so I got down off the train to walk around, and who do I see? My wife and the children! They were staying in a farmhouse, near the border station.

Because Chana Laja was from Poland and was only Belgian by marriage, the French border police refused her the right to cross into France and go to Paris like she had wanted. Avram was bewildered. What was happening? Yesterday he was in a sanitorium where they were taking care of him like a mascot, and now he was here where there was no food and not even a bed to sleep in. He was ecstatic when he saw me. Papa was there and everything was going to be well. But Eliane was drinking milk cut with unboiled water because there was nothing else. Being that she had just been weaned a few days before, she had gotten entritis, inflammation of the bowels, and she was very sick. There was nobody to help because of the chaos.

Because I am a person of action, I don't stay in one place. If I cannot get what I need here, I'll go over there. I did what I had to do. We calmed the little one—she had diarrhea and all that baby stuff—and then I cleared up Chana Laja's problem with the border police. When they understood that she was the wife and mother of Belgian citizens, they allowed her to cross the French border with us and the other Belgian refugees.

Instead of getting off in Paris, though, we took a train to Vichy, where the government had decided we should go. Chana Laja had wanted to go to Paris because she had living there a brother-in-law in the French army and two older sisters. Unfortunately, although the train stopped in Paris, no Belgian refugees were permitted to disembark. When we arrived, my brother-in-law, Maurice, was on the platform of the station to meet us, dressed in his French uniform. He was proud of that uniform because he was proud of the defense of the Maginot Line, and he was on furlough for a few days so he came to look for us. With him were my two sisters-in-law, Topje and Brandel. But we couldn't get off the train, so we kissed and hugged through the window and said we'd write to each other.

Our train left and we crossed L'Allier, the river that separates the southern part of France from the northern part. On the other side, we were happy to see the French flag, which we didn't see in the north because the Germans were already progressing. By this time we were very tired. Then we came to Vichy.

Vichy was like a small New York when I was there, an elegant city on the edges of the river L'Allier. Before the war, Vichy was a spot for wealthy nobilities and kings of the universe. Kings from Egypt, kings from Rumania, all the kings came there to rest and drink from the healthy waters to detoxify their livers from the good libations they had during the year. France was very xenophobic then. They disliked every stranger, even if he came only five miles from another village. But in Vichy, the people were more sympathetic to strangers because they lived with a lot of folks of different nationalities. In season, Vichy had 200,000 to 300,000 people; off season, there were 10,000. In May, Vichy was not in season yet so they opened up their arms to us and we had a good reception. Later, when we learned our king had abdicated on May 28, we received a lot of sympathy. They did nothing to discourage us or insult us. On the contrary, a lot of them were sympathetic and pitied us because of the behavior of the king, even though under the circumstances he could not have behaved differently.

So when we arrived in Vichy we were taken to Concour Hippique, the racetrack. Being that we were a family of four, we were given a clean, private stable with straw. In the halls of the racetrack they put long tables and they served us very well: wine, cheese, milk, bread. They treated us like brothers; the Belgian was the brother of the French.

Nevertheless, I was a Jew as well as a Belgian. I was not aware then of the concentration camps and the campaign of extermination against the Jews. But I knew from the refugees who came to Belgium that by remaining Jewish who knew the fate I would follow? So I figured, let me be positive and not negative.

On our third day in Vichy, while having our meals, when they came out asking, "Those of Hebraic conviction, please take care to tell us so that we can feed you kosher food," we decided altogether that it was each for his own and I decided that we could no longer be Jews. I said to Chana Laja, "We are Protestants" and she followed my lead. There was no discussion. That was the only way we would not have to look over our shoulders all the time. Of course, we were in danger of being found out by security police, but in that way we were no different than any other Belgian refugees.

There were maybe twenty or thirty other Jewish families there at the time; I don't know how many made the same decision. Afterward, I lost contact with them completely. And I was a "Christian" through the whole war.

Avram was six years old but he was no child. He was more like a young juvenile. I sat him down and I explained to him that it's war, the Nazis are hunting the Jews, and he should now behave as a Christian. Being that he was young, I knew he could be forgiven for not knowing exactly if he was a Catholic or a Protestant. But, I told him, "You are no longer a Jew, and that's all." I explained to him his circumcision by telling him that when he was three years old he was operated on. And, I said, "Your name is not Avram now, but Armand." And that's the way it stuck. He took it and he never flinched. He was six years old, and it was sad to see the seriousness of that child at that moment. He had no youth. He had no childhood years. And that's what I attribute his seriousness to today. Oh, he is anti-fascist absolutely. He is a very liberal person.

Eliane was just one year old. Her name we took from Belgian folklore. When she was born we had a lot of Gentile friends, and their daughters had names like Christiane and Eliane. We loved Christiane but it was very un-Jewish, so we went to Eliane, which was from the prophet Eli. Later on, she added to Eliane Denise, which is a typical French girl's name. Yvette is called Yvette Rollande, which is a typical Belgian name, although she was named in France. Chana and Laja were both common names so we didn't have to change either. In fact, when we were living in Volvic later, we found out that there was a village called Laja and a forest called Shana, so it was not strange to hear those names. Because she had an accent, I told people she was from the Flemish region, and most of the time I spoke for us both, and we managed. My name, Bernard, was not typically Jewish. The name was a translation from Boris, who was the uncle of one of my parents. My Hebrew name was Dov, or Ber.

After a few days, more and more Belgians came. Soon there were 15,000 to 20,000 of us. Every day the call for help would come in over the loudspeaker, that they needed a tailor, a baker, a shoemaker, and I was holding out because nothing came in my profession, until one day, a week after I became a Christian, I heard, "We need a butter and cheese man." I figured butter and cheese, it's war time, it's hard to get food, and I would like to get out from the horse stable. Also, I had decided to be positive. Never say no. If you needed a tailor, I was a tailor. You needed a cheese maker? I was a cheese maker. I had a good memory, and I was a good observer. Teach me and I learn. So I went to the office and said, "Yes, I am good at making dairy products."

Although our profession was written on our identity papers, nobody had time or the mind to look at the papers, so they accepted your word. If you could produce, they didn't care if you held the title of the job they were looking for. So they sent me to the owner of the cheese and butter factory.

I saw when I arrived that on one side was a store and on the other side was the plant. I met the owner in his store. I came in and I said to the man, "It's nice." The man said, "Where are you from?" I said I was from the borough of Brussels, and my father and mother were in the cheese and milk business. However, I said, "Being that we are from two different countries, everybody has his way of doing things. You show me your way." You don't have to have a Ph.D. to work. Just put your mind to it. He said, "Good."

However, I said," I've got a question. Why do you want me?"

He said, "I had to give up my other man." I asked what he had done wrong. "Oh," he said, "he worked for me for many years. He was stealing butter. Every day he took a half pound of butter. Now that we need it, there's an influx of people, I cannot afford for him to steal."

I said, "With me you can be sure I will not steal." Then he showed me around. In the store he had two young ladies and in the plant he had a lady and a man who manipulated the milk. As he took me through the plant he was wearing high boots and a little shirt to not get wet because he was always walking in warm water; very hot water was used to clean the cheese mold, and to wash the machinery and the milk cans so they were clean for the next collection of milk from the farmer.

The next day, at 3:30 in the morning, I started working.

Working with me was a Dutch girl. That was the first time in my life I saw a lady wearing slacks. I never saw it before. She could swing a can of milk like nothing, and she would collect the milk in a certain region of the mountains from midnight until 6 in the morning. Then she would bring it to the dairy plant and we would put it on a platform. There I would open all the cans and go through them extremely quickly with a scoop measure to measure the milk and test it.

To test it, I used a special rennet-like chemical called *pressur* that we got from the Scandinavian countries and Holland. *Pressur* is the lining of stomachs of calves, dehydrated and pulverized and sterilized, of course. I would put a drop of that chemical in a spoon of milk; if the milk turned red, we knew the cattle were not contaminated with anything and the milk would be fit for human consumption. If the milk remained white, I would make butter and cheese out of it.

On a long table covered with straw mats were rows of long aluminum molds. After I put the rennet in the milk, the milk would gel. Then, with a scoop, I would fill the molds with the gelled milk. Whenever I shook the table, the liquid at the top of the molds would spill over and run off into drums. I would push vats on wheels across the length of the table and collect the liquid for the farmers, as skim milk to feed their pigs.

From the molds I made the cheese. It was a very rich product. First I had to wait a few days for it to dry. Then I would add more milk and let it dry again. Then I would salt it, let it stay, turn it over, salt it again. On the third salting, I would put it in closets, closing it up on clays so mice would not contaminate it or flies touch it, and I would let it dry and ripen. When the cheese was ripe, I would roll it in paper and put it in the store for sale.

The finished product was magnificent, so I gave myself maybe eight ounces of cheese and a loaf of French bread—this was 3:30 in the morning, mind you—and a bottle of wine, because this was a wine region and we had many bottles in the store, and I could have all the cream I wanted.

The name of the cheese was Saint Chevremont. Saint Chevremont was a cheese that you could compare today to a Brie, very tasty, schmaltzy. We also made cottage cheese and ricotta cheese, but that was the only kind of hard cheese we made because it was going like hotcakes. We didn't have enough. Don't forget, from a city of 10,000 to 15,000, suddenly there are 200,000 families. Not only Belgians came; they came from all over France. And we didn't have distribution until we installed it ourselves. You couldn't get more than a half a pound of butter a day. If you wanted more you would come back the next day and get another half pound. Butter was very rare.

From my nature I was a butter lover, but I didn't steal it like the old Frenchman who came before me. I would eat butter from the churner while I was making it. I would pour heavy cream in and let it churn. After awhile the butter would solidify, and I would put in carotene to color it yellow. The butter came out nice and golden. Delicious! Every time I had to taste it, I would take a small amount on the tip of my fingers like maybe two spoons of butter. And if you take enough two spoons of butter during the day, your half a pound is very easily swallowed. Plus you swallow a little heavy sweet cream and a glass of milk and a couple of cheeses. So I would say that during the day I must have had my three thousand calories on cheese alone. No wonder I have a cholesterol problem today.

But I satisfied the owner because I worked very hard from 3:30 in the morning until 5:00 in the evening, and I was able to take what I needed for the family. During the day, my son would come in and buy his cream or milk, which we put in a metal can. And he would buy a half a loaf of the long French bread and, for his sister Eliane, who of course was a baby, little cookies.

Then one day the girls in the store gave me an idea. They said, "You know what? Why don't you fill his can with heavy sweet cream, and then we will cover it with cottage cheese." After that, Armand would buy a can of "cottage cheese" for twenty-five cents. Actually it was all heavy sweet cream left to be made into butter. I didn't steal it; I just took it. I paid up front. Then, when I got home late at night, I would beat it up with an egg beater and make butter. So it was white. Who cares? My children had all the butter they could eat because I was there. And like this I fed my family.

And so we adjusted. No, you don't adjust; you roll with the punches. If you sleep on straw that is uncomfortable, you take another pile and you make it comfortable. And an adult, if you don't sleep, it's *nich ge fehrlecht*, not terrible. I think from the sight of the war I learned not to sleep long at night. Four hours rest is plenty, and five hours is a nice sleep. Still today, that's how I sleep.

Being Gentile gave us some security that we did not have as Jews. We adjusted to it easily because we didn't speak of it and others took it for granted.

We received from the refugee organization a room in a hotel, Source de L'Hospital, because we were a family of four and I had a job. The lady who owned the hotel was an old French aristocrat. She was most generous and she received us with open arms. She knew the sorrow of what it means to run away from home. One night, I came home from work and I was exhausted. She saw me come in and she said to me, "Let me do something to perk you up." At that time they were still drinking real absinthe, alcohol that is forbidden now in France because it destroys human beings. She gave me a glass. I never drank it before and I was thirsty. I drank it and it hit me like an electric shock and I barely made it, crawling on my four limbs, to the second floor. I rolled over and I don't remember anything after that. That was the kindness of her. She would bring the children little dishes, little desserts. She always had a good word: the war will be over soon; everything will be all right.

Twice a day, Chana had to visit the huge kitchens at the race track, where she would receive our food rations. I saw my family very little, leaving for work early in the morning and going to sleep soon after dinner.

And every day Armand would come for his butter—they never missed it—until I was working there about six weeks. Now we are coming to the end of July; we received the sad news finally, because we had no radio or newspaper, that the king of Belgium had abdicated six weeks earlier, on May 28. King Leopold III was a paternalistic king for the country. His first wife, Queen Astrid, was liked by the Belgians because she was a gentle lady from Sweden. After she was killed mysteriously in Switzerland in 1935 in an auto accident, Leopold married a commoner whose father was a Nazi sympathizer, but the king was still popular.

I remember as a child his father came out to Brussels in 1918, when he came back from four years of exile in England, and he visited our schools to thank us for our patriotism, and we were proud like everything. I was only eight years old or so, and to see the king, it was something. There is a legend among the Jews that if you see a king you will live seven years longer in your life. So, if you are entitled to live to a hundred you will live to 107. I will always remember that I came home and said to my mother, "We saw the king," and mother said, "You're gonna live seven years longer in your life." So now I'm living my seven years.

When Leopold abdicated, among the Belgian population in Vichy it became like a funeral, and we thought the king was a traitor. We had manifestations protesting the king's behavior. One day, thirty or forty Belgian refugees gathered in the center of Vichy in front of a monument to Belgians killed in the first world war. The crowd swelled to a couple hundred and then they paraded around the monument waving Belgian and French flags. I was unable to attend because I was at work at the time, but I saw it pass our plant. Of course, I would have attended if I could have. I was a Belgian!

But who walked in his shoes? He had been told by the Belgian government, when they went to London, "Come with us." But he had said no, he wanted to stay with the people, because we had already lost all our men to a stronger Nazi army. Later, Hitler made a deal. Leopold must surrender to the Nazis and then Hitler would let the people alone, and that's it. Hitler said he would cross quickly, and later on, after the war, pay the Belgian government for usage of the road and for the damage he would create. This was a unilateral deal he made with King Leopold two weeks after the war started, on May 28.

Later on, history showed that Leopold did the right thing. He didn't want to give in but he had no alternative to save the life of the Belgian army. He had a knife on his throat. He didn't bargain for anything because there was nothing to bargain for. Hitler was strong and certain, having traitors, quislings, in every land of Europe. Leon Degrelle was a quisling, so Leopold became a prisoner in his own castle, and Degrelle, the Rexist, took over the government. But Leopold saved the Belgian population from domination by the Nazis, who had no heart whatsoever. They had no pity.

In the meantime, I received a summons from the French government that I had to present myself in Saint-Liguaire, near Niort in the state of Sèvres, about 600 kilometers from Vichy, and that's where I was supposed to work in a chamois factory making a certain type of glove for the manipulation of ammunition and all kinds of other implements. On the summons was stamped e"Secret." I took the document—I had no alternative. I had to follow orders. I was a soldier. I said goodbye to my wife and children. Armand fell into conniptions and he had spasms and said, "Papa, Papa, don't go away." But I had no alternative.

The moment I was ready to leave the house there was an alert. The sirens started blowing all over Vichy. Some English from the Royal Air Force had come to bomb Vichy because there was a concentration of Germans already. The Germans had come to establish their authority over the free zone of France. Finally I tore myself away and went to the train station. I had free passage, of course, to go to Saint-Liguaire.

CHAPTER 8

I RISK MY NECK TO MAKE LADIES' EIGHT-BUTTON GLOVES IN SAINT-LIGUAIRE

The train to Saint-Liguaire was filled to twice the normal capacity with fellows from all walks of life: refugees, soldiers, regular travelers. But nobody knew anybody else or what was going on, because in a war you don't talk too much, not knowing with whom you talk, and this was wartime. We were given the means to travel; that is all. We had to bring along something to eat. But that wasn't the worst part. The trip, which should have taken five or six hours, took me fifty-five hours.

Usually there is a straight line going from one town to another. The Frenchmen are very smart. They cut corners. They try to avoid roundabouts and mountains so they had made straight lines and express trains that could make eight hundred miles in four hours. But because of the war and bringing back wounded from different battle stations, our train was hindered. We rolled it on side tracks, and we had to allow trains coming from the front to bypass us. Then there was an alert: We had to jump from the train because planes were going by and we didn't know whose they were. They didn't do anything, but in the meantime we lost time.

Then we made a detour that took us to Angers en Touraine. Angers is called the Garden of the French language because there is where they speak the most beautiful and elegant French in all humanity. The train stopped there and, knowing I had to be in Saint-Liguaire on government orders, I got off the train and started looking for another means of transportation. I found nothing. Fortunately, after a couple hours, as we were milling around trying to find out what was going on, my train started moving. This was the only train going to Saint-Liguaire and I had a paper with "Secret" written on it. God knows what a "Secret" was. A "Secret" was I had a job, so I ran and I jumped on the train and I caught it.

Finally I arrived in Niort, which is the big city to Saint-Liguaire, in the state of Sèvres. I arrived in the evening to find I was in the center of a reunion of thousands of refugees from Normandy, and from all around the Parisian Region, where the Nazis were approaching rapidly. They came, complete households, with huge horse-drawn wagons, and the government of Niort had put up huge tents to give hospitality. But I had followed my principle never to look like a derelict. I always tried to look like a banker, an old habit of mine, at least in the older days.

So, as I was coming down from the train, wearing my one suit and my one tie, they told me they were going to give me room to sleep in a tent. "Excuse me," I said, "I need an executive." So a higher level officer came. I took out the blue paper from my pocket and on the paper in the corner in neat letters was written "Secret." "You see that document?" I said. "It does not allow me to be with anybody, and I must go to Saint-Liguaire immediately."

"Oh, that's something else," he said. "I'll place you with an inhabitant." He made a few phone calls and I was sent to a home in an old part of Niort. That home had no telephone, so to reach them the officer called the post office, and from there a messenger was sent.

The owner was a lady with a grocery store and a daughter. The lady must have been in her forties and the daughter in her twenties, and they were so glad to finally have a man in the house. They hadn't had a man in the house for two years because the French army took away the husband.

I told them I was a Belgian and I had family and I was going to Saint-Liguaire to work in the factory. They treated me royally. They gave me a room to sleep. In the room, the wallpaper was all flowers and colors; miniature paintings hung on the wall. Picture for yourself a room from the seventeenth century. The bed was like a virginal bed, piled high with goose feathers and covered with pink sheets. To relieve themselves they used a chamber pot instead of a toilet. We from the big city weren't used to using chamber pots, so I felt a little embarrassed. How could you leave all your waste in the house? But to them it was natural. In the country of any city they live a more natural life because they see nature in action. In America, when you see two dogs jumping each other, here is the ho's and ha's. But over there, in Europe, you take a goat or a rabbit to get inseminated and you wait until the mate is finished, so you see what goes on. Everybody there was a midwife, everybody knew the facts of life, and it was pure. There was no hypocrisy.

That night I thought of my family: my wife, my children. I was frightened for them and for me, and I was wondering what tomorrow was going to bring. As I was wondering, I could see little mice climbing up and down, and up and down. The store was a grocery, but there was no cat, and I was figuring, my heaven, I have only one little suitcase to keep my clothes in. I was afraid tomorrow in the morning I wouldn't have anything in my bag.

I woke up early the next morning. When I came down, the lady and her daughter were already there. They had prepared a great breakfast, just what I needed. Food was to me the morale builder. Jewish tradition. "Eat, my child." So I ate. Then they showed me the road how to go to Saint-Liguaire.

After saying goodbye to those good people, I began my walk, which was about ten kilometers, six miles roughly. Being the month of July, it was already hot. I had on my heavy coat, but I was wearing sandals. As I walked I was saying to myself, the road is not wide but, my God, is it long. But I kept walking. There were no cars, there was nothing. Suddenly I heard the rumble of a machine, and I took myself to the side of the road. Along came a heavy truck. The truck stopped, I looked, and I saw the truck had solid rubber tires but no springs, and it smelled terrible. It was coming from a tannery loaded with sheepskins to go to the plant where I wanted to go, so the driver was glad to give me a ride, and I was glad to receive it, but it took me awhile to become accustomed to the odor.

As we rode, he explained to me how from sheepskin they make chamois skin by treating it in seventy-two large drums each the size of a room. They throw 1,200 skins into each drum; then they throw the drums into a big vat that contains a thousand gallons of herring oil imported from Great Britain or Denmark. Wood hammers inside the drums bang the skins and the oil penetrates the skins. After sixty hours, the skins are hung in the air and covered so the sun won't hit them. When a skin is dry, they take it into the factory and the working people stretch it on a special kind of knife with both hands, pulling it up and down, up and down.

I knew how to cut the skins in two because I was a specialist in splitting skins. You have a knife eight inches wide, twelve inches long with a handle, and you hold that handle in your palm. Then you hold the skin on the blade, and the other side of the skin, the fur, you press against the marble. Then you lift up the marble and pull the ends of the skin real tight between the table and the marble, and you take the knife and you scive, piece after piece, until you remove all veins of the flesh of the animal, leaving only the skin, the beautiful skin, nice and soft, that you see in kids' shoes. The skin is actually about a quarter-inch thick, but after you finish sciving it's half of that, an eighth of an inch, and very soft.

But what did I make? Later on, I worked with the fellows on the bench making special gloves with a double thickness of leather which were used to manipulate explosives. But first they asked me to make ladies' eight-button gloves, long evening gloves. I said, "Is this the work? I came to make ladies' gloves?"

Well, they explained they had orders for America that they wanted to fulfill before the ships stopped traveling. I was outraged, but who was I to speak? It was an order from the government. So the owner said to me, "They're crazy. I don't need anyone." I said, "Look, I just came away from my wife and children. I had to risk my neck in trains with bombing in different cities with all kinds of problems, and you're going to tell me to go back?"

All right, he was a compassionate man. He said, "Stay and work." The fellows in the shop were very happy to receive me, and they admired my dexterity and my knowledge of the leather.

The whole village of Saint-Liguaire was about 3,000 people. Because the land was divided by rivers, it was called the Venice of Vendée, which is a state near Niort. On the river were barges where they sold groceries and baked goods and where they transported cattle from one grazing field to another. In the ponds they would raise trout and other fish that were used to seed the lakes and ponds belonging to the French government all the way up to Paris. Fish raised in Saint-Liguaire would fill the ponds of Versailles and the reservoirs of Fontainebleau. The ponds were like swimming pools with their fishlets.

During the war the employees of the fishing department were unable to collect the fish to distribute them, but the fish still grew. One day going to the factory I saw some fish swimming. I had a desire for a trout so with my full strength I threw pebbles in the water and two fish came up belly up. I grabbed them and I rolled them in my handkerchief and took them with me to the factory. The fellows laughed, but one of them took it home with him at lunch time. His wife made a matelote, cooked it in white wine. Exquisite. A French dish.

The people were very friendly. Whole families were involved with that factory. The husbands worked in the factory while the women remained at home, working with the cattle on the grazing land and sewing the gloves by hand.

For relaxation you went swimming with the fish. I was amazed seeing the behavior of those lucky people. They were gentle. They didn't grow their own wine so they had to buy it. There is a difference between when you must buy wine and when you make your own. When you spend money, you buy two liters a week. Maybe four. When you make your own, you have a barrel a day. For every collection of grapes, for every crop, you put away barrels, one for the wedding of this child and one for the wedding of that child, one for the birth of that child, and you have a collection of barrels that you touch only on special occasions. When the war was finished and I was living in Volvic, those barrels started getting opened. The people of Volvic had a different mental attitude. They saw everything in pink.

But in the community of Saint-Liguaire, we drank wine, but not wine we made ourselves. So, because they had to buy it, there was less libation and less drinking. But in those days I didn't analyze where they were coming from or why they were as they were. I have always enjoyed living as best I can in any circumstance. My co-workers were very helpful and sympathetic to me, being away from my family. Practically every night I ate dinner with another fellow, so I didn't have to worry for my dinners.

I lived near a family named Duval. Louis and his wife, Marie, were both in their forties. They were generous to me, and Marie took me under her wing. She would make lunch for me when she made lunch for Louis. I felt comfortable with them.

One day I was invited to visit one of their children who lived on a little island. We went by barge pulled by a mule on the canal, like in the old days. That evening we went swimming under a waterfall. The fish were jumping all around us. When it came time for me to leave, we were extremely emotional. We said "Adieu."

The mayor of the village was the owner of the factory where I worked and of practically the whole village as well. He had a paternalistic attitude toward all the people. When a child was born, he was the godfather; when somebody was getting married he would bring a nice gift. He rented the houses. And he was gentle and understanding. He wasn't angry at me for being there; he was angry at the government for sending me there. Why did they send people to work for him? Maybe five years ago he needed somebody to work, he said. But like every government, there was always tremendous disorganization in the French government. Now there was real panic in the government also, and many directives made no sense, but we the little people had to follow orders.

Being that I was a reservist sent by the government, City Hall gave me lodging in an old round castle. In that castle was a tower that had immense rooms that were roped off in five-sided, pie-shaped quarters to give many refugees a place to live. I received one of those quarters because I was expecting my wife and two children. I was entitled to two bundles of straw, and I received two kilos of sugar and a box of candles. I also received a hygienic pail because there were no facilities. The pail had a wide rim on which a person could sit to do his needs. When you were finished, you emptied it in the fields, where it was used as human fertilizer. I also received blankets and two sheets, made from pure handwoven linen, that felt like rough burlap. This was all provided by the mayor of the city of Saint-Liguaire.

I took that room and arranged it, and I went to work every day, and every day I saw refugees who were passing through on their way to Paris or beyond. They came from all over the Parisian region and also from other states—Normandy, Vendée, Sèvres. They were bewildered, tired, disoriented. Their only aim was to run away. It was heartbreaking! Luckily, it was a hot summer, so people slept where there was room. The city of Saint-Liguaire had organized as best it could and the villagers were helpful.

And I was hoping that one day my family would join me. Of course I had heard that they were on the way because I had received by miracle a letter from Chana Laja.

In the letter, she told me that, while they were waiting for their permit to join me to arrive, the hotel manager, a compassionate lady who loved the children, had allowed them to move into the maid's room in the attic. The floor was made of mahogany that was as shiny as metal. When I was with my family, whenever I bought salad oil, if I had nowhere to put it I put it in a basin. While I was away, Chana Laja did the same thing. One day while I was in Saint-Liguaire, Chana Laja had to go get the daily food in the cantine, so Armand remained with Eliane in the room. While Chana Laja was gone, Eliane made in her pants. Armand, thinking the oil was water, rinsed her diaper in the oil. When he put it on the floor it made a tremendous spot, and oil on mahogany spreads like wildfire.

When Chana Laja came back she said it was a catastrophe. She went down to the landlady but the landlady said, "Don't worry. What will I do if a bomb falls and destroys everything? This is only a spot." Remember, I was told that; I didn't see it.

But she remained there, with a group of Belgian and French refugees, and she did okay in the sense that it was a home. She remained in the attic for four weeks and then she received free tickets to join me in Saint-Liguaire. At least this is what she told me in her letter, but I waited and waited and no one came. Then, one day going to work I saw a lady with two suitcases.

We were always speaking very friendly one to the other in Saint-Liguaire, like a large family. We asked even strangers, "From where did you come? Did you see anything? Are the Germans far away?" So the lady says she's a school teacher from Paris. She was on her way to Normandy when she learned the Germans were coming to Normandy also, so now she was going back to Paris, and Niort was on the way. She was tired, but she didn't know where to sleep. I explained to her that I was waiting for my family and I hadn't heard anything from them. "If you want to," I said, "in all honor, I can share with you what I have. I have a room, I have straw, and if you wish you can share it with me."

"Oh," she said, "so generous, so nice," and so on.

I said I had to go to work but at night I would meet her. I told her where to go, and to wait for me there. She went and she waited. I came in that evening and said to her, "Here we are."

She said to me, "Listen, you are a man; I am a woman. Are we going to sleep in the same spot?"

I said, "Madame, listen. You are not in my mind, not in my thoughts, not in my desires. You don't want to sleep, don't sleep. You want to sleep, you are welcome." How old do you think that woman was? She was eighty-four years old, and still afraid for her virginity. I was impatient the rest of the night. It's a good thing she left the following day.

The fellows were very kind to me all the time I was in Saint-Liguaire but still I wondered what I was doing there. I didn't see myself doing anything for the war making gloves for ladies to go to the opera in New York. But I had no alternative. The man was paying me.

Then one day we heard that the Nazis were advancing from Normandy and weren't far away. We already saw smoke from the reservoirs of gasoline that they had torn up or that the Resistance had sabotaged and started burning. My employer said, "Bernard, you will have to make plans to go back where you come from because I'm going to close the plant. I don't have any more raw material." I said, "Thank goodness for that. Let me go back to my family."

In the meantime, I received a letter—I don't remember how that letter came into my possession—from my two sisters-in-law and my nephew who lived in Paris in Monmartre, where they were well known. With about thirty other Jewish people, who lived in the same courtyard, and a man who was a mover with a wife and two children, they had left Paris in a huge truck because they were afraid of the Nazis. And they came to Mairie Bousaix.

CHAPTER 9

"*SEIG HEIL*, I'M A BELGIAN AND I'M PROUD OF YOU"

I was leaving Saint-Liguaire for Mairie Bousaix, which was sixty miles from where I was, along the way to Vichy. Like always when I went on a long journey, I hid in shacks during the day and walked at night in order to not get caught by the French police or the German Gestapo.

I made lots of friends along the way—three friends, four friends, it was always a few—and with them I would make exchanges. I had sugar, they had sardines; I had candles, they had tobacco. We were friendly, we always exchanged food, but we told few stories and we never exchanged names. I called those men, "Hey, my friend." We were afraid to become too friendly with anybody. First of all, you were suspicious of everybody. Second, you were afraid to become too attached because you would have a short encounter and maybe not see them again, and that's all. After a while, they would take a different direction and others would join you on the road. It was a moment of panic, and misery loves company, and we were in the same boat. We were all trying to escape being caught by the Nazis or the French collaborators. Most knew their way in the night, having lived for a long time in that region, so we walked from sundown until we were tired and then we would find a place to rest.

One night, a summer storm kept us in a stable where a farmer had hidden his goats, so afraid was he that somebody should take them. I was starving because I couldn't live on sugar and sardines were so rare I wanted to save them for the children, so I grabbed a goat and I took its udder and squeezed. Then I washed from it the dirt and the feces and the urine and I took it in my mouth and suckled it like it was a breast, and I filled myself with milk. Many fellows did the same thing, but we had a taste in our mouths later on—let me tell you it was not pleasant. However, we were hungry and that was one of our adventures.

I remember another adventure. We stopped in a store on the road one evening and we asked the woman what she had to sell. She said she had some apple cider, so we bought a bottle apiece. As we opened it the whole doggone thing spurted out; it was fermented cider. We were glad we didn't drink it; we would have been made drunk by it, and because of the danger we could not afford to be drunk.

So anyway, such were the adventures on the road. As always, I was walking in open sandals. I had no stockings, my toes were bleeding from the pebbles on the road, the heat and the aggravation and everything combined together so that I didn't realize how horrendous it was, and I didn't know if I should be thankful that I was alive or cry that I had such a lousy destiny. For me it was worse than for the others because I was Jewish and nobody knew it. And in this manner, trusting the fellows to know where they were going, I think it took nine days, and I came to Bousaix, where my sisters-in-law and nephew were hiding out.

When I came to the outskirts of Bousaix, as I was walking on the road, I heard lively voices but I could not understand what they were saying. I looked very discreetly and saw young German soldiers, half naked, all naked, bathing in water that was hot. It was now the beginning of August or maybe the middle of August. I lost dates, and, of course, I wasn't thinking of keeping records. I just wanted to see my family again, but I wanted to stop in Bousaix to see my sisters-in-law first.

Finally I arrived in the middle of a main road where a truck was following me, so I stopped him. The driver picked me up but as we drove he told me the town was infested with Nazis, and he wondered what I was doing there. When I told him I was trying to find my sisters-in-law and nephew, he said okay, and thus I came in to the beginning of Bousaix. He had to go one way, I another, so he let me off and continued.

As I got out of the truck, my nephew David was wandering around aimlessly nearby, and so by coincidence he was there to greet me. With tears in his eyes, he told me that they had left Paris with a Mr. Sandler, who was the owner of a huge eight-double-wheel moving truck. Unfortunately, only the outside wheels were in good shape. The inside wheels were all flat, and they had just barely enough gasoline to keep going.

My nephew took me to the farmhouse where I found my sisters-in-law. With them were thirty people: elderly ladies, newborn children, young women, Mr. Sandler and his son Albert, Albert's wife and daughter, David's mother Teresa, whom we called Topje in Jewish, and Topje's sister Bertha, or Brandel.

I asked them, "What's happening? How come you are here?"

David said, "We were running away from the Germans but that's all the gasoline we had, and now we don't know what to do. These farmers are exploiting us because we're refugees. They are bad people. I am working hard in the kitchen, feeding all the people, and mother is working like a slave, and Aunt Brandel is transforming clothes as a seamstress, and there is no way of getting out."

"Oh," I said, "there is a way. Don't worry." Because they spoke French with an accent, those farmers were taking advantage of my family, knowing they were Jews. So I went to those people and I said, "As of tonight we are leaving, and that's it. We are going back to Paris. There are orders to go."

They said nothing. They were, I suppose, intimidated by my bitter outlook because I was very angry. I was an angry man. So we prepared the truck and whatever food we could buy from the farmer we did. Then we brought the food and the milk and cheese and butter, and we took the road to Saumur, where we were supposed to get gasoline.

Along the way, to conserve gasoline, when we were going downhill we would cut the engine and coast until we would be moving really slowly going up the next rise. Then we would put on the brakes and place stones or blocks of wood underneath the wheels to prevent the truck from sliding backwards. I was standing on the side of the truck, ready to jump when the brakes were put on, and on the other side of the truck was Mr. Sandler. Then Mr. Sandler would turn on the engine and we would travel the rest of the mountain. On top of the next mountain, we would cut the gas again. And like this we cruised along until we found gasoline. And so we arrived in Saumur.

Saumur was an historical city where there was a military school. That city was built under Napoleon Bonaparte—not built but, I mean, embellished. Military schools were begun then through his effort, and to be a graduate of the school of Saint Cyr was a big honor, like being from West Point in America. But the Nazis had torn down their gorgeous antiques like tapestries and paintings, and they had defecated on marvelous woodworks. They made a mess.

When we arrived, we saw a long line of cars full of refugees from all directions around Paris, and big cars and trucks and large families and single families. So I said to Mr. Sandler, "Let's take the containers and go see about gasoline." As we walked, other refugees greeted us. We greeted them back. They asked where we were from, we asked where they were from, and we arrived near the pump.

The pump was guarded by German soldiers and Belgium Gestapo agents. They were wearing their brassards, their armbands, so I went up to them and I said, "*Seig Heil.* I'm a Belgian, and I'm proud to see that you are here defending us on the French front. I would like some gasoline because we are on our way to Paris and my wife and children are in Vichy, and I have to go from Paris to Vichy to pick them up."

"Well," they said, "you know what? Don't you get gasoline tonight. First of all, we aren't giving it anymore tonight, but also our gasoline has been tainted with water. You come tomorrow, at 4:00 in the morning, and we'll have fresh gasoline and food, special provisions, for the refugees."

See, the Nazis were interested in keeping people off the roads and back in the cities to keep the roads open for military traffic. We didn't need to show any I.D. They trusted us. There was much confusion anyhow, and if I did show them my documents, I would have showed them my Belgian identity card because I had nothing else there. The only thing was my mother's name and it was erased, like a smudge, so you couldn't read it. Naturally I did that on purpose because that name was of Jewish consonance: Lanzman. My father's name didn't mean a doggone thing: Mednicki could be Italian, Rumanian, anything, but not particularly Jewish. And I didn't have the Jewish appearance. I was bland. I looked like a plain person. The Jew often has the characteristic of special intelligence, a special outlook, brilliant eyes, richness of lips, wider nose. Not that I have a small one, but I wasn't a typical picture of the Jew made by Hitler, and that's what counted.

That fellow, being proud that I was a Belgian going back to Belgium via Paris and Vichy, picking up my wife and my kids, said to me to come back in the morning. As I was walking away, I saw people going along the wall on the other side of the street, sneaking into a small door in a café, and I knew something was happening. Otherwise, why should people disappear very quietly? So, looking like a Frenchman with my beret and jacket and everything else, I snuck myself into the door. As I came into the café I saw mountains of bread and butter and coffee on the table, and people were eating all they wanted for a fixed price. Well, I satisfied myself first, and then I sent in David and Mr. Sandler. Then I sent Albert with Teresa and Brandel, then women one right after the other. By 11:30 at night everybody from the truck was fed.

Afterwards they slept in the truck because I didn't want them to sleep in the hotel or the castle that the authorities had prepared for the refugees. I told them, "Please be very quiet with the children. Don't let anybody cry. Our lives are at stake. Nobody knows we are Jewish." Anti-Semitism was very strong then.

All night I walked around guarding the truck to see that no stranger would try to steal anything. Stealing was tremendous. They could unscrew your wheels and steal the motor before your eyes. Mr. Sandler stayed up with me, so I walked one way and he walked another, and nothing happened.

At 4:00 we reported to the pump with our canisters. I think we paid something like eighty francs, which was a lot of money, but we had four canisters of gasoline when we got back to the truck. After filling it, we took the road to Paris.

In order to get to Paris, you had to cross the River Rhone, a tumultuous river that was as wide as the Hudson in New York. The bridges had been blown up and in their place the Germans had put pontoons that wobbled when you walked, following the movement of the water in the river, so you had to be very careful. The width of the pontoon bridge was only about the width of the truck so so many trucks would go one way and then so many would go the other way.

When it was our turn to go, I said to Albert, who was frightened stiff, "You know what? I have a rabbit's foot in my pocket." The rabbit's foot was really the cap of a bottle of white ceramic with a piece of iron that I had attached to the wheel. "When you drive and you hold the wheel of the truck, look towards this and it will bring you luck. You will have the certitude that nothing will ever happen to you." Then I said, "Follow my direction. I'll be right in front of the truck. But don't deviate. When I make like this, go here; when I make like that, go there. Okay?"

And so he held that amulet in his hand, and he drove, and we did arrive, but at a certain moment my heart almost fell off because he was practically on the edge of that pontoon. When we came to the other shore, there was a little mountaintop to climb, but in order to climb it you couldn't take it at a slow speed. You had to take it with a lot of energy. So as we were coming to that side I said to him, "Albert, now when I give you the signal throw yourself and all your strength into it and climb up." He was paralyzed with fear but he did it, and we came out alive on the other side. The Nazis were there on the other side of the bridge flirting with the girls. Whenever soldiers come, there is always a group of young girls who receive them with open arms. To them, whoever it is is of no importance; it's a man. Of course we were intrigued, but we kept our opinions to ourselves, and we took the road to Paris.

Mr. Sandler knew a way to get into Paris without going through the important official checkpoints that were kept by the Nazis to control the people coming in. So we snuck into Paris by underways near cemeteries and through fields of corn and other greenery, and we went back to Monmartre. Monmartre was the artistic colony of Paris, and home to many nationalities. The people lived there as furriers and as cobblers and tailors and as merchants. Chana's sisters lived at 64 Rue de Poteau, in a house in a court.

After seeing that they all were well settled, I didn't even spend the night with them. I didn't know how many Nazis were in the area. I did not take time to judge. I wanted to join my family in Vichy. So I said goodbye to my sisters-in-law, and I went to the train station.

When I arrived at the Gare d'Orléans, I discovered that they were not selling tickets to Vichy, only to Orléans, so I took a ticket to Orléans. In the train I didn't mingle with anybody. I was very tired and sad. I felt completely miserable, although I always tried to keep my morale very high. I had to. Always I was optimistic but sometimes it took me awhile to get that way. I was in a position now to not speak, so I closed my eyes and I didn't look at anything.

CHAPTER 10

CADAVERS ON PHONE WIRES, *SCHLEPPERS* ON THE TRAIN, AND I ARRIVE IN RIOM

We arrived at Orléans just after a bombardment by the Royal Air Force from England. Pieces of cadavers were hanging on high telephone wires, radio emission stations, electrical wires. I saw a house that was completely bombed. In Orléans, which was old France, the walls of houses were sometimes four feet thick. On the edge of one of the walls of one house, on the top floor, a piano stood in equilibrium, staying there from the explosion after it was hit and sent there. The dust had not settled yet.

At the train station, I discovered they did have tickets to Vichy but they couldn't sell me one because I had to have a document of permission from the *kommandantur* of the Nazis, who was at the City Hall.

The *kommandantur* was like the commanding officer of a legion in the first world war. He would listen to your request and ask the reasons why. When I met him at the City Hall, he said to me, "What's the big idea to go to Vichy?"

I said, "My wife is there with my children, and I am from Brussels, I am a blood brother, and being that the *führer* is on the way to winning I want to take them to go back to Belgium."

He said to me, "Why don't you go to Belgium, give me their address, and I will send them back to you? When you arrive in Brussels they will already be there."

"She's a sick woman with two sick children. My son just came out from a sanitorium," I said, and I pleaded with him.

But he said he could not send me on the train to Vichy, and I could see he was in a turmoil because so many people were coming and going because of the bombing. So I said it was all right, and I would think about his offer and come back later.

I went back to the train station and started milling with the fellows from the yard. I said to them, "Hey, how does one go to Vichy?" One fellow said, "Look, you see that group over there in the back of the yard? You go and speak to them."

And that's what I did. The men explained to me that they were waiting for trains that would be sent over empty to unoccupied France because this was a very rich region, and the Germans would bring cattle, wheat, dairy products, and all kinds of vegetables back to the occupied zone. They must have had an agreement with the French government in Paris then, because Petain was in charge at that time, and he was a collaborator with the Nazis.

At night when the trains went by, going slowly with their doors open, the men would jump in. Once they were inside, they would go to the back of the car and hide under burlaps and papers. So with a group of six or seven or eight, I jumped in the train when it went by, and we hid, and we rode like this most of the night until we came to the river L'Allier.

At the river, a thorough check was made to see if there were any hobos or unnecessary *schleppers*, so we jumped off and slipped along to the edge of the river. From there we saw the French flags on the other side of the river. It was by now the end of August or the beginning of September, I guess, and the river was very low, so we removed our clothes and made bundles to carry on our shoulders. Then, in underwear or naked, we went into the water. Where we could walk we walked; where we had to swim we swam. And we arrived at the other side.

When we came onto the road in free France, non-occupied France, we were met by people who hugged us and kissed us and brought us wine and coffee, and rags to dry ourselves with. And they were proud and happy that more Frenchmen would come to non-occupied France.

I asked them, "How do I go to Vichy?" and one man told me I could take a train, which I did. I don't remember the amount of time I was in the train but I arrived at Vichy the next afternoon. I knew Eliane would be taking a nap so her mother must be in the hotel room. Fruits and vegetables were in abundance so—I was always a *schlepper*—I bought a basket of peaches as a gift for the children and my wife—Papa was away for such a long time.

I looked miserable, with a red, unkempt beard. I wasn't a bearded man then, and I was faintly brown from the sun. I catch the sun very quickly. Even though I walked at night, the little bit of sun I got was enough to make me darker. I was wearing a pair of sandals, no stockings, and I was carrying around my winter coat on my shoulders like a pack, and *schlepping* that peach basket. Looking like that I went to the Hotel Source de L'Hospital, where my family had moved after I left for Saint-Liguaire.

As I passed the kiosk where they sold newspapers, the man said to me, "Hey, Belgian, what are you doing here?" "Ah," I said, "I just arrived and I am going to see my family."

"Your family?" he said. "They left long ago to join you."

I said, "What do you mean they went to join me?" "Well," he said, "they went to where you were in Niort." When he told me that, I just collapsed.

So they brought me to the hotel, which was about two minutes from there. The lady from the hotel very cordially accepted me and set me down, poured me a drink, and said to me, "My poor friend, how come you are here? You know your wife is in Riom."

In the commotion, I could not distinguish between Niort and Riom, and I was already half drunk from tiredness anyway. So I whipped out my map from my pocket and laid it down and began tracing the directions from Vichy to Niort, which was five hundred or six hundred kilometers away. As I started marking the villages I was going to have to go through, she said, "No, no, your wife is in Riom, which is only ninety kilometers away, and she is well. They are all right. In fact, I can call for you and tell her that you are here."

Oh, I was so happy! I figured only a couple of days and I would be there. I began marking a new route on my map. "No," she said, "why don't you just go to the main bus station. Of course you will need a special permit from the police or from your employer, but ask the people and explain to them that you are a husband who is looking for his wife and children and maybe they will squeeze together and give you a room."

And so it was. When I arrived there, I didn't look good at all. I was tired. I looked like a vagabond, and I was now amongst people who were wearing ties and nice clothes. "Ladies and gentlemen," I said, "I just came from far away and I hear that my family, whom I miss very much, is in Riom. Please, allow me to ride with you."

The consensus was yes, I could ride with them. They were very sympathetic. They made a collection, gave me a few francs, somebody put cigarettes in my hand, another one put a bundle of foods in my hand, and I was very happy. I paid the driver the price of a ticket, put my luggage on top of the autobus, the good people squished together so that I could have a seat, and like this I arrived in Riom.

CHAPTER 11

FAMILY REUNION, COLORED WATER, AND EGGS ON THE CROSS

When I arrived in Riom, I went directly to the place where my family was. When they left on the train from Vichy, they had intended to go to Niort, but before arriving at Gannat the train was bombed by the English Royal Air Force, who did not know that the train was filled with refugees. While the train was stuck there, the refugees jumped from it and hid in the culvert. Armand grabbed a valise that was not ours. Then trucks from different sides of the city came and took all those people to the first nearby big city, which was Riom.

In Riom, my wife was received by a lawyer who saw that she was not a working man's woman. She was not a rough woman. She was a very distinguished woman, very well educated, of a very delicate behavior, and the children were well kept. So the lawyer took pity on her, and, because there weren't too many people, gave her hospitality in a little room, where everything was done for her.

The home was one of the famous old mansions that belonged for centuries to the same family of magistrates. I knocked at the door and the maid came out. When I explained to her who I was she said, "Oh, Mr. Mednicki!" She made me come in and she called to the lady of the house, who said to me, "Oh, yes, Chana Mednicki, she came here just a few weeks ago with two small children. Your son wasn't well at all, but the little one, she was very well. I kept them here until my doctor looked over your son, and then I placed them with the other refugees. The doctor said your son was too young to worry about; he just needed food and rest and the care he didn't get, but he will be all right. Unfortunately, many trains arrived with a lot of women and children from different parts of France and we had to give them all hospitality, so we had to clean out the stable where we kept cattle and horses. We put in cots and straw and we gave hospitality to five hundred women and seven hundred children. There is no room for men."

Then she said, "You know what? We will give you a private stable." Across from the long stables where twelve hundred women and children were sleeping were little stables where they kept goats and donkeys. I received a goat stable, only now it was filled with hay and straw but no goats. The war was already a few weeks old, so people were disposing of their animals. Those people always had somebody high in the mountains taking care of their cattle in the summer. In the winter, the cattle would come down, but in the summer they would be grazing in the mountains, so the stables were empty.

But I couldn't find my wife. I went into the long stable and there looking at me were all these women. They had not seen a man for weeks. "Where did you come from?" they wanted to know. I said, "Please, ladies, I am looking for my wife. I have just come from Vichy; I came from far away. Where is my wife, a lady with two children?"

They said she had gone to the train station to look for me. Because the train station was just across the street, you could walk over to it in five minutes. As I turned around, ready to go out to meet her, about one hundred feet from me I saw Armand looking at me and he was screaming, "Papa!" He ran and grabbed me and attached himself to me, and he cried with such a spasm I couldn't contain my tears, and so we both started crying. In the distance, I saw Chana. She left Eliane alone and kept walking faster until she grabbed me and she kissed me. And Eliane was walking. When we left Brussels in May, she was one year old and she was not yet walking. Now, four months later, she was adorable and cute, and she was walking. She didn't remember me because she was a baby, but seeing her walking, my heart was just breaking that I missed her first steps, so I grabbed her and I cried and they all cried.

At that time, Armand said to me, "Papa, I have to go to the bathroom but I cannot go here." I said, "What do you mean you cannot go here?" He said, "You want to see something?" And he showed me a hole in the ground that they used to relieve themselves because there was no sewer system. Feces were all over the place and maggots the size of your thumb were crawling around on the walls. The odor was so terrible I could understand my son's revulsion, so I took him into a nearby field and he satisfied his need. At that time Armand had scurvy because there was not enough vitamin C, and I was very scared for him.

"Look," I said, "now we are a family together. Let's stop crying and let's be confident that things will work out." Then I said, "Where do we eat?" Chana said we would eat in the hospital. She explained that they fed thousands of refugees there three times a day.

I asked, "What kind of food do they provide?" and she said, "Don't ask. It satisfies the hunger."

I figured to myself, a hospital cannot give bad food; they must follow certain hygienic rules. So that evening I went over for dinner with my family. We sat at long tables with other refugees, and here came four sisters from Saint Vincent de Paul. Two were pushing a huge bucket with soup, and in that soup were celery and potatoes, lamb bones, lamb meat, lots of liquids, unpeeled string beans. Everything was in that soup.

We ate the soup out of metal plates. One of the sisters gave us a scoopful of the soup, and one sister gave us each a piece of bread that was three or four days old. Later I was told if they gave you fresh bread you would swallow it too fast, but old bread takes longer to digest and longer to chew. It made sense to me, but when I saw what was cooked up in the soup—it was heads of sheep and bones, but it was food, and edible—we closed our eyes.

But when Armand asked for another piece of bread, and the sister said, "My child, you cannot get bread again," ooh, that strangled me, so I shared my plate with Armand. After eating I said to my wife, "Do you know what I'm going to do, Chanala?"—that was what I called her. "I need a job. Let me go and ask for a job here in the hospital."

I went to the director and said to him, "I need a job and I need money. I have a wife and children." He said, "I need a dishwasher." I said, "Good."

And he explained my duties to me.

I went to work at 4:00 the following morning. The wages weren't that big but, as you know, when you work near a bakery you always receive a small piece of bread. Working near a kitchen, I was sure that my family wouldn't be hungry, and in war time this was the main thing, not to be hungry, because, when you are hungry and your teeth are itching and your navel touches the bone of your spine and you see starvation in front of you, you will eat anything, anytime.

So I accepted the job. The first task I did every morning was to polish the utensils that the chef used in the kitchen. To clean the huge brass milk pots where we boiled the milk and the big copper kettles where we would mix soup, I used pulverized brick and vinegar, and scrubbed. It was a very labor-involved job, the scrubbing and everything else, but I wasn't a delicate person. I was a strong worker. When I was finished working I had to go into the kitchen area. That area was 150 feet long from the dish room where I worked to the dining room where the sisters ate. I would walk the length of the room with heavy dishes of hot, fresh food, come to the window of the eating room where the nuns would be sitting and waiting, knock on the window, and put down the food for them. Then I would go back and forth as many times as I had to until all forty sisters had eaten as much as they wanted.

Later in the morning when the refugees were finished eating, I had to wash the pots and pans as well as all the dishes from the refugees. That's thousands of metal plates that I had to wash three times a day. The forks and spoons they kept in their pockets; if they had no forks and spoons they received no food. In the morning, work was easy because the refugees had only coffee, bread, and butter, or bread and cheese.

Any leftovers I would pour into barrels to feed the twelve pigs. Underneath the kitchen of the hospital was a water pool made for pigs to wash. Pigs love cleanliness. They were pink like in a picture, and they were so fat that every evening the veterinarian had to take blood from their tails so they wouldn't have a heart attack. One sow lay on a board with wheels because she was so fat she could hardly move. She had a lot of piglets that she was feeding, twelve or fifteen at a time. I had to get in, with my feet in the water, and scrub them. These pigs were food for the hospital.

The sisters were trying to practice what they had been taught: charity, kindness, and devotion. But while working in the kitchen I learned that the sisters had made vows of chastity and poverty. The only thing remaining for them was good food so they ate good food. The best of it.

In the hospital they had a hierarchy. First they would take care of the sisters with the first coffee they would make. The second coffee, made from the same grounds, was for the maternity patients and those who had to pay to use the hospital. The third coffee—that means they kept pouring water through the same grounds—was for the general patients of the hospital. And the fourth one was for the refugees. So the sisters drank pure java, but by the time it came to the refugees it was like colored water that you couldn't compare to coffee.

The sisters had fresh bread; we had stale bread. When cans of milk came from the country, they removed the cream to make fresh butter for the nuns. The nuns received the best cuts of meat; we got the bones and the heads.

Maybe they deserved it. Maybe. I don't know. At that time my feelings about the nuns eating better than the refugees were very divided, because I thought that Christianity meant suffer with those who suffer. Evidently they needed their strength to suffer for us.

So I said, "I'm gonna do that? The hell with them." Well, I figure my family is entitled to have. For my labor, I was paid something like a couple dollars a day because I fed my family, but I was able to skadoodle everything I needed. I filled a handkerchief with sugar, and I would slap steaks on my body. The chef would boil eggs that I would put in my pants pocket, and I wore a belt with a bag attached on the back of my pants in which I put pieces of bread and whatever I could put my fingers on.

When Armand came to visit me, in the pocket of his clothes I would insert a handkerchief with sugar in such a way that nobody would catch him. Then I would remove the steaks from my body and roll them in paper and put them in the back of his pants and attach it with a belt. He had a little container that, instead of putting coffee in it, I would fill with milk. I taught him at age seven to be sneaky. That sneakiness must have saved his life. It wasn't easy because you have a mind of straight living, without any need of being sneaky, and suddenly you have to look for devious ways to remain alive. But I saw to it that my family had food to eat.

The chef was a young fellow, twenty-four or twenty-five, from near Gascogne in France. He was a terrific fellow, very jovial. By the second day we had become acquainted and friendly. That morning when I came in he said, "Are you hungry?"

I said, "Don't ask." He said, "Wait, I'll feed you." I had told him the first day that I was a big eater and whatever he gave me to give to the nuns I thought I could put away. So that day he made me an omelet out of a dozen eggs, and a two-pound steak, and maybe three pounds of french fried potatoes, a loaf of bread, and a hunk of cheese. He put a bottle of milk in front of me—the good milk; the cream wasn't gone—and a bottle of wine, and within half an hour, maybe even less, I polished everything off, because I was afraid it would be taken away; or maybe it was a dream.

The guy was astonished. I was inhaling the food; I didn't chew. I swallowed because I was so hungry, and then I said to him, "I need food for my children and my wife."

He said, "Don't worry, Bernard, you work hard but you eat well." And this is a trick that my father taught me when he presented me to a master to learn a trade. "Let's have dinner first," I would say, "and according to the way I eat, that's the way I will work." Everywhere I went, they loved me, because I cleaned the table off.

I remember one day when I was young, twenty-one years old, I ate two ducks at one dinner. Yes, sir, I ate. Like I told you, we were a small group of Jews in Belgium. The children grew up like brothers and sisters. Four other young men and I learned our trade from the same master. When we married, we remained like family. One Chalamoide Pesach—one of the minor Jewish holidays where you still may cook and earn a living—we decided that for the first time in our lives we would eat in a restaurant. To celebrate, we made a challenge. What was the challenge? Whatever you eat, I eat. Whatever you order, we all order, and the first one who stops ordering and eating pays. Well, they had the right guy in me. I can eat. And we ate. The other fellows stopped on the third meal. I ate the fourth. I ate a fifth. We were, of course, stuffed like geese.

This was in 1931. At the time they were beginning to speak openly of syphilis. Until then we never did speak of venereal diseases. Now the movies were showing pictures of what syphilis and other venereal diseases looked like. Somebody from our group had the crazy idea after a meal like that to go see that movie, so we went into the movies and we saw the chancres and the green blisters and that pus running. Three of my friends started throwing up their guts; they were heaving like pigs, and I had a job to keep everything down. It was a shame to throw up all that good food. That was when I was young.

Now, ten years later, I was still a good eater, but I had more sense now. I had responsibility for a family, and it was a time of danger. One day the chef received a delivery of fresh eggs and he started a battle of eggs with me. There was a big Jesus Christ hanging on one of the walls and he said, "Let's see who can hit it right in the face," because he was a left-wing sympathizer, an atheist.

I said, "But this is Jesus Christ." "So what?" he said. "Let them take him down." So we tried throwing eggs, and from there we started throwing eggs at each other. We must have ruined six dozen eggs at least. And then I realized the immense stupidity of what we had done. The cook didn't care because he didn't know hunger, while I didn't know if I was going or coming. I had declared myself to be a non-Jew, which weighed heavy on my heart. It was really tearing apart my people, who, to save their lives, had to renounce their heritage.

But this was a different situation. Here we were hoping that Hitler would not survive the pressure of the war and that, between France and England, he would be crushed. We didn't know his strength. We didn't know that he would circumvent that Maginot Line. We didn't know that he intended to bomb England. We didn't know that he would climb into Belgium, crush Poland, annihilate Europe. We didn't know the brutality of that man, of those people. It was something we could not fathom, even. So I worked in that kitchen, unaware of the terrible danger ahead, and I did that for quite a few weeks.

PART III: THE MOVE TO VOLVIC, AND THE BEGINNING OF LIFE IN THE RESISTANCE

CHAPTER 12

LIFE BEGINS IN VOLVIC

During the time I worked in the kitchen we were still living in the stable. At the pharmacy I had bought a little alcohol stove, the kind with a plate underneath in which you poured alcohol to make fire. It was rudimentary, very rough, but I could cook steak on it. I had eggs; I had butter. On the roof was a window to let the aroma escape, but the people would still smell the food and become excited, so I would only cook in the middle of the night. I ate very little before leaving for work.

My son would come to the kitchen during the day, for breakfast at 8 and lunch at noon. For dinner I went home with them. The sisters knew I worked in the kitchen, and that I knew they had good food, so they treated me nice. In this way, I saw that my family wasn't hungry.

But in the stable were rats, and the rats smelled the food. I remember at night fighting off rats the size of big cats. Then Armand started getting fevers. He got sicker and sicker and I tried to find a place to put him. The hospital where I worked was overflowing with people from all over France so they couldn't take anymore, and the patients were all adults. Also, I wanted Armand out of my sight because instinctively I knew that the children were in danger. I didn't know the Nazis had plans to take children but I felt it in my heart.

First, I tried to place him at a sanitorium near Riom, but nobody wanted him because they were full with refugees from other cities and we were aliens.

Then I stood in the middle of a road with Armand at my side and stopped a huge truck. The truck driver said to me, "Who in the hell do you think you are to stop a truck?" I cursed him back. "This is a sick boy." I told him I had to go to the sanitorium not far from Clermont-Farrand and needed a ride. Then I opened the door and put my son in. The driver was flabbergasted that I had so much *chutzpah*, so much nerve. Today when I think of it, I cannot believe it.

He took us to that sanitorium, but the director said, "I regret I have no room whatsoever." I said, "My son has a fever and he is very sick." I showed him a certificate from the doctor at the hospital where I worked.

"I'd be glad to take him," he said, "but I have no room. There is no bed. There isn't a spot." I said he could sleep in the hallway. "The hallways are taken already," he said to me.

And my heart was broken.

I stopped another car. But where could we go? Only back to our stable. We went back to our stable.

One day, five or six weeks later, I complained to a co-worker at the hospital, Marie Lessmaine. Marie was a very kind woman. She said to me, "Bernard, it worries me that you and your family live in a stable. I own a house up in the mountains in Volvic, not far from here. If you want, I can rent you a room very cheaply, twenty-five francs a month." At the time, I worked for minimum wages of ten francs a day but paid no rent at the stable. The food I could obtain was compensation for the small salary, so my family was not hungry. But I didn't want them to remain living in a stable, and twenty-five francs wasn't that bad.

So I went up there with her. Volvic was five miles away, and the going up took us two hours. I was much younger and had a good step. She was pushing a bicycle so she could sit coming down the mountain. When we got there, she showed me her house. It was better than what I already had, so I said we would take it.

But how was I going to get my family up that mountain? In Riom, I went to the commanding officer of a French regiment that was still stationed there and I said, "Mon Comandante, I am a Belgian. My son is sick. I have a wife and a baby. I have found a room in Volvic. Would you please be so kind as to have somebody drive me up there?"

He said, "Well, I cannot do anything, but being that your son is sick the Red Cross will help you."

I was pleased to hear that because the Red Cross had already been helpful to my family. While I was still in Saint-Liguaire, Chana Laja took the children to the Belgian Red Cross in Riom with the documents that proved we were Belgian refugees. From the Red Cross, she received a weekly stipend of twenty-three francs, which is today about eight dollars, plus meat for the children. There she had met M. Robert Duhin, a native of Brussels who was born to French-Catholic parents. M. Duhin saw that Chana Laja was from Brussels, and Armand was a beautiful child, and Eliane was a gorgeous baby of fifteen months, and so he took to the children and he did special favors for her. Why was he sympathetic? I don't know. There were many war children. Since we were hiding that we were Jews, he saw in us good Belgian Christians and he fell in love with my children. Chana Laja had nothing so he gave her little underwear for the children, a pair of shoes for Armand, a pair of pants for Eliane. When I came back and she told me about a M. Duhin who was very nice, at first I felt a sense of jealousy because she was a very pretty woman. I had no reason to be jealous, but it was instinctive, you know. Somebody looked at my wife. She told me that he would have liked to meet me, but I could not possibly go to City Hall because I worked late at the hospital and he never came down to visit us, but because of him I had faith that the Red Cross would help us.

The commandant called the Red Cross and they sent an ambulance to drive us to Volvic. In my hurry I forgot my luggage and I didn't remember it until the truck left. Not that I had much—I had received, from this one and that one, *schmatas,* which means rags. But I had nothing now. So after the ambulance took us to Volvic and my family got settled, I had to walk down, collect the *schmatas,* put them on my back, and walk back up to Volvic.

And I was sad but I couldn't afford to lose courage because my family was looking to me and I was their courage giver. Eliane will tell you today she doesn't remember missing anything. She doesn't know in Volvic she ate beans with maggots. She doesn't know that she ate a rabbit that was killed three days before, because she was very young, and she was hungry, and that was a fact.

We moved to Volvic in September of 1940. Volvic was a stone-cutting and grape-growing city that you had to go through if you wanted to go to Clermont-Ferrand to the south or Vichy to the north. It was started in the year 1100 by Comte de Tournoël, who reigned there. Comte de Tournoël had a castle and in that castle in the dungeons he had built a room from lava of Volvic as a wine bar. In that wine bar, he kept 11,000 gallons of wine so that in case of a siege he would have his wine. The spigot of that room was the size of the waist of a child. Its opening they filled with straw coming from oat. Because that straw was very thin, they twisted it and made a cork out of it. Of course, when we saw that castle it was already a monument.

Volvic was a town in the midst of caves and mountains. We were 3,000 meters up a huge mountain that must have been 10,000 meters high. The town had one main street with homes on either side. In addition, the people had a library, a public school, a post office, the gendarmerie, a pharmacy, two grocery stores, a baker, and two butchers, until one of the butchers left for Germany. We lived at the end of the village near a disaffected railroad.

In the olden days, before the kings of France, the railroad led up to the quarries, where they mined the lava from the volcano on a small scale. That lava was like glass. During peace time, it was sent all over the world to be used in the construction of chemical plants and for monuments and buildings. In one mountain was a natural spring that ran into the town through four different fountains in different points of the village. The fountain nearest my home was about two hundred feet away.

But Volvic was still very primitive in the sense they never had a sewer system for toilets. Soon after we moved there, when I took my first walk at 4:30 in the morning, I smelled an odor like stables and I figured, well, the cows, the pigs, and so on and so forth. But then I heard somebody taking care of business. I moved away and, whoosh, here comes a piss pot through the window.

Where we lived, human waste would be used in the fields for fertilizer. The Catholic church was built into the mountain so that the cellar was forty feet below the church. There they had built a latrine that was about forty feet long. Six huge barrels lined one complete side of the cellar, and on the barrels were boards with holes where you sat down to do your business. You brought a handful of leaves or grass; paper was unknown. When the barrel was full, the people of Volvic would bid for the right to use the fertilizer on their fields. They had the best crops in the world.

And so you had a hygienic pail in your house. The pail had a wide rim so that when you sat down you wouldn't catch your flesh. But it was used mostly for women and children. Men would go to the field, do their business, and that's it.

The blacksmith, for instance, had a little vineyard in front of his house and a big vineyard far away. In the yard he kept a shovel and you could dig a hole in the ground, make your deposit, cover it up with soil, and go. Like this you would fertilize the ground while you relieved yourself.

We rented a room on the second floor of the house. A door led outside to a balcony that had only a platform, with no rail around it for protection because the house was never finished. If you opened the door to the balcony you could go out and break your neck, so we never opened that door. Inside were a spring and mattress on the floor, a stove, and on the side of the stove a container to heat water while the stove was burning. We had a little closet, a few pots and pans, two chairs, and a table. Period. And this she rented to me for nearly eight dollars a month.

When I was in Vichy on May 15, I wrote to America, to my father's brother in Philadelphia, Boris Mednick. I didn't have an address so I put down Mednick Photography Studio, Philadelphia. I told him what was happening and gave him six pages of history. I wrote in French, not knowing any other language, and I figured yes yes, no no. He gets the letter, I have an answer. He gets no letter, I get no answer. But I didn't count on anything.

But one day, six months later, I received a reply. The letter was delivered to me in Volvic by the Quakers, who are an international organization. My uncle had gotten in touch with them and they had found me through Marseilles. In his letter, Uncle Boris said he regretted deeply that I was in such a terrible situation and that he hoped things would turn out all right, and he sent me a check for fifty dollars. Those fifty dollars were like the Taj Mahal. To cash it, I went to the local post office, because there was no local bank. In the post office whatever happened everybody knew, so they all knew that the Belgian had a rich uncle in America.

Fifty dollars! Those fifty dollars helped us live maybe more than a year, more on reputation than actual value. I was fortunate enough because I had given up working at the hospital when we moved to Volvic three weeks before. In Volvic, I had not yet found a job, except for occasionally helping neighbors to pick grapes in exchange for grapes, which I would hang on threads in the attic to make raisins.

I was also fortunate because, six days after we arrived in Volvic, Armand became very sick again. He had a high fever, 102. Oh my God, what do I do now? I was told there was a sanitorium in Saint Jean Den Haut, near Enval, about six miles from the town of Volvic but higher up in the mountains. For Eliane I had received, like a miracle, a carriage on loan from a neighbor so we wouldn't have to *schlep* her on our backs. But Armand was already too big for a carriage. So I carried him on my back and, using a solid branch as a walking stick, climbed those mountains.

On the way to the sanitorium, while Armand was on my shoulders, I spoke to him and explained that it would be very dangerous for people to know we were Jewish. I said, "Armand, remember, you are not Jewish. You are a Christian." Armand was a very brilliant and open child. He had a vivid mind, and he understood, and he asked me questions. I explained to him that his real name was Avram but that from now on he must be Armand and say that we are Protestants. After nearly three hours we came to the sanitorium.

At the sanitorium door, the guardian did not allow me to enter. But when he went back to his cabin, I opened the door and followed him there. He saw that I was angry and worried, so he changed his mind and allowed me to come inside, where the doctor received me.

I explained to her that my son was very sick. Of course, she could see that he was sick, so she said, "Let me examine him." I was afraid that if she examined him she would see that he had been circumcised, but I said nothing.

When she was finished with her examination, she said to me, "Was he sick or anything when he was a baby?"

I said when he was three years old he had had an inflammation of the penis and had to be circumcised, and that was the reason why the child was as he was. She accepted my explanation, so I arranged to leave Armand there with her. I never told her he was Jewish, but I think she must have suspected because she was herself a Huguenot Protestant, and the Huguenots were an oppressed branch of Protestantism. It was strictly a woman's sanitorium but, she said, "Because of his young age I will accept him here and I will keep him until I make him better." We thanked her, I came down alone to the village, and we were entitled to visit him whenever we got a chance. Of course, his mother was heartbroken. But she had Eliane to compensate while I scrounged around to see what was where and when and tried to know the townspeople.

Now, Volvic was a village of 3,000 people, all related. Cousins, and after cousins, and between cousins, and cousins, cousins, cousins. For 3,000 years, people had never moved out of Volvic, not even to visit the city eight miles away! People who were ninety years old, I spoke to them. Go to the city? What for? They didn't even know what a Jew looked like. They thought it was a frightful thing, with horns, and a tail, and spitting fire. That was the image of a Jew they had. It confused them. And I kept quiet because it was not smart for me to try to teach them at the time, or be too much of a wise guy or too smart.

Also, the people had a reputation for being very hardworking, very economical. I wouldn't call them stingy, but if one could cut a nickel in seven he would. They were of swarthy color and black hair, and they were garrulous, but slow with giving friendship to strangers. Because of this, and because the French people of Volvic were very entwined and family, for me to receive their confidence and for me to get sympathy from them took three years, even though I worked with them and struggled with them and showed them that I was not a lazy man.

But slowly I got to know them. Next door to us was a man named Jean L'Aime who worked in the quarry. *Laime* means "I love you," and Jean L'Aime means "I love John." Jean L'Aime had one daughter, who was very pretty, and a wife. His wife was a retarded lady, but at that time we didn't recognize retarded like we would in today's sense. Then, we considered her to be a little slow, not smart. And he accepted me very roughly.

There was also a baker who lived with his wife. Le Grossalle in French means "the heavy dirty one," and that was his name. He was very suspicious and never took to us, but when I would take Eliane and go to his wife for a small piece of bread, she loved Eliane and would break a piece of bread to give her, and we found grace in her eyes. Mme. Grossalle was a frustrated, childless woman. It was impossible for people to believe that Mme. Grossalle would be good to a child. Having Eliane was a tremendous help to our survival because a child opened many a door. I don't have to tell you!

But not for everyone. Underneath us lived a poacher named Le Moine, the Monk. Le Moine had a wife from Auvergne who was a bitter woman with a dark complexion. She never spoke a word, always stared. She had two sons who were also poachers. They lived out of poaching, that's all. Once in awhile, the father would go and chop wood for people but he never had an organized job.

Mme. Le Moine resented that we lived upstairs, so she gave us all kinds of little miseries. For instance, to get upstairs we had to go through a common front door, so she would lock that door with the key and we couldn't get inside. Or, she would take human waste and throw it in front of the door, as if a cow or a dog had done it, and then the odors would go up to our room. One day, very nicely, I said, "Would you mind throwing your waste in the back of the house?" She got very angry that I was asking her to be a little bit more hygienic. I said, "I have children. You know the odor of human waste. Then that excrement, what happens when a little bit of rain hits it?" Well, we had a disagreement but, seeing that I could not reason with her, I left without the argument that she was looking for.

Across the street from us was a shack, which I was permitted to use as part of my rental agreement. In the shack were all kinds of farm tools. I found two two-man saws to cut trees. They were very long, maybe six feet apiece, with huge teeth, and I had files to sharpen them. I also found axes to chop wood, a saw horse on which to cut wood, hammers and an iron wedge to split the wood, and a little bit of kindling. But I had to seek permission from City Hall to get more wood because by October it started getting cold and the winters were very tough. The snow was always high. In fact, the winters were so cold there that when we heard explosions in the middle of the night we were told that the bark was exploding off the trees.

At City Hall they told me that Comte D'Hérauville was very kind to the refugees and would allow us to cut acacia trees on the mountain belonging to his estate. Acacia is a very hard wood. The villagers used that wood to make supports for wire and vines that lasted for many long years. Other wood would rot but this didn't. On acacia trees there are long "sticking pins" of wood that you can break off and use to replace a nail, or you could use it for a needle. They are a real weapon. Years before the mountain had burned but the trees remained standing.

I didn't know that a burned tree was very hard to chop down and acacia was already very hard. You had to saw it down and I was using an ax. I would swing hard, because I was strong, but the ax would bounce back. I could not bite into the wood until I understood, and then I brought a saw. Chana and I sawed that burned tree at the bottom and only by strict, fierce energy were we able to topple it. Then we *schlepped* it down the mountain to Volvic and to the house. I carried the heavy part on my shoulder and the rest of the branches were hanging on the ground. Chana stood on the branches to hold me back from running too fast, until finally we came into the railroad yard near where we lived. In the yard we threw the tree down and we cut it. It took us a week to cut the tree with the two-man saw. Eliane, who was warmly dressed, thanks to M. Duhin, sat on the trunk of the tree while we were sawing, working all day cutting, back and forth, until we had enough wood to last us the winter.

And so I learned a lot of things then. I was told not to pick mushrooms; I was told to be extremely careful never to take anything from gardens. I was a city slicker from Brussels, but thanks to a few of them who had learned to give me their confidence I learned which mushrooms were good and which berries were edible, and they showed me tricks to survive. I was able to put up rabbit traps and catch squirrels. The meat is good. I remember climbing trees with a young refugee from Lorraine and together emptying the nest of young crows. It was edible. Later on, that was all that mattered.

CHAPTER 13

THE EYES OF THE BULL

Armand remained in the sanitorium about a year and a half. During that time, because food was short there, we had to provide it for him. I had saved some money from working in the hospital in Volvic, so I was able to buy food for Armand in the grocery store. I bought wine because wine was thought of as food. On the way to the sanitorium, going up through the mountains, we were able to pick chestnuts, apples, and walnuts. This was all counted as food. Then, from the house we brought what we could share with him.

Armand was fortunate in that, being the only boy, and he was a youngster, the ladies around him kept him like a mascot. They all took care of him. But it was a full-time job for me to bring food to him. Until I found my first job, we would go every day, five miles up and five miles down, to visit him. After that, we went once a week and brought food for the whole week. I said already that a neighbor had loaned me a children's carriage in which we could put Eliane. I would pull the carriage while Chana pushed it and like this we would climb the mountain. We even discovered shortcuts.

After Armand started getting well, the doctor gave him weekend passes and he would come home with one of the ladies from the sanitorium. At home he was able to play with the other children from the neighborhood. Then he would go back with the lady.

Near the end of 1941, after Armand was better, the doctor arranged for him to be sent to La Bourboule, to a preventorium for little children. He spent time in the sanitorium and preventorium between the ages of six and a half and nine, and then he started going to school with all the children. He adjusted well.

One day, Chana wanted to go see Armand, so we took the bus to La Bourboule to visit him. Imagine! Armand was completely shaved. He was wearing a uniform like all the children, like a convict, and a little blue hat. Although he was mature for his age, and he looked good because he was well fed, he was bewildered because he had been removed from the adult ladies and here he was with children.

He knew he wasn't a Jew officially but he remembered that he was a Jew actually. He looked like a nice little boy. But when he heard expressions about the Jews, the propaganda of anti-Semitism, even at his young age he had to hold it inside and it made him a bitter person.

It must have been a long time since we had last seen him, although I didn't know dates. I asked him how he was feeling and if he was eating all right. I said, "Have they asked you why you were circumcised?" But I don't remember what else was said. His happiness at our being there superceded all conversations. When he said he wanted to come home with us to Volvic, I explained that here he was eating food that we could not give him, and with a little patience he would be coming back with us. I was able to keep him there one year and a half with the help of the doctor at the sanitorium.

I began working in the quarry in December of 1940. By then I was getting short on money. I decided with Chana that it was no good for me to do nothing, and the only industry in Volvic was quarry work. The quarry in which I worked was one of many owned by M. Channeboux and his son. They also owned a cheese store in Volvic, where Mme. Channeboux worked. The job came to me because I asked around. One day when I was buying a piece of cheese, Mme. Channeboux said to me that I should speak to her husband or her son, and thanks to them I received this job. They were pleasant people to work with but you had to work hard. They did not indulge fooling around.

The men worked in the quarry and the women worked in their store on Main Street where they sold cheeses that were like pearls. The store was on top of a mountain. In the mountain were natural caverns. Also, they dug a lot of cellars, at different depths of cellars. For instance, three flights down, which was a depth of ten feet, would have been the wine cellar, two flights down was the cheese cellar, and one flight down was the cellar for the root vegetables. Another cellar was for meat. In the cellar for cheese, the cheese came out with little mushrooms on top. The rarity! The deliciousness of it! That cheese was of worldwide reputation for cheese eaters. It was made of regular cow milk, but cheese that is kept in the mountains can stay for long, long years, and the older it gets the more vintage it gains. Ah, I speak of it and I'm drooling, so beautiful it was.

I worked all morning in the quarries. Because I worked five days a week, we could only go to see Armand on Saturdays and Sundays. On those other days, we would give packages to neighbors who would go off to the sanitorium to visit their family members, and we would collect what we could: the fruit and the food and the bottles of wine.

To go to work, I would leave at daybreak and climb the mountain because the quarry was not near our village. I followed the other fellows until we came to the quarries. Then everybody would go to his own mine. We did mostly heavy work, swinging a sledge hammer, pushing, pulling, collecting small rocks, large rocks. There were maybe fifteen or twenty guys working there and we were paid a living wage for our efforts. We worked from 8 in the morning until 4:30 in the evening and took an hour for lunch. Because we worked in the field, the fellows working near trees would tear off branches and make a shelter and there they would unpack their lunches, which were very nourishing. They always carried a gallon bottle of wine. Of course, I didn't have all of that luxury so I ate my meal and it was a pittance, and once in awhile one of the fellows would give me a little of whatever meat he had.

In the quarry at the depth of the old volcano, about 1,500 meters, we would knock out a block of lava the size of a small bedroom but, you see, it weighed nothing because it was porous. Two workers could pull it out from the bottom of the quarry. We hauled it on blocks of wood, very primitively, yet we did it, with the help of a team of oxen. It was dangerous, but you had to work, so I worked.

Lumberjacking was also part of the job. Over a period of many, many years, trees had grown on the edges of that volcano, so to get to the lava we had to remove the trees. To remove those trees you would attach one end of a rope around your abdomen. The other end you would attach to another tree so you wouldn't fall down the mountain while you were chopping.

Then, with hatchets, you chopped the trees beginning with those closest to the rock. You would start cutting from the front of the tree and make a deep cut. Then you'd cut the back a little and automatically the weight of the tree would knock it over. It would fall down the side of the volcano to the fellows below who would chop off its branches and make nice logs. Then we waited for trains to come in so we could load the logs onto them.

One day when I was helping to load the trains I was standing on top of a mound of logs when suddenly the logs started rolling off the train. I saw myself getting crushed so I jumped and I fell and somehow I got underneath the train. I was protected by the wheels of the wagons, but I hurt my back and legs and the other workers had to carry me home. Everybody was scared thinking the Belgian had been killed, but I wasn't.

Another time, in the winter, working at the bottom of a mountain I found a piece of rail. It was about three meters long and weighed a thousand tons because it was steel. I knew the blacksmith would give me something for it. But how do you *schlep* that piece of steel? Luckily there were holes in it where they put screws to tie the rail. I took my red handkerchief and slid it through the holes. Then I pulled that steel rail until I came to the mountain. I pulled it up from the railroad bed, up the ravine. I pulled it up, I pulled it up, until at the top of the mountain I came to the road. On the road it slid down on the ice and snow and I brought it to that blacksmith.

The blacksmith thought I was a giant. "How in the hell did you carry that piece of steel five meters?" And he gave me four bottles of wine and a half loaf of bread in exchange, because to him a piece of rail was useful. Mind you, when a young couple got married in Volvic they received stamps from City Hall to purchase a couple plates, a couple forks and knives, a pound of nails, and a few appliances for the kitchen. The Nazis took everything else. Although you could get all you wanted on the black market, these items were very expensive.

Up until now—it was already four months—we had no limitations on food from the Germans. We could still buy our food any way we wanted. The few grocery stores had enough to supply the population. And my family received financial help from the Red Cross so we were not yet experiencing extreme hunger.

In Volvic I was considered some kind of an intellectual. I didn't mix, I didn't go to the café, I didn't brawl around, and I shaved completely—in Volvic they shaved every two weeks. And we tried to stay clean, so Chana would wash every day at the little laundry in town. To them, these were signs of my intellectualism. One day two months after I began working in the quarry, the mayor, whose name I don't recall, approached me, and he said, "Mr. Mednicki." We spoke very correctly; there was no first name calling for anyone unless you worked with a fellow. "Mr. Mednicki, I know that you are from the big city." He knew that I had finished school and evidently I must have told them, not having proof, that I had gone to a higher school. Having read extensively, I had a phraseology that was a little bit out of the ordinary.

So the mayor asked me if I would be kind enough to help out in City Hall. Because I was an alien—we were the only refugees from Belgium—I had no legal right to work for the village, but with the influx of refugees, my volunteer help was useful.

I said, "What would be my place?" He said, "Mr. Mednicki, we have received an order from the prefecture"—"Prefecture" means the headquarters of the city, from the big capital, Clermont-Ferrand—"that rationing is going to start soon. It's the end of abundance of food. We will have to give out food stamps. There are 3,000 people in Volvic. How am I going to do it? I have nobody to take charge of it."

"But," he said, "you are from the big city. Would you please help me?"

"Mr. Mayor," I said, "to the extent of my means I will help you, but I don't know what I can do. What would be my place?" "Oh," he said, "you can do so much. You can count."

Then he explained to me that he had 3,500 books to give out, and it was to be done within one week. Every member of every family was to receive his own book of stamps to last six months, and the five hundred extra were in case we made any mistakes. However, having the stamp did not assure that you would find what you wanted in the store. Every stamp had a designation: milk products, bread, meat, groceries. But children got a smaller amount in their books, and working men got a different amount in theirs, and a nursing mother got a different amount in hers, and it had to be done in a week. Also, the mayor had received a sheet of instructions that said, for every mistake above five percent, the people would have to pay a collective penalty.

I thought to myself, if I keep three percent for myself and say they were mistakes, I will have ninety-four books, including the four books my family would receive anyhow from the ration. So I said to the mayor, "Of course I'll help you."

I went to M. Channeboux and he said, "Okay, Bernard, if the mayor wants you, go"—because the mayor was also a part owner of the quarry. Then I went to City Hall and the mayor gave me the book with the names of all the inhabitants and he gave me the sheets for stamps. I counted the books. Then I started making the distribution.

But first I took down the amount of books equal to three percent because I had my sisters-in-law and my nephew in Paris and I had my family to feed and I had no one else in Volvic to turn to, like the farmers, who all had somebody in the mountains to give them extra food. Higher up in the mountains were large flocks of cattle, and, although it was forbidden to slaughter any animals, the people were seldom short of meat or food.

With the dollars I received from my uncle plus those ninety-four books, I was able to buy food and send bundles to my sisters-in-law in Paris. The train still accepted bundles, so I would send non-perishable beans, rice, and whatever else I could find.

And I guess I helped the mayor. In fact, when I was finished giving out the stamps I only missed three percent, so we really didn't have any loss because everybody was checked thoroughly by me.

Oh, they were so thankful. "The Belgian is a genius." The mayor was very proud of me for doing the impossible because everybody there had the same name as someone else. For instance, there was a Jean Laime who was the son of the baker and there was a Jean Laime who was the son of the alcoholic. There were maybe twenty-five Jean Laimes because the population were intermarried and inbred. Between those stamps and the letter I had received from Uncle Boris, we were able to push through, but food was still always scarce and I had to be creative in finding ways to have food for my family.

One day, working with the fellows, I heard them talking amongst themselves and saying that they wanted to kill a bull and that the mayor was in on it. He wanted to buy a piece of that bull. The Nazis forbade the killing of any extra cattle or poultry or rabbits or pigs. If you wanted to kill an animal for meat, you had to tell them, and they would remove from your rations as much meat as you were going to kill. So we killed a lot in a clandestine way.

The bull they wanted to kill was a huge bull from Cantal, a longhorn, six-foot tall, like a monster. He was a regular reproductive bull, and they were afraid of slaughtering him because the noise he would make might arouse the

Nazis. He had a pair of huge testicles. In his nose was a ring, and by twisting that ring you could control the bull. But they didn't know how to kill him because of the noise he would make while they were hitting him with a sledgehammer or the noise he would make while being shot in the brain. They didn't know what to do.

So I spoke to the fellows and I said, "Who is in charge of this business?" They said the mayor. I went to the mayor and I said to him, "I have a way to kill your bull. Give me three or four days, and I will kill him. Nobody will hear a note, a word, a peep."

He said, "How will you do that?"

I said, "Leave it to me."

He said okay so I went to Pere Pougeon—Father Pougeon. Pere Pougeon was the old blacksmith of the village. He knew his business. From nothing he could make something. I went to him and I said, "M. Pougeon, I need a knife at least twenty-four inches long, and I want it shaped like a razor—that means a very thin cutting edge, but very thick on top. I want it very sharp and I need it in three days."

He looked at me and he knew I was not speaking foolishly because I was not a foolish talker. I said, "What I have I can give you. Would you like wine or brandy?" He accepted my wine and brandy and in three days I had a twenty-four-inch knife that he had worked out on the anvil.

I spent that night honing the knife on a whetstone, so that when you took a piece of paper and let it fly over the knife just the weight of the paper would cut it. It was an extremely dangerous weapon!

The next morning, I went to the mayor and I said, "I need six strong men, and whenever they are ready I am ready."

The next morning very early, we pulled that bull into a barn. That barn was near a stream that ran down the mountains and into a river. That water flowed to Clermont-Ferrand and then into the Plain of Limoge. We were near that stream, so I figured after we killed the bull we could shovel the blood away to the stream.

We threw a burlap bag over the bull's head to keep him completely quiet. Then one fellow controlled him with the ring in his nose while the others attached ropes to his four legs. When you twist the tail of the bull, you can dominate him because the pain is horrible, so one guy was twisting his tail and the bull did exactly as we wanted. He remained quiet the whole time because by twisting the nose he didn't come out with a sound.

That bull was a heavy one but, by throwing the ropes over the main support beam of the barn, the men lifted his back end up so that the front of his body and his head, covered by the burlap, lay on the floor. I jumped on his head, pulled his head back by the horns, and I slit his throat. But I cut so hard, back and forth, that my knife remained embedded in the spine at the back of the head. He started thrashing but he was tied and two legs were in the air. His thrashing stopped immediately. And he never made a sound.

Then we pulled him up and with the same knife I slit him open, his whole abdomen. I was ready with burlap bags to collect the intestines, the stomach, and everything. Then I very easily removed the skin. Once I cut around the knuckles I started punching the skin down. Where it didn't go, I made a slit with the knife and kept punching. It's like when you peel a chicken. When you can, you pull and it goes down. When you can't, you take the knife and start cutting and it goes down further.

I gave the men who were with me the liver, the brains, and the tongue. The rest was all mine. They remained with the carcass, of course. But the skin was mine, and the four hooves from the knee down, that was mine. You know, one hoof is enough meat for a week because I removed the horny part of his foot. I had learned from my mother to boil it, and after it becomes soft you insert a screwdriver and just fluff it up. Then you cut off the toes and break off every joint. With the hammer you can also crack the bones to get the marrow out of it. It was a hard job, but I had food for four months.

The distance from that slaughter place to my home was, I would say, at least a thousand feet. I left the men alone because after I cut the bull open they had to hack it apart, and I was carrying bags on my shoulder. I made four trips with full burlap bags. The juice was running because of the humidity and because the intestines weren't clean yet.

In the house was a slab of lava that ran from the kitchen to the wall, where a hole led into the gutter outside. Our fountain of water from the spring of Volvic ran constantly. I cleaned the bull's intestines on that slab and I brought water by the buckets from the spring, which was sixty feet from the house. Chana and I washed day and night until we cleaned up the meat.

I took the skin from the bull. But having no alum powder or anything, I had to bury it in the ground to cure it. The walls of the house were four-feet thick, and chopped out of those walls were cabinets that had hooks and a little curtain, no doors. In those cabinets in the wall I stuffed the meat. I rolled crushed garlic into the meat and that's all. I had no salt or anything to preserve it, but I had baskets and baskets of garlic that I got from the neighborhood. They grew a lot of garlic there.

See, in Volvic we were big garlic and onion eaters. All of Volvic smelled of garlic. They were Auvergnat. That means they were near the sun. They were people who stayed outside. Garlic to them was like eating pizza pie in America. Everything was garlic. The meat from the bull's carcass was quietly distributed throughout the entire village.

And Yvette and Eliane played marbles with the eyes of the bull.

CHAPTER 14

"DO YOU KNOW HOW TO STEAL?"

And like this life continued. After working at City Hall those two weeks distributing ration books, the mayor slipped me fifty francs and I went back to work at the quarry for two or three more months. Then, Chana took sick with a miscarriage and had to go to the hospital in Clermont-Ferrand. While she was there we managed. Three houses from us was a Polish refugee family by the name of Kosicki. They had children about Eliane's age so I could leave Eliane with Mme. Kosicki for the day while I visited Chana.

After three or four days I brought Chana back from the hospital. That day, which was in the beginning of May, I received a letter that said I had to present myself in Clermont-Ferrand to be sent away to work for the German war effort. My address had been sent administratively to the main hall from the Volvic City Hall, where I had been required to register. At the main hall, the Germans had noted my address.

In that letter, I was ordered to bring a three-day supply of food and clothes. Well, that order caused consternation. We knew from other neighbors that their sons and husbands were being forced to work very hard in Germany for the Nazis. I wasn't concerned about working, but I didn't want to leave my family alone in a foreign country.

According to my orders, I was to present myself to the German War Department, which was employing alien help living in France or Germany. I dressed myself up in the only nice clothes I had, which was a suit and tie, because I didn't want to look like a laborer, and I went to Clermont-Ferrand.

In Clermont-Ferrand, when I was asked directions to the German War Department, I learned that thousands of people in working clothes were milling in front of the sport arena, ready to go to work, with shovel and pick and bags on the shoulders. A group of French police were keeping order, and the people were sullen and resigned.

As I arrived, however, they separated and opened the rank for me, thinking that I was somebody famous—because I always believed that nice feathers make nice birds and "the clothes make the man." That means whatever you wear you may look like. You may be the best and most noble, but if you look like a *schlump* you are a *schlump* until they know you.

So as I came up to that big building they opened the door, and I walked into the Rotunda. In the back were all the functionaries of the Nazi government from Belgium, from France, from Holland, from all over occupied Nazi territory. All around them were tables with girls and books and all kinds of documents. I spoke to the first girl on my left. Showing the letter to her, I said, "Do you know what this is? Do you know who I am?"

She probably thought, "God knows who he is." She looked at my name. "It says Mednicki." I said, "That's right." "But," she said, "M. Mednicki, those are orders for you to go to work."

If I had gone to work as those orders said, I would have been a laborer. If they had found out I was Jewish, they would have killed me. So I said, "But I am not fit to work in Germany." She said, "Wait a minute," and she rattled the pages. Finally, after a few minutes, she said, "Look, would you know how to work on pocketbooks?" I said, "Of course," because I never said no to anything.

So she said all right, and she gave me four addresses of pocketbook makers. I told you previously that the job of the Jews in Belgium and France was pocketbook making, all leather work. On the address list were three Jewish names and a Monsieur Orléan. Orléan was not a Jewish name. Maybe in Poland it was Orleonski, or Orlovich. I have no idea. But in France it was Orléan. I chose him to be my employer.

I went to M. Orléan's place on top of a very hilly street—Clermont-Ferrand is all mountains. I walked into the plant. The men were sitting down, working. My heart was beating fast. What the heck did I know about pocketbooks? So there came M. Orléan, a typical, beautiful type of Jew according to Hitler: big, rich lips; very eminent, curved nose; black, rich eyes; and sturdy hair. He said, "Yes, sir?"

And I said to myself, "What? That's it. You try to avoid them but you can't. They are my people." So I said, "Here is a requisition for you to give me a job. I am a pocketbook maker."

"Oh," he said, "it's for work. Wait a moment, I will send the foreman."

I figure, I'll see what's going to happen. The foreman comes in, a beautiful young man, very elegant, nicely dressed. "Yes," he said. I said, "I have an invitation to get a job from you, and I'm a pocketbook maker." He read: "Bernard Mednicki, Brussels, Anderlecht, Belgium."

He looked at me. I had a moustache then. And I had hair on my head. Of course this was forty odd years ago. He looked at me and he said, "Bernard Mednicki, did you live on Rue George Moreau in Rue Des Vétèrinaires in Anderlecht during the first world war?"

I said, "How do you...yes, but...." He said, "Did you live on the fifth floor?" I said, "Yes, I lived on the fifth floor?"

"Who lived above you?" he asked. I said there was a Zlotnik family: a husband, a wife, and two children. I said in 1918 they left for Paris.

"That's right," he said. "What was the name of the boy?"

I said, "His name was Roger." "Bernard," he said, "that's me!"

And we fell into each other's arms, crying. The coincidence of twenty years later finding each other! I explained to him, "Roger, I'm not a pocketbook maker. I'm an orthopedic technician. I know leather, but not pocketbooks."

He said, "Don't worry. I'll teach you everything you need to know. The main thing I want to know is, do you know how to steal?"

Now, I thought he'd cracked up. I said I never did steal and I didn't feel it was necessary unless it was to steal food for my children and wife.

He said, "No, no, no. You see, we make pocketbooks for the women of the German army. The Germans deliver the skin and the metal, the nails, and the thread, and everything needed to make pocketbooks. They tell us every skin has to make so many pocketbooks. We twist and turn and we make about thirty-five percent more than they demand. All those extra skins and nails and cotton and threads and linings and everything else we steal from this factory to sell on the black market. That money goes to the Resistance. I live across the street. Every night the fellows from the shop come to the house and unload what they have stolen. Some take skins around their bellies. Some fix material around their bellies. Nobody has a package in his hands because they are afraid, there may be Gestapo watching."

And that's the first time I heard the word "resistance." Before that time, I knew something was going on, but I didn't know what it was because just a while before I had hidden my identity, and I was afraid to be too inquisitive because if you are inquisitive they can be inquisitive.

At this time, the Resistance was a passive movement. There was no armed resistance then that I knew of. If you could do harm to a Nazi you were lucky, because the purpose of every little act was to break the war effort of the Nazis, like when we stole merchandise from the Nazis. Resistance meant to help those who were hidden and looked for by the Nazis. So with money from the black market we would buy the necessities to help those who were hidden. Maybe they were organizers of a stronger Resistance, in need of food for themselves or more weapons. It was all those things.

The fellows in the shop were all members of the Resistance, practically, everyone in his own way. But nobody knew who else was in the Resistance because nobody asked questions. There was tremendous fragmentation for the sake of security because we lived in an unknown world where events kept us apart. Me they knew as "the Belgian." It was all anonymous.

For instance, I would steal wire that we would string up from our city, through the forest, to another city just for Resistance activities. The fellows used this means to bypass regular city telephone lines for official Resistance conversations that were naturally hush-hush. The guys who worked on the railroad were Resistance. The policeman, the postman, everybody was Resistance. But only two men in twenty knew how we were connected. It was a secret. I never questioned Roger or asked him where his link was in the chain of command. I never wanted to know more than necessary.

Naturally Roger knew I was Jewish because we grew up together. He was Jewish also, of course. I think our families mingled and went to the same synagogue, but I was only eight years old when they moved to Paris.

One other fellow knew I was Jewish, a young chap from Paris named Goldstein or Goldberg. We became very close, although we never socialized out of work. One day he said to me, "Besides working here for the Nazis, nobody knows I'm Jewish. I didn't give them my real name, so I can go out with a lot of non-Jewish girls."

I said to him, "Then how do you make out? You go to sleep with them. Don't they see you?" "They never see me," he said. "It's always dark." Period. You had to be very careful.

Thirty people worked at the factory; ninety percent must have been Jewish. We knew one from the other but we never said it. The others suspected we were Jewish but they didn't know for sure because we never spoke. What you did I didn't know, and what I did you didn't know, and I didn't want to know what you did and you didn't want to know what I did. We did not go too deeply into friendship because we were afraid of friendships. We already had had the experience of heartbreak, of losing a good friend. So we settled for factory camaraderie. We never asked, "What does your family do?"

Still, in a distant way, we became family. I never told Roger that I was posing as a Christian, and he never told me his role in the Resistance, but he taught me the trade. After three weeks, I had a couple of apprentices working for me and every evening whatever I could I would roll around me—a skin or a bolt of material—and bring it over to him.

We were very much involved with thinking about saving our families' lives and our own lives. We worked instinctively in the sense that it was a job and God knew if tonight going home we might not be arrested by the Gestapo. So we never concentrated too much on the job, you did not do a polished job. We did not make it too *chachkadik*. We did the best we could, and we tried to get along with everybody.

One winter day, I remember, I was chatting with the fellows. It was toward the end of lunch as we were going into the shop and an elderly man from the bottom of the street was trying to push a wheelbarrow with coal up the street. I could see he was an elderly Jewish man. You could recognize if you knew what to look for. So I said to the fellows, "Ya know what? Let's play a joke on that guy," because it was good to play jokes on elderly people. I was young then, and never knew I'd be old one day. I came to the man and I said, "Are you going to tell me you're going to pull that wheelbarrow up the street?" I pushed him away very rudely and I said, "Watch me do it." Then I ran up the street with it until I came to where the street was equal, and I left it there. When I passed the man at the bottom of the hill, I said loudly, so the others could hear, "You see what I can do? Who do you think you are?" And that's the end of the story. I went back into the shop feeling good. I had done something good, but I had done it by acting nasty, and the fellows were thinking, "Bernard is a regular guy. He makes fun of elderly people."

You see, I was jovial. If you say it's green, I say let it be green. If you want it white, it can be white. I never contradicted anyone because I could not afford to be in any uncomfortable situation.

Here is another example. It was very hard for me to go up and down the mountain every night. At the factory, I worked with a Spanish woman whose husband had been killed in the Spanish revolution. She was gorgeous, like a Madonna, and she lived with her father and mother and her two children. One day she threw an eye on me and said, "Bernard, why should you go up the mountain every night? We have a spare room. Why don't you sleep in our home?"

I came home that night and I said to my wife, "Do you think I should do that?" She said, "It's up to you." I said, "You know what? Listen. If the weather is really bad I'll stay down. When you see a bus that I am not on, you will know that I am sleeping at Dela Rosa's."

The night I went there, her parents gave me the highest respect, and she was sweet on me, but I never made an approach to her because I respected her and I was afraid for myself. So I tried to forget that I was only a man and she was really gorgeous. In the shop we were very friendly but I never again slept over after the first night.

But overall, life was now bitter, and we were hungry. Hunger is a subject that is very hard to talk about. Some people are never hungry because they are not eaters. Some people glorify food. Some people are born natural eaters. To them, anything that is chewable and digestible is food. That doesn't mean they are not discriminating under normal circumstances, but when circumstances demand, if it crawls and you can cook it, it's edible.

So I remember that we were hungry. Today Eliane and Yvette don't know of the hunger. Eliane will tell you, "I was four years old, and I remember, but I don't remember being hungry." And that, when I hear it, makes me feel good. But the hunger gave us sleepless nights. Sure we drank well to fill our stomachs but there wasn't enough that was nourishing. I must have weighed 145 pounds. I think I was born weighing 120. Whenever I had a chance to eat

I could eat for four people. I could sit and eat, if nobody bothered me, for two hours. Most of our food was rations from the government. You were entitled to three ounces of beans a month per person. The beans we received were full of maggots. You could see them moving around. I would cook them, puree them, mix this with chopped onions and a little of walnut oil, and not say anything. What you don't know you don't know. I crushed the maggots and we spread them on bread. Children were allowed farinas, children were allowed a half a liter of milk a week, but the milk was cut with water, so that it was almost not white. I was lucky. I had received canned milk for the children from the pharmacist before the rations began.

The inside of the cow—liver, spleen, brain, lung, the tail—was premium meat. You couldn't get it unless you received a prescription from the doctor for your children, but I was able to get it from the butcher in exchange for what I received from the Red Cross. I received three warm shirts; I gave him one. I received three pairs of socks; I gave him one. He would give me three weeks' worth of food. He knew if I had any needs I could trade with him further. You know, the promise of tomorrow was important. Whatever I received I would give sparingly to the children. We adults ate a rutabaga and we killed a crow or we had a squirrel or a rabbit, and that was good enough. Children are not like that. They must have something to hold them up.

When the wheat was ripe I would go to the fields with Eliane on my shoulders and we would break up the ripe grain of the wheat on the end of the plant, and I would fill my sweater with it and come home. Then I would take the grain out from the chaff and I would grind it in a coffee mill. When it was ground, I would cook it in water like cooked cereal, but I had no salt, no pepper, no sugar. It would come out hard like a piece of cement, with no flavor, the flavor of water, but I would eat it anyway. I was hungry.

At the end of 1941, we moved from the house by the railroad to a house by the church. In front of our home was a shack that I was not allowed to enter. It belonged to a Frenchman who had stacked there bags of potatoes and wood and all kinds of provisions.

Early one morning, I was looking up at the shack roof and I saw something hanging, like a tongue from a cow, only heavier. I wondered, what could that be. I took a stick and carved the end of it like a harpoon. Then I removed that string and brought down what I saw were the penises of porkers.

As I told you previously, you threw nothing away from the pig but the oink. Everything else could be used. The feces was fertilizer; with the intestine you could make casings for any kind of sausage; from the tail you made soup; from the head you made cheese; and from the heart you made bacon. Even the hair could be scraped and used in a brush factory. There is nothing to throw out from the pig. So when they kill the male pig, they take the penis and dry it. Then, when they go in the forest to cut trees, the penis greases the saw so the resin or sap in the wood will not hold back the saw.

Well, I stole those penises. At the time, we were desperate. We had nothing. We had received two eggs; they were rotten. We had received three ounces of butter for each child but the butter was so rancid you could mix half a pound of garlic with it and the garlic would be rancid.

So I took those penises and I thought, "What the heck can I do with this?" First I washed them well and I chopped them up and I boiled them. After I boiled them I removed all the impurities, all the dirt, and I rolled them in a piece of cloth—we had no paper then—and dried them. Plenty of pots remained in the house where I had moved so I put the dried penises in a large pot. I rendered the fat and the fat started smelling good.

Now, we had collected quite a lot of walnuts from the forest during the fall. With Eliane on my shoulders, I would go out singing a song: "The sun is hot/The wind blows in my ear/And I take the nuts and give them to my papa." When the farmers saw her, they would say, "Oh, it's okay. She's a child. What can she take? Two nuts? Big deal." I had a sweater six sizes too big that I had received from the Belgian Red Cross, so when I came home I had something like thirty pounds of walnuts on me, from everybody's trees.

At night, we burned wood on the stove and we sat by the light of that stove cracking the nuts and putting the flesh in a bag. In the morning, when I had something like twenty pounds of flesh, we would go to the mill, to the oil presser, and from that twenty pounds we would get three liters of oil. This I mixed with the fat from the penis of the pig, and I had a product that was delicious. I didn't tell my family what I made it from; they would not have eaten it. In the meantime, I had three large pots of fat that they could eat. The dried walnut meat that remained the farmers would normally give to cattle, but during the war I would mix it with a little saccharine and a little red wine and we would have a nourishing meal.

For my fruit and vegetables I still thank all the Volvic farmers. Although I was assigned a piece of ground to use for my own garden, it was at the top of a volcanic mountain and had no soil. How do you grow food when there is no soil? Early every morning on the way to my garden, I would pass the gardens of real farmers and I would borrow a little bit from every farmer so that the damage would not be noticed. For instance, potato plants grow nice green flowers. When they are ripe you pull the whole plant out. But I would make a deep slant hole underneath the potato plants, remove the potatoes, but not touch the plant. Then I would fill the hole, and the farmers would say, "The rats ate all my potatoes." I learned how to dig up scallions without disturbing the ground. I learned how to take out carrots without anyone knowing. I didn't take that much from any one farmer but I would come home with large baskets of carrots and onions and potatoes and whatever I needed. "The

Belgian has a gorgeous garden," they said because I always had food, but nobody ever came to see if I grew anything. The only thing I grew in my garden was nice and brown.

The baker was a real businessman. If you brought him five kilos of flour, in the five kilos of flour he would always find that you had two kilos of bran. So he would take a kilo from your good flour and give you another kilo of bran. Like this he accumulated lots of flour. He had a flourishing black market, and the bread we were able to make filled our stomachs but it was horrible. The bread would be so wet the water was still running out of it. So we took the bread and squashed it to make a pancake, then put it on the hot plate of the stove to boil. We had to practically carbonize it.

On the counter in the front of his store was a jar in which he kept his customers' stamps. He wasn't interested so much in the stamps because he had as much flour as he wanted, being from that region. So I would put my hand into the jar, take out a lot of stamps, and I would have bread for a little longer.

One day, I came to his bakery and there he was standing by his pastry table, half naked, working on the dough. He was throwing it over and over to mix it with the yeast and he was perspiring. Suddenly he took a piece of dough from the drawer, wiped his body with it, and threw it back into the drawer. I said to him, "What are you doing?" He said, "Oh, the fire will clean everything out." Being with them you learned that everything was so simple. Everything was so *rudimentaire* that you would not even be fussy if somebody threw up on the next plate while you were having dinner.

I would leave my home in the morning after I would have my *rudimentaire* bit of bread. Then I would take the bus. The driver of the bus was La Pierre, a tall six-footer, a jovial fellow, who was bald like a billiard ball, with a face that was completely without hair. All naked. He was another Kojac, and he always had a cigarette at the corner of his mouth. We riders needed that driver, so we always saw to it that he had something. He was a big wine drinker; he always had a bottle of wine. He lived near me with his three daughters and his wife. In fact, his wife and my wife were very compatible, and when they saw each other they spoke.

To run the bus, there was no gasoline. Instead, the bus ran by a new means of transportation in France called *gazogène*. In the back of the bus was a drum filled with charcoal and the fumes of the charcoal would activate the motor. The bus was built to hold fifty people but because it was war time they accepted one hundred, so we would squeeze together. Instead of three on a seat, we might have five—two small ones and three normal people. Lucky for me the first stop was almost in front of my house so I had a good seat. We stopped in every village until we came to Clermont-Ferrand, so people were always coming and going. Often we would push the bus to save fuel.

I would come down to work every morning from Volvic and every night I would catch a bus to go back home. I made a lot of acquaintances with people who also went down every morning from Volvic and the villages in between: Maloza, Chamaillere, about ten stops altogether. One day on the bus a young lady said to me, "Are you a dentist?" I knew that young lady because she would ride with me quite often, although I never knew her name. She was from Alsace-Lorraine but lived in the last village before Clermont-Ferrand. I always reserved a seat for her because she was a tiny woman and an agreeable one and she smelled good and a good smell was important in the morning. So I said yes. I didn't know what that meant but I thought it must mean something, and, like I said previously, I never said no. Instinctively I said yes to see the end of it. If I made a mistake, there would be time to repair it.

She whispered to me there was going to be a Seder in the mountains in the Pui de Volvic, which was not far from us, maybe three hours walking higher up in the mountains. Then she clammed up. When we got off the bus, all she said was, "Good day."

For the rest of the day, I was in a turmoil. I remember I took Roger aside. He was Jewish but he didn't apply any religion whatsoever. I asked him what was meant by, "Am I a dentist?"

He said, "I don't know if it is possible or not but I hear the words 'dentist' and 'Briton' have two meanings."

So you see, he knew already before I told him. That means the passive Resistance was widespread among the Jewish population. "Being a dentist" was like a code among the Jews. The code came from Resistance leaders in Paris, this I know. They had decided if you were a Jew you were "from Brittany" or you were "a dentist." But how were we to know? The newspapers didn't announce it. The dictionaries didn't define it. It was in the air. It was something that you didn't know where it came from. It came to you. How do I know that girl knew I was Jewish? I didn't have a yellow star. My zipper was closed, so she couldn't see my circumcision. So how did she know I was Jewish? We had an instinct for it.

That night when I came home I told my wife that there was going to be a Seder that evening, and I reminded her that I had made a promise to my father that as much as possible I would keep up my Judaism. "Because the Seder is a big part of Judaism," I said to her, "I would like to go to it. Who knows where we will be later on? Let Armand have one Seder." This was already April 1941.

She agreed, but she was afraid of course.

That evening I took Armand and we walked into the mountains. We didn't follow routes; we cut through the thickness of the underbrush, the *maquis*. We had already become very familiar with the woods because we often picked berries and set traps for animals, and I would gather wood to bring down. So, although all the trees looked the same, the forest was not unknown to us.

See, in Volvic on top of one of the mountains at the turn of the century, the townspeople had elevated a statue of the Virgin Mary that you could see from everywhere on the mountain because she was 135 meters tall. Once a year in the fall, they had a procession to celebrate the end of the grape harvest. Going up from Volvic in the morning, they would sing songs, make prayers and lights candles, and keep going into the night. We used that statue like a compass and we walked for about three hours until we came to a place up near the top where there was a shack.

There, we found a few fellows dressed like farmers walking around like they were busily chopping wood or carrying things over. When they saw me, one of them said, "You are looking for something?"

I asked him, "Are you a Briton?" "Oh," he said, "you're here for the Seder." "Yes," I said. He said, "Come along."

There was no light coming from the shack. When I opened the door I saw burlap bags hanging on all four walls, and people standing and praying, with tears running and much sobbing. Naturally it was a sad moment.

To celebrate the Seder, we had a few candles and a matzo. Period. No dinner, nothing. Some had an *hagudah* translated in French; most of us didn't. We had pages written by hand, the important chapters reminding us of the struggle of the Jews. Reminding us has kept us alive through the centuries. Reminding us of the oppression of the Inquisition, reminding us of the oppression of the Nazis who already were oppressing the Jews for five years in Germany and Poland, and all of these memories were now brought out. We relived the history of the Exodus but instead of speaking of Pharaoh of Egypt we spoke of Hitler of Germany, and we hoped that we would have freedom the next year. And that was it.

About forty people were at that Seder. A lot of tears, a lot of crying. Elderly men. Middle-aged men. I was the youngest, after Armand, who stood by me but did not participate because he was only eight years old. I was in the prime of my life. Most of them were in their forties and fifties. They were in their primes, too.

We didn't converse. We were afraid to know who was there because we had learned already from reading the papers that if you didn't know they could kill you if you didn't speak, and if you did know they had ways of getting it out of you.

At the end, we said, "Next year in *yerushalaim*," we said "*gut yom-tov*," and we left. Everybody left. We couldn't speak to each other. I never saw any of them again.

To this day, I don't know who organized the Seder, although I assume they were from the Resistance. I have no idea who the house belonged to. Maybe no one. It was just a shack. I assume the people were from Alsace-Lorraine.

Must be. Must be. You assumed a lot of things. Maybe it was somebody who knew somebody who had money enough to buy and to give him the shack for the night. That's all.

Afterwards Armand and I were both very silent. Going out I said, "Armand, God knows if we will have another Seder but in the meantime remember that, although I had told you that you are not Jewish, that Seder is the history of your people." I know he felt confused. Here he is not a Jew and I take him to a Seder. Here he was just a Jew called Avram and suddenly he is Armand again. That confusion has led him to look upon religion as an hypocrisy. He believes more about history than about religion. He knows that he is Jewish, he knows what his people went through, he knows that had our ancestors not been removed from Egypt maybe we would be slaves today. He knows all of that. But he doesn't believe that God was an instrument in that. He thinks only men make events happen.

After this we didn't speak a word. I put him on my shoulders and took to the woods. We came home around 11:30 at night, pitch dark. His mother was in the room waiting with impatience and fear that we made it.

That woman I saw again a few times but we never spoke together.

CHAPTER 15

"I AM JEWISH"

While I was working in the pocketbook factory, I never developed any close relationships, even with Roger, whom I had known as a child. At lunchtime I would often go alone to a café for a bottle of wine and a hunk of cheese. That was lunch, like the Frenchmen do. The owners of the café were beautiful six-footers. Marvelous people, and they loved me because I was a Belgian with a wife and children living in the mountains. They knew that when I was working in Clermont-Ferrand I didn't *futsel* around with the women, and they admired that in me. One day in February of 1941, I came into the café and there was M. Duhin.

M. Duhin, you will remember, was the man from the Belgian Red Cross who had been so kind to Chana and the children before we moved to Volvic. He had said to her that he would like to meet me one day but, because he worked in Riom and I worked all hours in the hospital, our meeting was not convenient. However, I did meet him one time when he came to see them. He congratulated me on the children and on my exquisite wife, and we became very good friends. Then we lost contact with each other until I met him again in that café.

Well, what can I tell you? The excitement! The surprise! Because we never thought we would find each other again. Oo la la. We were very enthusiastic about finding each other, and we started kissing and we started hugging. We had another bottle of wine and another bottle of wine and he asked about my wife and children, and he told me he was already married and divorced and had no children, and so on and so forth. Then I said, "I have to go to work." "Where do you work?" I told him I worked in a pocketbook factory but I didn't say I worked for the Germans. I had no choice, but I wasn't extremely proud of it.

"Oh," he said, "that's fine." He said he was no longer with the Red Cross but was now working instead for Marshal Petain, sending foreigners in France to Germany to be laborers in a war materials factory. "It's a tough job," he said, "because I don't like to send people away." But, he explained, he was helping the Nazi war effort because France had realized it had to be friends with the New Order in Germany.

When I heard that I figured, "Oh, my heavens, a collaborator." And I was afraid to get too close to him because, even though I knew he could help me because he adored my family, I had to keep away from danger and this was tremendous danger. Remember, I was a Jew in hiding—not in the sense that I was living in the basement, but my identity was hidden.

He told me his offices were not far from where I worked and that instead of going to the café at lunch time I should go to his office and meet him and his employees. I could not refuse. So after that day, I visited him there often after I finished my lunch. There I met his secretaries, twelve or fifteen of them, and every one was a beautiful woman. They were the daughters of ambassadors and of ministers and secretaries of state from the upper society of Paris. They were "high falutin," very high financial people. Oh, he was a womanizer, and there was a shortage of men because they were prisoners or in the army. He was always sleeping with two or three women at a time, but you had to fall in love with him. When I came to visit the office, all these people fell upon me like flies around honey—"My dear Bernard, my dear Bernard"—because I was a Belgian, and I was a friend of M. Duhin, and I didn't know if I was going or coming. I loved my wife; I had no idea of doing anything wrong.

From that time on, we renewed our friendship and became very good friends, but always as Christians. He was a very electric person, very magnetic, and a dominant person in the sense that what he wanted you to do, you did. You did not discuss it with him. His was the figure of a commander, and when he spoke you listened.

Whenever he spoke to me I learned something useful, and I went to his office quite often. But he knew in my eyes that I disliked his position. He knew I didn't like collaborators because my conversation was so careful. He knew I repressed my talking, my voice, because I never approached any subject that would have been compromising.

One day, M. Duhin said to me, "You know, Bernard, I'm going to Belgium on business and I would like to take pictures and a letter from you for your father, because he's entitled to know his grandchildren."

Oh, when I heard that my soul fell into my shoes. What was I going to do now? He knew me as a Christian, but my family had a Jewish outlook and my father was a bearded gentleman. Although he didn't carry the characteristics of a Jew, you could have assumed it. I didn't want to get caught in a hornet's nest like that. I was scared stiff.

When I came back that night, I said to Chanala, "What do we do now?" She said, "Bernard, listen. We must one day take a chance and that is a chance. Speak to him and tell him." Then she said, "You will see. You will find a way of speaking intelligently."

The following day I took, from our wine cabinet, a few bottles of wine, our weekly allotment, as a little gift for M. Duhin. You know the old proverb says, "Little gifts keep friendships alive." When I was alone with him in his office I said to him, "M. Duhin, would you mind if I lock the door of the office? I would like to speak to you confidentially."

"Very well," he said, and I went to lock the door. He was intrigued. What's happening? When the door was locked, he said, "Yes, what do you want to tell me?"

I stood in front of his desk. Hanging on the wall in back of him were pictures of Marshal Philippe Petain, and of Pierre Laval, who founded the Milice, the French secret police, and of Jean Louis Francois Darlan, who was one of the right arms of Marshal Petain. I said to him, "Now I am very concerned but before you go to see my father I have to tell you something that nobody else knows, but the information I will give you can end the lives of four people."

He said to me, "Did you kill someone?" I said, "No, worse! I am Jewish, and so are my wife and children."

When he heard those words, he stood up from his desk, came to me, and he grabbed me and kissed me on both cheeks. For an instant I thought maybe he's Jewish, too. Who knows?

Then he said to me, "Bernard, I have been looking for a man like you. You see, I'm chief of the Maquis, the Resistance, in Clermont-Ferrand, and I need a man to help me because I collect the weapons England is sending me by canister and I distribute them to the fellows of the Resistance all around this area."

See, we lived in a chain of mountains that is called the Massif Central. The Massif Central divides southern France, running north and south, like the Pyrenees separate France from Spain. They run a distance two times the length of Pennsylvania, but they are hard to climb because of the 6,000-foot mountains and deep valleys and many caverns and woods. Because of this topography, the region is known as *maquis*, which means "underbrush." Members of the Resistance who lived in those mountains were known also as *maquisard*. He said canisters were collected and brought to spots for him to distribute to members of the Maquis and to other groups and organizations from the armed Resistance.

Then he turned over the three pictures on his wall. On the back of each picture was a defender of the Resistance: Charles de Gaulle was in the middle and to his left was Marchand, the leader of the Resistance in the Massif Central, and General Marshal Philippe LeClerc was to his right. The three French Resistance leaders.

I could not believe my eyes. They swelled with tears. I remained speechless for a few moments. Then slowly I began to speak. In the revolution in Spain, the Passionara was one of the heroines. I said, "You know, during the revolution in Spain, the Passionara said, 'It is better to die standing than to live crawling on your belly like a snake.' I will be honored to work with you." Again he grabbed me and we kissed again, and that is the way I became part of the armed Resistance.

From then on, I remained in Clermont-Ferrand three evenings a week. I would finish working at the pocketbook factory at 4:30, have a bite to eat, and then go walking with him. We would receive canisters of plastic explosives and detonators and machine guns and bullets and other weapons that were dropped in the fields and picked up and then brought to him by friends of the Resistance. The weapons came in canisters weighing sixty kilos—130 pounds—but physically I was very strong and could swing a canister over my shoulder, carry it up the mountain to the road, and put it in his car.

From there, I would go with him up to the wealthy villa of Chamaillere, which was not too far from Clermont-Ferrand, but higher up Mont D'Or. Capitan Duhin lived in Chamaillere in a suite of rooms in one of the few selective hotels. When I saw how he lived I became a little embarrassed because then I could see that he had the means of being in such a wealthy spot.

In front of his door was stationed a Moroccan watchman and bodyguard by the name of Karma, who would have chopped me in pieces for M. Duhin. Karma later died of consumption because he was used to warm weather, from growing up in Morocco, and where he lived in Mont D'Or the weather was frighteningly cold and the food was bad. But while he lived in Mont D'Or nobody could approach Duhin without going first through Karma. When I met him he said to me, "You give him your trust. He needs trustworthy men. And if not...." He took out the dagger from his belt.

I said, "Karma, you don't know me. I don't know you. Only experience will prove me. Put it up."

When M. Duhin and I got to Chamaillere each night, we would open the canisters and hide the ammunition in different spots around the property. The next day, while I was at work, members of the Resistance would arrive for their needed ammunition. Some arrived with bags on their backs. They would fill their bags and then disappear into the *maquis*. Others drove in horse-drawn wagons filled with hay and loads of wood and rotten, dripping manure. Then underneath the hay and the straw on their wagons and in the loads of manure they would hide the canisters with all kinds of wood implements filled with ammunition that they would carry back to the Maquis. The Nazis were smart. They knew the Resistance was at work and they'd look in every bundle we had. But we were smarter. The men brought barrels with double bottoms. They traveled with forged papers.

During the time that I worked with M. Duhin, I never asked him if he knew Roger. I never asked Roger if he knew M. Duhin. In the Resistance, it was a rule never to talk or to confide in anyone. We lived in secrecy, in fear of the Gestapo and of each other.

I worked with Robert Duhin until that May, when through word of mouth I learned that the director of the water plant of Volvic was looking for somebody with knowledge of the world. I presented myself to him. I was from the big city of Brussels, the others were from Volvic, so he hired me. Also, he was a Parisian, and he liked the way I spoke French. The others, from Volvic, spoke Auvergnat. Speaking Auvergnat is like somebody from the deep, deep South in the United States speaking with an accent so thick that you can barely understand it. But being Jewish I had the talent to understand anyone. In me was a little bit of King Solomon, who understood the birds and the donkeys and the mares and everything. After I was there awhile, I was able to understand Auvergnat, and, being that I spoke excellent French, that administrator accepted me as foreman of his plant.

I had no problem leaving my job at the pocketbook factory because I was leaving it for another German job. Naturally I told Roger of my departure, and my employer Orléan. Also, I told them I could not travel anymore because my wife was sick and my children were not well. So the papers went through nicely. They gave me a slip saying I was leaving willingly to go to another German job where I was wanted, and they wished me well. But they didn't ask any questions.

The water plant was an assembly of many buildings. Much has been written about the quality of Volvic water. That water came to the plant from two hundred miles away through underground springs and rivers. At the plant, it would flow into a man-made chamber of gigantic proportions. Through its long underground run, its impurities were filtered out. Today, that water is exported to America. It's good for the kidneys because it's chemically clean.

At the water plant during the war, the Nazis took most of what we bottled for their use. The overflow they didn't take provided drinking water to the population of Volvic through fountains placed in strategic points in the village. When I stood outside the plant, in the distance I would see an immense fall of foamy water coming from around a dark corner, like a terrible cloud, crashing and thundering and then falling into space, and after a few seconds there would be quiet like a lake. Then it would run again, all the way to the Plain of Limoge southwest of Volvic.

In the region of Nice, in the Cote d'Azur, there grow lemons and oranges and fantastic fruits that were used strictly to make essence that they mixed with saccharine in water to make lemonade and orange juice. You know, my family was practically starving, but they never missed lemonade or orange juice or saccharine because I was the foreman there. The tips of my fingers always smelled of citrus essence.

I was foreman over a group of maybe thirty youngsters between the ages of fourteen and seventeen or eighteen. They were young boys and girls from the mountains of Volvic, far away from everything. In the summer, they would wash the bottles, scrape off labels, and seal the bottles by hand on a machine. A few times a week, with an engineer I would go down to the spring to see if everything was in working condition. Sometimes I would change an electric bulb or test the water coming out from the spring for purity.

Every now and then I would see a couple disappear and I figured they were going to the bathroom. One morning I saw three couples go out together. I was curious, and so I followed, very sneakily. What do you think they were doing?

In that village, there was not much social elegance, and sexuality was very natural. If you had a desire, you fulfilled it. If you had a request, you asked for it, whether you were male or female. It was very easily accorded and there was no shame. Wherever you turned you would hear exclamations of endearment, and kissing and hugging was natural and normal.

It was summer, and those young people had the instinct, the animal instinct. They were having intercourse. She was bent over and he was doing it, and it seemed like they would come back with froggy eyes, but they would not be talking.

I was in charge and I had a responsibility, so I took the boys aside and I said to them, "Look, if you want to do things, why don't you do it after work or before? You're not getting paid to screw around." One boy said, "That is nature. You cannot stop it. When I get an erection, I must find a hole to put it in."

Plain, logical Volvic. I couldn't believe it. And while one was outside fulfilling his natural urge, somebody else had to work faster. You had to produce, with no excuses, but no one complained. And I held that job for over four months. Meanwhile, in the village, I became known more and more, and I got to know them more and more.

Mind you, they had two baths for the whole village to use on Saturday and Sunday, but the baths were never full. Two bath houses. And they were never full. When I first went there and saw they only wore brown stockings, I was amazed that they only had one color. But it was not stockings; they didn't have any. Their feet were stained from working in the fields and in the quarry. Only when it was vintage time in the fall, when they would go into the vats and squeeze the grapes with their feet, did they wipe their feet. In fact, they never bathed because they worked long days in the quarry and in their vineyards. They would come from the field and go to bed tired and exhausted. In the morning, they would wash their faces, jump into their wooden shoes, have a drink of alcohol or wine to clean the mind, and go back to work.

I know this for a fact because when vintage season arrived, in September of 1941, I worked in the fields in my spare time for the farmers. I worked at the water plant each day from 4:30 in the morning until 1:30 in the afternoon. Then I would go around to the wine growers and see who needed help. I received no money. But I was entitled to wine and grapes, and I was allowed to partake of a free supper of lamb, bread, cheese, and wine.

I started on one row in the morning, collecting grapes with four women. The rows were so long that by night we were just finishing that one row. I carried a basket on my shoulders that reached from my neck to the top of my buttocks, the bottom of my spine, and the women would pour grapes in it. When it was full it weighed sixty kilos, 130 pounds. I would carry that basket to the road where there was a truck with a huge vat on it. Into the vat I would dump the grapes. Later, when the vat became too full, although my shoes were full of you name it from what I stepped on, I would climb into the vat and squeeze the grapes to make more room.

And as you stomped the grapes, you could snatch a bunch of grapes, put them in your mouth, suck out the juice, and spit the skins out. But you never spit on the ground; you spit into the vat because the skins could still be used, because how much juice could you suck out when you were working fast and you didn't have much time to suck?

I worked a few days and then they said, "The Belgian is honored today to go into the vat to crush the grapes." I was the Belgian. I got the honor. So I thought, just go into the vat and crush the grapes.

But no. They gave me an umbrella and told me to get undressed. Naked. I was to go into a vat where the grapes came up to my neck, and open and close the umbrella to chase the fumes of alcohol, which would knock you out. You had to chase the fumes while you kept stepping, and while you stepped the others drew white wine from a ten-inch spigot at the bottom of the vat.

At the front of the vat, in the spigot, was a filter made from oat straw. Being very fine, oat straw filters everything, and alcohol kills everything, so all the shit from my shoes, and all the excrement of the horses and the donkeys that I had stepped on in the field would never touch that wine that we drank later on. But if you drank too much of that wine, you would get a case of diarrhea that would make you see your great-great-grandmother before your eyes. That wine turned your intestines inside out! So I turned then to drinking in moderation.

After I was finished squeezing the grapes, they said to me, "Don't you dry yourself because the grape juice on you will preserve you from further sicknesses."

Now mind you, six of us were in that vat, and we were naked. We were supposed to come out and stay there stark naked. It didn't bother them, but I was very much bothered because I was afraid they would see I was Jewish. So what could I do? I went into the vat with my underwear. They couldn't understand. Was the Belgian so shy he couldn't show what he had? I said, "That's me. So what do you care?" Of course, I was afraid because of my circumcision that they would know I was Jewish. Only Jews and Muslims were circumcised in those days.

After we were dressed, we started drinking, and while we were drinking we filled an alembic, a mobile still that came through town in harvest season. But before that, when we finished squeezing the grapes dry, we took the squashed-out grapes that remained after the juice had gone through the press and been watered down and sugared. We made a hole in the ground, put all the grape skins in, and covered the hole with sand and with soil. Then we whitewashed the hole with a cement-like white powder to prevent the escape of alcohol and keep the strength of the grapes from evaporating while we waited for the alembic.

When the alembic was ready, we would break the hole open, and with wheelbarrows we would transport the grapes to the machine. The machine consisted of four big kettles like a locomotive the size of a room. We filled the kettles with the grapes. Through the kettles ran a copper pipe line of water. The mechanic made sure that all the spigots functioned. After cooking that grape mash slowly in a constant water drip, the kettles started to drip clear white alcohol about 200 proof. We were allowed to taste the first green booze, so we filled our containers. The longer it cooks the weaker it gets until you come to an average of 175 proof of alcohol. This was a legal way to make moonshine, and it was potent.

At that time there was no coal. We used wood. So we stoked the fire for the alembic and the steam would cook the mash. Volvic was a town like every town in America with a main road. The alembic would come up the mountain and stop at four spots along the main road. It remained at each spot for a few days while the farmers brought their leftover grapes, and the whole village would smell like a still. Just from the smell you could get drunk. Then the alembic would go on to Chattel Guylon and Riom and all over the region. This was the business of the guy who made the alcohol.

To a stranger, the people of Volvic appeared to be big drinkers. For them it was natural. You were raised on wine. My Yvette was raised on wine after her mother weaned her at age two. By the time she was weaned, Yvette was running around and she would say to her mother, "Sit down." Chana would sit down on the steps; Yvette would sit beside her on a little bench, and she would take her mother's breasts in her mouth. While she was sucking she would be turning around looking right and left. I'll never forget. Her mother would hit her and say, "You're biting me," because Yvette would take possession of the nipple, but while she was eating she was curious to see what was going on all around. I guess two years of having the breast was a long time. I don't know by what miracle Chanala had enough milk because the food we had was the worst. I would mix wine with sugar or saccharine and water for Armand and Eliane. That's what I did. After the breast, the doctor said, "Give her wine. It's healthy for her." So I fed Yvette wine, of course mixed with water and sweets, and she grew up.

I had a reputation: "The Belgian, ooh, what a drinker. He can put it away." I wasn't a drinker anymore than you are a ballet dancer. But what happened was they would give me a big eight-ounce glass of alcohol. If I had drunk that, it would have dissolved my stomach and my two kneecaps. So I took the glass, I sniffed it, and—pfft, threw it out—and held it up to my lips. I was very swift. "That Belgian, did you see the way he drank?" I'd cough and clear my throat and say, "No, no, that's enough."

During this period, I didn't work with Robert Duhin, but we stayed in contact. Once in awhile, he would come to the house on a Sunday when I wasn't working. He would come with a couple of secretaries. All of them were well-dressed girls, and the car had gasoline, and he had an official flag on the front of the car. So the neighbors opened their eyes and looked upon us, a refugee family from Belgium, very warily because they knew he was a collaborator. What's a collaborator doing at the Belgian's house? Nobody made any open move of hostility, but when we went with our food stamps to buy rationed goods from the grocery, they would say they didn't have this or that. And I told them I knew he was a collaborator but what could I do? He brought me food for the children. He brought us clothing. He had money and friends, and I had none.

And like this I worked until after the fall harvest, when I was told by M. Duhin that he had another job for me and he sent me a document asking me to present myself at a factory in Riom called Companie de Signaux.

CHAPTER 16

EMORY POWDER AND 1,001 NIGHTS

The Companie de Signaux was a government-owned monopoly that was created when the subways were built in the early 1900s. Before World War II, it was a factory that manufactured instruments to guide the system. When the Nazis began moving into Riom in 1941, they transformed it to meet their needs. The Companie de Signaux stopped making equipment for subways and started making sending stations that the Nazis used to receive signals from clandestine radios. In this way, the Nazis could find out about people who used radios illegally.

When I started working there, I received instructions through Duhin that I was to make contact with a fellow who was wearing an aluminum leg. He knew to look for me also. The first day I worked there, he came up to me and said, "Are you a friend of Duhin?" I said, "Of course." I knew right away he was my contact because Duhin wasn't that well known.

"Aluminum leg" in French is *pied d'alu*, and that was his name: Pied D'Alu. Pied D'Alu's aluminum leg was attached to a stump and at the other end was a stick on which he walked. When he sat down, that aluminum leg stuck straight out. When he brought his leg down, he would bring it down from the hip because he had no knee, but inside that aluminum leg was enough room for him to hide little packages of emory powder and diamond powder that he would give me every morning when I came to work. They never suspected him because he was an invalid.

The factory was a building with three huge halls. In one hall were drill presses and the lathe. In another one were electricians and wire works. In the third room, the rust of the wires was removed by bathing the wires in sulfuric acid. All this was in the control of the Nazis because everything went to them. Every hall had its own stove. It was not a modern plant.

My job was to keep the stoves supplied with coal and to sweep the floors. I would carry the coal in a wheelbarrow from one hall to the other. Being a laborer who was just doing his job, I didn't arouse suspicion in them because what did a dumb laborer know? So I had a chance to put powder in the little oiling pot, enough so that the machine would continue to run still for a few minutes and then it would burn out. By that time the powder was mixed in and would not be found. I poured powder in the oil opening on the side of the motors that activated the devices used to detect illegal Allied radios and ham stations. While I was sweeping the rooms, I would pour powder in finished machines, tractors.

The fellows who worked there before the Nazis came, I was told, had hidden all the copper and pipes and tools and everything else behind planks in the ceiling. Once in awhile, when I could, I would take a roll of that copper to the office of a Hollandish dentist across the street. He was a genuine, bona fide dentist and a non-Jew, and he received the stolen goods from the factory. Whenever we could steal, we'd say we had a toothache. "Go to the dentist." After awhile he'd give you some aroma to make you smell like he'd worked on you; *essence de girofle* it's called in French. Clove essence.

I was wearing a pair of pants received from the Belgian Red Cross that was maybe four sizes too big for me. Around my legs I had wrapped rags like the French soldiers during the first world war, so the pants looked like knickerbockers, and I had a pair of suspenders. With the help of a friend, I would attach a roll of copper wire around my abdomen. Then I would get a terrible toothache while I was working. The guards were German soldiers. I would tell them, "Ach, my teeth, they hurt. I go to the dentist for a minute." I must have been known to them, always working on different jobs. "Okay," they would say, and I would go over. In fifteen minutes, I would be back, with a piece of cotton in my mouth, and I smelled from dental work. The next day I would have another toothache because we could only get temporary relief from the dentist. There was nothing for fillings, just plain pain killers. In the meantime, the copper I gave him would be used to make communication devices for the Maquis through the region.

These were the major Resistance activities. We stole from the Nazis. We sabotaged. I helped divert special tools that took time to replace.

Working in the factory must have been hundreds of workers, but I have no idea how many were in the Resistance. Forty or sixty maybe. Like I told you, we kept everything secret. It was known that in factories ninety percent of the workers were collaborators and ten percent were passive resistance. But everybody hated the Nazis unless he was a collaborator who had goods. Rich people were collaborators; they were afraid that fascism would turn to communism and with communism they would have to share.

To get to the factory each morning from Volvic, I would walk alone one mile from the village to the beginning of the mountain. Then I had to take a steep road down. In the summer the walk was not a problem but I had to work most of the winter and the winters were frightening. Sometimes the silence was torn by faraway explosions. You heard the howling of wild animals in the forest and you didn't see any light whatsoever. Even the stars were hidden.

One morning in the winter I was walking down the hill, and I was crying about my dirty luck to be there when people in other nations, in other worlds, were sleeping in their beds. There were people who were quiet, who didn't know fear, and I had fear. I was walking and it was very cold and icy and I was wearing wooden shoes. Suddenly I slipped and fell with a heavy thud to the ground, right on my coccyx, and I cried and I didn't know what to do. I could not go home like a child going to school. I had to work. So I went down to work. The wind had frozen the tears on my face.

I came into the shop about 5:00 in the morning. Already other workers and laborers had arrived, and they said, "What happened to you, Belgian? You look completely haggard; you look lost."

I said, "I just fell and hurt myself badly on my spine."

"All right," they said, "you work slowly." Then they gave me a job where I stood in the factory without having to carry heavy loads. Instead, I rinsed metal parts to remove the grease and cleaned them with a rag.

One winter day I had the idea for making an electric heater because we had no heat in the three rooms of our home. I asked one fellow at the plant to do me a favor and make me some kind of a gadget with wires that I could plug into an electric outlet to make heat. Different fellows combined the skills of their different jobs and they made me a heater. They took elements, put them in a frame, and made it so that I would be able to handle it but very carefully. It was not for a child, because on the end of the cable were two prongs with a live wire. If I used more than three hours of electricity a day I would be penalized, so I stole electricity from the village by attaching the live wire through the third floor of the house to the main current and nobody knew.

My three rooms were one on top of the other. The third floor was Armand's room when he came back from the sanitorium. In that room, to keep his attention, I hung a chime I had made for him in the factory from pieces of metal. I had all lengths of different kinds of brass and aluminum and copper and steel that I attached with threads and put in front of him so that with a stick he could play music. Next to him he had shelves on a frame and there I put apples that I had collected through the season from the farmer.

Of course I borrowed: apples, pears, walnuts, string beans. I had no way of keeping vegetables for the winter so I tied them with a thread and needle and hung them up to dry. Dehydrated vegetables last a long time. When the string beans dried up, they looked like little worms. I had strings with grapes drying to make raisins. I had the patience of an angel.

Because my job required that I walk all around the plant, I received special stamps for extra food, which I would give to my children and my wife.

Sometimes the fellows would give me a bite from their own lunches because they saw I only ate rutabaga.

I remember an incident during the potato season—it must have been in September or October. The fellows gave the small potatoes to their pigs, so I spoke to Pied D'Alu and said, "Look, you're feeding your pig. We don't have potatoes for the children."

"Well," he said, "I'll sell you a bag of potatoes, fifty kilos."

To take it over from Riom to Volvic was a five-and-a-half-kilometer climb up the mountains. Because I walked to that factory for long, long months for the Nazis, I received special permission and tickets to buy hobnail boots. But five and a half kilometers with fifty kilos of potatoes? That's about 125 pounds. So I said, "How can I do that?"

He said, "I'll tell you what." He had a little two-wheel wagon that he attached to his bicycle. "I'll give you the wagon and you can pull it up."

There was no question that you couldn't or it was too heavy. You just did it. So I said fine, and he gave me the fifty kilos of potatoes for fifteen francs. The potatoes were all small ones that you would feed to the pigs, but I was tickled pink to have received so much food without stamps.

That night when I left work, I took out my red handkerchief, attached one end to the handle on the wagon, and I attached the other end to my hand to hold it so I could walk and pull it. It was cool and I was wearing a heavy corduroy jacket that the mountaineers wear, and I had on my head a big French beret. When the rain and the storm started coming down, I practically crawled on four limbs to keep going. The rain was hitting me and I didn't know that the dye from the beret was coming off on my face.

When finally I arrived home, nearly four hours later, my family was at the end of their wits. "What happened to Papa?" Because they knew I usually was home by 6 or 7:00, and here already it was maybe 9:30 or 10:00 and I wasn't there. They knew that when I came home from the main road I took a side road around the hospice and kept on walking, so when they heard the echo of my step they knew Papa was coming. But pulling the wagon changed the sound of my step.

When I came to the house and knocked on the door to go in, the storm was blowing. Already it had blown out the electricity. A single candle was burning so it was a Dante-esque picture: shadows, darkness, the children and Chana hovering together. And I knocked on the door.

"Who's there?" I say, "It's Papa." So they open the door and I come in with the force of the wind and the rain behind me. They stared at me. My face was blue from the dye from the hat and in the light of that candle they were frightened.

"What happened to you? You turned blue." I couldn't see myself so I rubbed my face and I saw black. "Oh," I said, "that's my beret." Then I said, "I have potatoes for you."

Potatoes! That same evening we took a bunch of potatoes and put them in a pot and we ate the peels and everything.

Later on we stretched the potatoes out. We couldn't make Bacchanal out of it anymore because we only had fifty kilos of potatoes. The children didn't need only potatoes. Chana and I rationed them, and they lasted five weeks.

Another time, after work, I was returning home from Riom. Coming back on the road, I had a habit of trying to pick up whatever I could. I always carried a bag to fill it with something. The region was rich with apples and walnuts and chestnuts and vegetables. Sometimes I would find a lost chicken. Many times the farmer forgot to clean all the fruit from his tree.

On this day as I walked, a big porcupine crossed the road. It must have weighed at least seven or eight kilos, a twenty-pounder. I took a stick and poked him and he rolled up like a ball, and with those huge stickers!

So what do you do with a porcupine? I took off my big farmer handkerchief and wrapped the porcupine in it and brought him home on the end of the stick.

I didn't know what to do with him, so I put him on the kitchen table. That's all the table we had. The children looked at him. They had never seen a porcupine before. I had a bottle of ether so I took a rag and poured the ether on it. Looking where the head of the porcupine was, I put the rag there. The porcupine breathed it into his nostrils, relaxed, and stretched out. He was three-feet long, and wide. All underneath he was white like a baby's skin. We carried it and we touched it and then we saw on the side of his flanks where the points started. While the children were playing with the porcupine, I went to my baker and said to him, "I have a porcupine. What do I do with it?"

"Bernard," he said, "this is like pork meat. We eat it. You take him as he is and you throw him in boiling water and the quills will come out." *Oy gevalt*, when I heard that.

So I said to him, "Would you exchange?"

He said, "Sure, I'd love it. Delicious meat."

So he exchanged it with me for a female rabbit. "Take this rabbit," he said. "She will make a lot of youngsters, and then you will have your meat."

In Volvic, everybody had fifty rabbit cages. I had mine in the hallway of that shack so when I came home I said to Chana, "You know, I have a gorgeous female." She was the giant of the Flanders. She weighed maybe fourteen pounds. And I said, "Listen, she is fertile and she is going to have youngsters."

One morning, leaving for work in Riom, I said to Chana, "Look, today is the day she is going to have her youngsters so listen. You stay here with her.

When she gives birth, put your hand in a rag and grab the babies and put them away in the other corner. When she is finished she will be taken care of, and later the babies will be our food. But if you don't take the babies away during birth, the mother will swallow them. She's carnivorous."

All right, I go to work, I come back at night, and Chana's crying bitter tears. I say, "What's the matter?" Chana was a city dweller. "*Oy*," she says, "you're gonna be angry." I said, "What happened?"

She said, "I could not reach into the rabbit cage and she swallowed the nine little babies."

I said don't worry. I took the rabbit, went back to the baker, and he gave me a rooster. I had a knife in my pocket, so I took the rooster, slit his throat, went home, and said we have a chicken. And that is the story of how a porcupine became a chicken.

In the fall a lot of young crows were born in the pine trees. I had been told you could catch them while their parents were flying around. Climbing a pine tree is easy because the branches are numerous, so I climbed the pine tree and I saw a nest full of young crows. You grab the little crow, twist its little neck, and pull.

My jacket had pockets on the sides, so I would shove all those little crows in my pockets and go down quickly, because I had been told, "Be careful. A crow can come after you." I always did those things while the children slept. I didn't want to show them the barbarity involved in doing those things. To me it was natural for survival.

After plucking the crow, you slit the back and peel the skin because that skin never gets cooked. There's an old saying in Volvic, "If you want to cook a crow you put it in the pot with a pair of steel pliers. When the pliers are soft your crow is finished." But if you peel it first, you get something better out of it. So I made soup for the children, we had pieces of meat I trimmed from the bone, and we ate.

Sometimes some of my friends in the neighborhood would send me a rabbit, and always I would carry a straight razor in my pocket so whenever a chicken was lost on the road I could take pity on it and take it home.

And I learned slowly because usually the thought of slaughtering is very repulsive. It is against human nature to see blood running. But after watching the ritual slaughterer doing it and if you must do it because you have to eat, after awhile it's nothing. It is absolutely nothing anymore.

One day I went to Jean the baker, Jean Eguillon, and there was no bread. "You know, Bernard," he said to me, "we have a woman here, Marie Jadoville, and she is a nymphomaniac."

The word "nymphomaniac" we understood then to mean that she never had enough men. She had eleven children from forty-four fathers. Every day, her husband would go away to the fields to tend his cattle and turn over the land. While he was gone, other men would come and satisfy his wife.

So Jean Eguillon said, "Bernard, if you want bread, why don't you go and see Marie Jadoville. She wants you in her bed."

So Marie Jadoville had an eye on me. It was not in my mind to be unfaithful to my wife, but for food.... I spoke to Chana and said, "Listen, let me try to get out of this by a thousand and one nights. You know the story. Let me try. Making love is not only the sex act. Let me try my charm."

The next day I told the baker, "Tell her I will come tomorrow, early in the morning." He said, "Bernard, try to be there by six."

The next morning was Sunday so I didn't have to be at work, but I had to walk four miles to where she lived. I took the largest basket I could find. I put in it six empty bottles for the milk that I was hoping to get, and I was on my way. I came to her farm about six a.m., and she received me in a robe. She was very charming.

I said, "Where is M. Jadoville?" "Oh, he is in the fields," she replied. "Would you like to look over my house?" I said, "I would be delighted. However, before we do anything, how about breakfast? I'm hungry. And you know, we don't have much food because we are refugees." "Oh my god," she said, "I forgot. Please come in."

I went into the kitchen. Hams and baloneys were hanging. It smelled of fresh bread.

"Well," she said, "what would you like?" I said, "Whatever you put on the table, I will eat."

Now in France people had large, long wooden tables, handmade from oak trees or from walnut trees, and each table had a drawer the length of that table. I pulled out the drawer and in that drawer was a crown of bread, like fifteen pounds, and there was a basket of walnuts, a large piece of roast beef, a big cheese, a piece of ham, a piece of fatback—what Americans call bacon—and all the things you could dream of. And she said, "Come on in, sit down, and eat."

Well, I ate until I felt the seam of my shirt busting, but I felt good. She was sitting and watching me with a smile of satisfaction. "Can I show you the house?"

"Look, before you show me the house, how about filling my basket, because after you show me the house," I said, "we will go on to serious things and nobody will have a mind to fill that basket. We will be too tired or too involved. Let's fill the basket first."

She said, "What do you want?"

I said, "Whatever you can spare. One of this and one of that and that looks good." I knew she was impatient and wanted already to taste Belgian lovemaking. I was in no special rush. We filled the large basket.

"Let's go upstairs," she insisted.

I went upstairs with her. I said, "Don't remove your robe yet. Sit down with me on the bed and let's talk. Let's talk." She sat on the bed and put her arm around me.

I grabbed her by the side around her waist and I said to her, "Listen, Marie, you're a beautiful woman, and I'm a man. You had many, many men, I know it, and you know it. However, you never had a man like I am, because I'll tell you why. The sex act takes a second, like a rabbit. But let me tell you, you are so beautiful, your eyes are so expressive, and your lips are so gorgeous."

I gave her a peck on the cheek. I never kissed her lips because who knew what she might carry. And I had to keep my marbles in my head. I was a married man. I loved my wife. But I needed the food. And how do you cross the river without wetting your tail if you are a cat?

So I kissed her cheek and I spoke to her of her charms and I told her of her beauty. And I told her what would happen if we already were finished. "Tomorrow I cannot look at you and the day after tomorrow you are ashamed of me and it would be an embarrassing situation."

"Remember," I said, "I'll tell you how beautiful you are, and what marvelous moments we could have spent together if we were twenty years younger, and how regrettable it would be later on if we were to do something foolish now."

I sat with her maybe an hour and a half and told her the dreams that we could have had, had we been younger, had it not been the war. I said how charming she was, and how beautiful she was. "What great sorrow I feel," I told her, "that I cannot marry a woman like you, having a wife and children of my own already, and being a refugee."

After speaking to her, her heart was beating fast because she was excited, from just my words. I kissed her and I hugged her and I embraced her, but I remained clean. And I explained to her, "You know what you do is not because you want to do it. It's because nobody told you that you shouldn't do it. But you're doing no better than the female rabbit because basically you're getting jumped, and that's it, and the men go away in five minutes."

She looked at me and I said, "You know, we have been busy an hour and a half. I've told you how charming and beautiful and adorable you are and how lucky and rich you are having your family and your husband and your children, and all your fortune around you. And do you know what you did by helping me now, by having food for my children?"

And the woman really melted away. She understood. She said, "In a short while, we will be killing a bull, and I will have a lot of fat, but I need soap." Then she kissed me and said, "If you want to, when I kill my next bull, will you make soap for me from the fat?"

I said, "Of course," because the Belgian had a reputation. I knew it all. I never said no. Naturally I said yes.

That night when I went home, I said to my wife, "You know, I am now like when I left you. The only thing is I *acht a chinek*." That means, in Jewish, I filled her ears full of a thousand and one nights of stories. And she knew I was sincere.

Meanwhile, in the village, it was known that Bernard and Mme. Jadoville were in love. Of course, in the village it was nothing abnormal because they had no moral idea what abnormal meant. One-third of the village were illegitimate children. Cousins with cousins and uncles with nieces and aunts with nephews. Everything went there. But having done nothing bad, I wasn't feeling embarrassment yet, so when they said to me, "Hey, hey, you with Marie!" I would say, "Ho ho, Marie! Oh boy, you should see that."

In Volvic was a good fellow by the name of M. Cotton. M. Cotton was a tailor who lived with his wife and daughter about six doors from the church. At that time, it was forbidden to kill a pig. The Nazis declared, "If you kill a pig, you will get less stamps for food." But M. Cotton was raising two pigs, and he had no electricity in his pig sty. Being that I was near copper wire and he knew of that, one day he asked me, "Bernard, would you like a side of pork?" I would have eaten—you name it, I would have eaten it. I said sure. He said, "You know what? You install electricity in my pig sty and hang it on one of the municipal lights to bypass my meter and I shall give you half of a pig."

Fine, I said. I knew from electricity like you know from *modernala boodishkeit*. That means *goornisht*, nothing. I knew that two wires connected to two more wires and if it was right you got light.

So I undertook to make that wire system, and I connected it to the lights belonging to the municipality. When I threw the switch the lights went out in all of Volvic. We started laughing. "What the hell did you do?" I said I don't know. So we switched the wires around but an electrician came and fixed it properly. That was an adventure. And for that he gave me no pork. Instead, he made a suit for me out of a cheap wool material. Wearing that suit one day, I got caught in the rain and it shrunk. I had sleeves ending just below my elbows and the legs came up to my knees. Experiences I'll never forget.

Times were tough and made worse because the rations we received from the stamps were already gone because I had sent a lot of packages to Paris where my sisters-in-law and nephew still lived in the court of Monmartre. Whenever we could correspond we did, and so I learned that they were worse off than we were. In Paris you could find nothing. Brandel, the youngest, was hiding from the Nazis in a broom closet. Only at night did she come into the room to limber up and remove the stress from her body.

At least here I could find something with which to go up to the mountain and make promises. I promised a farmer that I would fix the lock on his closet. The closet was made from a piece of massive oak wood that must have been five hundred years old. The lock was hand-forged iron, and I had the audacity to promise that farmer because he gave me food in payment. Every couple of weeks I would come to measure that closet and get more food. He had food! But I had promises.

Even today, forty-five years later, I'm still in love with food. I reminisce a lot. Sometimes when thinking of it I get very hungry, ravenous, and I became disorganized. And what do you think, I lost 3,500 pounds in America. I could tell you stories of eating that are not even human practically. I can sit down and finish everything on the table: a pound of butter, a loaf of bread, a jar of ... you name it, I ate it. I always carry food in my pocket. I'm always afraid of being hungry. I never carry fancy food, just a hunk of bread, a bar of chocolate, or a piece of meat. I would not stop in the street to buy food. That's not a habit of mine. I would always leave the house with food. Even today, I cannot travel without food. And when you are invited to dinner by friends, you don't want to show that you are a famished individual so you eat with elegance and care. My friends, knowing me, say, "Bernard, eat to enjoy." When they said that, "Eat to enjoy," I eat. I have made a lot of people marvelously surprised to see the way that I can ingest food. Oo, I could eat a storm.

That lady I told the stories to, Marie Jadoville, told me she would bring me fat to make soap because she knew I could do anything. One day she brought me two bags of fat, maybe 150 pounds of fat, from her cattle. I looked at that fat and I knew I could make delicious meals out of it to feed my family.

So when I got that fat, I bought potatoes to make french fries for the children. I rendered the fat by mixing it with walnut oil that I had received in exchange for one of the woolen shirts I received from the Red Cross.

When you mix fat from cattle with walnut oil, it makes something like chicken fat—very smooth—and it doesn't harden in your mouth. Ooh, I learned all kinds of tricks.

But then I had to give soap to the lady. In the region where we lived, we slept on old pure linen. Some of it was woven by hand a hundred years before. When you slept on this linen, you did not need a massage in the morning. It was like sleeping on burlap. But it was linen and the Germans would send it to be washed by my friend who had a laundry factory in the mountains, in the town of Sayat on the road to Clermont-Ferrand.

My friend got electricity by using the water coming down from the mountain, and he had a dynamo to create current. In the quarries, the slabs of stone were cut with a special saw. The dust from cutting made pozzolana, or pumice powder. The owner of the laundry received good soap from the Nazis to wash their laundry, but this he kept himself and instead used pumice, the cheap soap. If the laundry fell apart, he would blame it on the war. In the meantime, he sold or traded the good soap to get food for his family. So when I needed soap I went to him. One time the Belgian Red Cross sent me eight wool shirts and a pair of knickerbockers. For one of those wool shirts, he gave me twenty kilos of soap. Good soap. I took the good soap and went to a grocery store, and for two kilos of good soap I received ten kilos of artificial soap. That soap stunk.

And that's the soap I gave to Mme. Jadoville. So I had fat and I had good soap and everybody was happy. I had no alternative. That's the way you had to do it.

CHAPTER 17

VIALS OF DISEASES

Just before Christmas in 1940, while I was still working in the quarry, a Belgian banker arrived in Volvic from Paris and brought his bank with him. In the main street of Volvic was a mansion, whose name I forget, but only a banker could afford it, so magnificent it was, and he rented it. Because he was a Belgian and I was a Belgian, he called upon me. Two nationals together is something important when you are somewhere else. To be nice, he invited my family for Christmas and to share a goose. I said very well. Food anytime. He said, "You know, I know what to do. I'll cook the goose myself. You just come to the table."

But in my heart I knew that he knew how to kill a goose like you know how to whistle the Marseilles through your left ear, so I arrived early at his house. When I got to his house, the man was in a shack and he was trying to kill the goose like he had seen in comic books. The goose was running around half killed and half alive. Finally I caught it and did the job myself, because as a child I had observed how the ritual slaughterer killed chickens, beef, calves, lambs, oxen. I did the same, and that saved a lot of food for us. The banker was very happy. We had a good meal.

Two months later, in February 1941, my wife became very sick with bronchitis and had to go to the hospital in Riom. Fortunately, she was not there long, but in September of 1942, she got sick again. Although Armand was no longer sick, we were keeping him at the preventorium because he had good care there and I would bring him food. But during the time that Chana was at the hospital, Armand was home on furlough. So he remained with Eliane while I was working at the Companie de Signaux.

I didn't think at that time that the Nazis would kill children. We didn't know that a million and a half children had been killed by the Nazis because we lived in ignorance. We only had a little newspaper from Pierre Laval and this I did not want to read because it was not palatable to me. Once in awhile we would hear of someone having a baby and London gave as news only immediate news, and news that we were happy to hear.

But our village was patrolled by a lot of Gestapo because it was located at the entry to the *maquis* and it was a known nest of the Resistance. Most of the people were in the Resistance, because most of the people were against the Nazis and Resistance meant doing whatever you could do to not obey them. You didn't have to blow bridges or kill Nazis to be Resistance. You just resisted everything. There was an inborn hatred of the Nazis.

Mme. Martinon was the head of the Resistance fighters in Volvic. She and her husband had eight or nine children. It's written up in the history books of France. They are national heroes in France.

When Chana got sick the second time, from an allergic reaction, an ambulance took her from the house. I remained with the children. After a few days they sent her back. But during the few days she was away, the village was raided by the SS and the Gestapo, who attacked the Hotel Martinon where a group of executives of the Resistance had come down from the mountain for a reunion. The Nazis shot two men and arrested the mayor and the council. The rest escaped by jumping through the windows, crossing the narrow street, and running on roofs past the mansion, which was six hundred yards from the hotel on the main street.

Just coincidentally, the raid took place on a legal holiday, so I was home with the children. I had Eliane in my arms. Armand was standing on my side. Yvette was not born yet.

We wanted to get out to see what was happening or run away from the neighborhood. However, in front of the door stood a Wehrmacht, a regular German army soldier, a man in his forties. He carried a machine gun in his arms. When I tried to leave with the children he gave me a dirty look and said, "Get in the house." Then Armand said to me, "Papa, ask him if we could go out from here." I said to Wehrmacht, "I have two children here and my wife is in the hospital and I would like to get out."

That German looked right and left but he didn't say anything. Then he said to me "*Schnell.* Fast, run out." I don't know why he did that. Maybe he was a compassionate person. He was not regular SS or Nazi; he was regular German army. That was Wehrmacht. To this day, it's a mystery to me why he was compassionate. Perhaps because he was an adult man and understood better the tragedies of life. Look, was every German a Nazi? There were many of them, like in our Vietnamese War, who didn't want to go but they were in Germany and they didn't know where to run. Many of them joined the Resistance. Maybe that German was one of them.

And so I ran to the home of the Belgian banker who was living on the main street of Volvic. From there we saw the hotel burning, so I left the children with the banker and ran to the center of the village to see if I could help put out the fire.

When I arrived I saw that nobody could go and help because it was forbidden by the Nazis. Not until that hotel was nearly consumed did they allow men to make a water bucket chain from the fountain to the hotel, but there were no firemen. We made a chain and started throwing water on the hotel but it was too late. It was burned. I don't recall if the Nazis took any prisoners then, but later on Mme. Martinon was a prisoner of war. M. Martinon was taken also. I don't know how many of the eight or nine children were taken.

Later on I found out that they were sold out by a woman who was a collaborator. She was a wealthy woman who hated communism and all the people who were the real patriots. She loved the Germans because they were able to keep order. Yes, order. There are a lot of crazy people who believe in fascism. Later on she paid. Her head was shaved and painted with mercurochrome, and everything she had was taken away. In the village she had to creep, and she couldn't show her face. The government removed everything she owned and gave it to the orphans of the Resistance. All her fortune was sold and they condemned her to death, but because she was so old, they allowed her to die in peace in jail.

I left Companie de Signaux in October of 1942, a little over a year after I began, when Capitan Duhin told me he had a more important job for me working for a M. Streisguth from Strasbourg. You could not leave a job that you were assigned by the Nazis unless you had a major reason, like if you lost your head or an arm or a leg. But I had to leave. I had orders.

At the time, my job was to move equipment in a wheelbarrow from one room to another by pushing it along a large platform that was raised four feet from the ground and extended along all the walls of all the rooms in the building. One day I loaded that wheelbarrow very heavily with a lot of steel pieces. I waited until there were officers nearby—there were always officers in the factory. When I got to where the main engineer was talking with an officer, I turned over the wheelbarrow and the noise caught their attention. As they looked I was on the ground screaming and holding my abdomen. Right away people came, called down the nurses from the second floor, and they carried me upstairs. Nobody could touch me; the pain was terrible; I was dying.

In fact, I was not hurt, but I played the comedy. In previous years I had played theatre and I knew how to make the *meshuginah kintz*. That means I knew how to be crazy if I had to. They took me upstairs. There was no doctor, just nurses, so any time they wanted to touch me I screamed like a wild man until they decided I had a double hernia, a tear of the muscles of my abdomen. Because I was no longer any good to them, they gave me a document specifying that due to a working accident I could not do anymore lifting and I could not work for them. After receiving a lot of certificates and affidavits, stamped and signed by the German bureaucracy, they drove me home in a truck.

At home, we immediately called Dr. Blanc, who was with the Resistance. Dr. Blanc was about five feet by five feet and he arrived smelling of wine, with bloodshot eyes. He certified that I actually had a rupture and I received a ticket to buy a hernia truss for 175 francs from the pharmacist in Volvic. The pharmacist in Volvic was also in the Resistance, so he took that paper and he gave me two cases of milk for the children and a bottle of saccharin. I never bought that hernia truss because I didn't need it. After two weeks the doctor gave me a permit to go back to work but I could do no lifting. And that's when Robert Duhin said to me, "Now you will go to Clermont-Ferrand." I must have gone there by the end of '42, the beginning of '43.

M. Streisguth's shop in Clermont-Ferrand was actually two stores. One was a shop where sixteen ladies made cosmetic items for other ladies: undergarments and brassieres and girdles. The other was the orthopedic shop, where I worked with M. Streisguth and one other man making arch supports for the Luftwafen. I dealt with all kinds of disabled people and many of them helped me to live, because in the store I was able to get all sorts of things other people might need that they could never get anywhere else.

Take, for instance, condoms. We received an allotment of three dozen a month. You could sell three dozen just like that. So when a farmer would come to me needing condoms, I would say, "Unless you give me three kilos of butter I can't give you two condoms." He understood that he had to pay me because I don't run the store—I'm only an employee. But two condoms were really worth two kilos of butter. The third kilo of butter belonged to me because I was smart enough to ask for it. One fellow from Saint Etienne made me a pair of scissors in exchange for condoms because I was working with lousy tools and Saint Etienne was a center of knives and scissors.

A lady came in one day, very chic, and she had a prescription for a pair of varicose vein stockings that had to go from the crotch all the way to the tip of her toes. I said to her, "Ma'am, I regret deeply but such stockings are very hard to get. They're elastic."

"Oh, Monsieur," she said, "my husband is the chief of the administration of food for Clermont-Ferrand. If he wants to cut off food tomorrow, nobody has any food, and if he wants, tomorrow everybody will have much food."

"Ooh," I said to myself, "that is some potato—hot, hot, hot."

But she was nice and elegant. Usually we had men fitters and women fitters: a man fitter was more able to be professional than a woman, who was sometimes squeamish. I said to her, "Should I measure you or should I call in a lady from the ladies' department?"

"No, no, no," she said. "I know that a man is much better."

So I asked her to lie down so I could measure her. To me, the human body was only something for me to serve, to work, to help. I was an orthopedist. But as I was measuring her, evidently she got ideas and she said to me very gently, "Do you live around here?"

"Oh," I said, "no, Madame. I live in Volvic."

"My goodness," she said. "So what are you doing at night?"

I said, "I'm going home at night—and being that food for you is in abundance, would you mind seeing if you could help me for my two children? I have a very weak wife and my two children could use some food."

"Monsieur," she said, "with pleasure."

You see, you get a special intuition when it comes to saving your life. You know you can get maybe something for yourself by just being nice and by telling the customer that what she wants is hard to get but you will sweat your head off to get it for her. So it was hard to get elastic stockings at that store. But in Lyon, where we had another store, it was easier to get. I called them, they made the stockings, and in ten days they sent them back to me.

In the meantime, the lady brought me food every time I called her in for another fitting. I didn't have the stockings but I would measure. I'd say, "Come in the morning right after you get up so I can see the swelling of your legs." Then I would have her come to me in the afternoon: "I'd like to see the swellings of your legs."

And again in the evening. I did this a half dozen times because I was able to give her a stocking to try on. Every time she came she brought me a little box with powder milk or farina for the children, all kinds of ingredients that could save my children's lives.

When the stockings were finished, she called me on the telephone. "Monsieur," she said, "if you don't mind, would you please deliver the stockings to me? My husband won't be home. He'll be in Vichy for three days. So would you please bring me the stockings?"

Now what does that mean to you? When I was trying the stockings on the lady, she would press her lips in my hair and I would make believe I didn't feel anything. I said, "Madame, it will be done."

That night, I took those stockings, put them in a box, wrapped them up, and I said to my wife, "Chanala, I'm not coming home tonight. I must play the *meshuginah kintz*, the crazy game."

When I told her I must play the crazy game, she knew food was coming. So I went to that lady. She received me dressed in a thin, elegant robe. And she smelled so good—oh, my goodness. She made breakfast for me with two eggs. And she said, "Would you like to have supper with me?"

I said, "Madame, at a time like this, to have supper with you is an honor."

She prepared the finest of suppers: roast rabbit and fresh vegetables and wine and aperitif. After we finished eating, she asked, "Would you like to put on the stockings now?"

I said, "Your stockings are to be put on in the morning before you get out of bed. Now your legs are swollen, and you are tired." She said, "You know what? Tomorrow morning if you don't mind you can put them on."

I said, "I regret, Madame, but I have to go back."

"Oh," she said, "you can't go home. It is too late. We have a curfew, I meant to tell you. It's already after 9:00. That's it."

I said, "Madame, I regret that I cannot stay with you." "Oh, Monsieur," she said, "but I have a desire for you." I said, "That's very, very complimentary to know that such a beautiful woman has a desire for me. After all, I'm the father of two children. And I'm a refugee and a hungry man and I don't know how to tell you how I appreciate what you have done for my children and my wife." I did not let her forget that I was married. "But," I said, "you know what? Let's sit and talk."

And again the same story. I told her how beautiful and marvelous her lips were, her eyes like a deep lake. And I told her such a *bubbameinsess*, such a tall tale, that I started believing it. And that was dangerous. But what I said came out sincerely and she understood that I could not cheat on my wife. To her, being from France, that was not cheating. It was only an affair and an affair was no big deal, like drinking coffee with me. Do you only drink coffee with your wife?

But she understood, and she drove me to Capitan Duhin in Charmaillere. Capitan Duhin had women who were just—my goodness, in America we have never seen women like them. But let's not speak ill of America. There are gorgeous women here, too. But in Charmaillere I wasn't afraid to sleep because I had Karma to watch me.

When I started working at Streisguth's, the store had just been sold to him by M. D'Astugue, a nobleman from Gascony who had inherited the orthopedic shop of his father. M. D'Astugue was ninety years old when he sold the shop to Streisguth. He once told me, "My dear Bernard, now I have lived my life. Until a few weeks ago I still had a sexual life, not often but once in awhile, but now no more. I have no more interest in life." And that was his philosophy. Then he moved away and we remained in the store.

When Streisguth took over the shop from M. D'Astugue, while we were cleaning and throwing out, we found a lot of apparel that you couldn't find anywhere, but we didn't think to put them away just because they were antiques. An antique was a vanity. I'm certain that you never saw a chastity belt made from silver. I saw it. But because it was silver I crushed it and I kept it to sell. It was money. We had old broken-down wax dolls. I crushed the wax, we rendered it, and we made candles because that way we had light.

M. Streisguth's partner in the store was Comte de Brequeville, who lived in Lyon. Comte de Brequeville was the main owner; Streisguth was the minor owner, but Streisguth was the one who worked at the shop. I became the right arm of M. Streisguth. I had a key to the store because I was responsible for the orthopedics department. I sold hygienic apparel, such as, for instance, special pockets for people having a new iliac operation. Because of cancer, the rectum would be closed up, so an opening in the abdomen was made to allow the waste material to discharge in a bag carried on a belt. I would wash those bags for older people and they would pay very dearly because those bags smelled terrible. There was no plastic then, only pure rubber, red rubber.

So the farmers would bring me what I asked them for. Food was what I needed most. One day, a farmer came down and he was resting his own abdomen in a wheelbarrow. He had a big hernia and all his intestines had fallen into his scrotum, and the scrotum was dilated like a huge balloon. He was in terrible pain. I reduced his hernia by putting him on the couch. Then I maneuvered all his intestines back into his abdomen and put on a hernia belt, which is a spring with two cushions that close the opening where there is a tear in the muscles. However, by putting back all the organs in place I didn't realize I had squeezed his testicles up into his intestine. I put the belt on and he went away.

Six hours later he came back, and he was blue with horrible cramps. It's a miracle that he did not get any kind of infection. By checking, I found out that one of his testicles wasn't in the right place, so I opened up the belt and—bloop—it came out. I fixed him and he was relieved and very happy. I told him to come back to see me the day after tomorrow and to bring me some butter, a piece of bread, and some milk for the children. He did.

And I shared whatever I had with M. Streisguth, because he also was in danger because of his Resistance activities. Whatever happened in the store was only a cover-up.

Streisguth's daughter was a doctor working for the Nazis, but she was Resistance, too. She was the one who had to check all the aliens going to work in Germany. Of course, thanks to her and Robert Duhin, I was given lists of people to see, and vials containing germs for all kinds of diseases not allowed by the Nazis.

The Nazis didn't allow people into Germany who had certain diseases, such as venereal disease and tuberculosis. So I would bring the workers those vials of those diseases. Whenever a worker whose name appeared on a list in Duhin's possession had to go to an examination, I would come to him and say, "Tomorrow, you have to go for an examination, right?" He would say, "Right." I would say, "Before you go in, take that vial and rub its contents on your handkerchief and when they want to give you a test rub that in whatever they want to test. If it's sputum they're testing, take it in your mouth and spit it out and rinse your mouth later on with alcohol or whatever you have in the house." They were happy for the help and did not ask questions. I was giving these men a chance to be syphilitic, to have tuberculosis, to have a rare communicable disease.

One guy who had a wife and four children was told he had to go to Germany. He was a strapping man, a six-footer, but he didn't want to take any specimen from me. Instead, he put his hand in front of a saw and cut off three fingers and he didn't go to Germany.

His wife, Marie, was very heavy. She had a pair of breasts like my buttocks. Sixty pounds of breasts. When I came to her she grabbed me and squeezed me to her breast to kiss me for saving her husband's life.

I said, "I didn't do anything. The poor devil, he cut three fingers off." "It doesn't matter," she said. "We have enough money. He doesn't have to work. And to make children he doesn't need fingers."

So when she squished me in the underbreast, I figured, "Oh, my God, am I going to get out alive?"

When I came home, I told my wife, "Chana, you know what's happening to me? Look at my face." She said, "I see nothing."

I said, "I thought my head was squashed together." When I told her that woman had breasts like my buttocks, she started laughing her head off. She said, "You are lucky to be in one piece."

It was a moment of laughter, because we looked for laughter in the tragedy in which we lived. Sometimes you almost lost the habit of laughter. There was nothing to laugh about. At home I tried to keep things on an even keel, to keep morale high and not to let my family suffer because of the consequences of my life.

That woman with the big breasts and I remained good friends. I wrote to her for many years after the war.

One day when I came back from work in Riom, I found in my home a Portuguese and he had an eye on my wife. He wanted to get sex from her and he thought, because we were refugees and he had lived in Volvic for thirty years, that he was entitled to certain graces from the refugees. Chana was scared but she fought back. I had big knives so I took one knife and I said, "If you don't go I'll cut your throat." In French, I called him everything in the book that's not nice.

Just being menacing was enough to scare the hell out of him, so he said, "Oh, I didn't mean any harm. I just like your ...." I said, "You like a little too much. Touch my wife once more and I'll cut not only your throat but your you know what."

Because Chana was an elegant woman. She had square shoulders like Gloria Swanson and she was beautifully built. She had an interesting grace and she was gentle. She was completely the antithesis of me. I was like a storm; she was like ice cream, nice and smooth and cool. We made a good couple.

The children said, "Papa, Papa! Don't! Don't!" He said, "All right, all right, I will leave." And he never came back.

I was more scared than he was that I would do something. But you know what? You become strong when you are in an action. Before an action, your heart is fluttering, your strength is leaving you, and you are nauseous. But once you are in an action, nothing bothers you. No wonder our youngsters can kill. We have taught them so. And it's natural. The instinct of madness. Your fear disappears and your pituitary glands start working and you find in yourself a reserve that you cannot believe.

PART IV: FROM MAQUIS TO AMERICA

CHAPTER 18

THE MAQUIS

After I had been working at Streisguth's for just over a year, I came down to that infamous day at the end of the summer when the Gestapo was waiting on the bus and my two friends were taken away.

I don't remember the exact date, maybe it was already November, but it was a day like every other, where one had to remember that his life hung on a thin thread. In the early hours of the morning, after a lean breakfast of some imitation coffee and a small piece of bread, I kissed the children and their mother goodbye. At the bus, I greeted the driver, Monsieur LaPierre.

There was not much talking on the bus, but there never was. The passengers all worked in Clermont-Ferrand and would commute every day. We would make room for new passengers coming onto the bus from the maybe ten stops between Volvic and Clermont-Ferrand. You could feel the seriousness of each person, never knowing what the day would bring.

I traveled on the bus every morning with two friends. One lived in Volvic, one in Saya, a village on the way to Clermont-Ferrand. We did not openly know each other. We would just be polite without showing closeness. One was working in the airport near Clermont-Ferrand. The Nazis had occupied the airport in 1942 and were using it as a base to train young recruits from the occupied countries of Europe to fight on the side of the Nazis. My friend worked for them there as a translator between the German and French workers. On the way to work, he got on the bus with two more people.

At the bus stop in Clermont-Ferrand, we stepped off the bus, first my two friends and then me. The Nazis were there and arrested them, but not me. We found their bodies later in the forest. The interpreter was so tall he couldn't fit into a standard box. So they broke his legs at the tibia and bent them under to fit him in a box, and then they buried it. I don't know why they put him in a box.

But coming off the bus in Clermont-Ferrand that day, when they didn't touch me, I felt relieved and I ran to the shop. As I went in, on the right side were about fifteen ladies from the foundation and fine lingerie shop and on the left in the back was the one other man beside Streisguth and me from the orthopedic shop and fitting room. At the end of the hallway stood a man I didn't recognize. I thought he was an Alsatian from Lorraine who came very often for a little relief, until I saw that he had his hand in his pocket, and my heart started beating faster because I knew he was Gestapo.

We knew already what the Gestapo looked like. They always wore long leather black coats, or green grey coats with wide pockets, and always they had their hands in their pockets as if their hands were cold. But, in fact, they held their guns in their hands.

I said, "Good morning, Sir. What can I do for you?" The man said, "Herr Streisguth!" I said, "No, I am not M. Streisguth. He is not here. Who are you?"

And as I was saying that M. Streisguth was not in, M. Streisguth came up from the basement where he had just made a plaster body cast for a patient.

When he came up, the guy from the Gestapo grabbed him and slapped him practically into the ladies' department. Streisguth tried to cover his face but he said nothing. When I first met M. Streisguth he had just gone through the removal of his larynx because of cancer. When he spoke to me, the highest he spoke was in a soft whisper and I read his lips. He would give me mostly written orders because he couldn't speak.

The ladies didn't see what was happening because they were under surveillance in the lingerie shop. We men said nothing. When a Gestapo takes two guns in his hands and slaps you around, you say nothing. You don't play heroics. But all attention in the hallway was on Dr. Streisguth so I was able to sneak into my store. I was relieved to see that I had nothing in there that would jeopardize me, just some packages an Alsatian had left for Streisguth, and that I had everything in order. Nevertheless, I was scared. I waited for the sky to fall on me.

Suddenly a Gestapo opened the door and said, "Please come into the other side of the store." I took my key, locked the door, put the key in my pocket, and went to the other side. I felt my heart sinking. Previously, when I came into the store, I was diverted by the Nazis' abruptness and did not notice their number. I could see now that there were about ten Nazis in uniform—Belgian Nazis, French Nazis, German Nazis—plus some in civilian dress. They herded all the workers into the corner and interrogated them and asked them if they knew about the activities of the owners of the place.

Seeing Belgian Nazis, I started speaking the vernacular of Belgium while making a *Seig Heil*. When I made a *Seig Heil*, the women of the shop looked at me, and I could see by their eyes they were disgusted with me, thinking I was a collaborator. They were not collaborators I am sure because only rich Frenchmen were collaborators. A poor Frenchman had nothing to defend but his country and his honor, while a rich Frenchman had to defend his money, too. Were they Resistance? This I don't know because I never asked them. Like I said, it was dangerous to make friends so we were civil to each other but nothing more.

I showed one of the Belgian Nazis my identity card from Belgium that said my name was Bernard Mednicki and I was married to Chana Sztroch. You know, those names didn't mean a damn thing to those men. And my mother's name, Lanzman, which is very Jewish, was half erased, as if from being handled extensively over time, although I had done it deliberately. Then he spoke to another Nazi and said, "Yes, this is a regular Belgian, a good blood brother." Then I told him, "I want to go home when my child is out of the sanitorium and my wife gets better. Belgium is a very happy place; the *führer* is on the way to making it a happy world. *Seig Heil*." He said okay.

Then he said, "Wait, we can only take so many in the truck." The truck could hold maybe twelve. They pushed in Streisguth and all the workers, and took them away to the *kommandantur* at the Gestapo for questioning. To me, being that I was one of them, he said, "You wait here until we come for you." I was the only one left behind.

As soon as they left, I made a phone call to Lyon and I spoke to the Comte De Brequeville. We had arranged that I would use a simple code language to communicate over the phone because the Nazis were always suspicious. I said, "You know my grandmother is very sick. What should I do?"

I knew only a little about the Comte, only that he was Resistance in the sense that he was against the Nazis, but he was also a wealthy businessman with many enterprises in non-occupied France so he didn't take part in active resistance. He said, "Close the door and go see her. When you are finished come back."

So I closed the door, slipped the key in the mailbox, and went to see Capitan Duhin, who was still working as a director of employment for aliens in France. When I told him what had happened, he said to me, "Okay, I am in communication with the Maquis by telephone." He made a call, then said, "You go to them." We embraced and said farewell and that we would see each other again if we were lucky. Nothing was said about living arrangements in the Maquis or what I could expect.

From then until the end of the war, my time was spent between the Maquis and Volvic. In the Maquis, I made raids throughout the region but we never went to Clermont-Ferrand.

I learned after the war that the French Red Cross found M. Streisguth somewhere in Majdanek, which was a women's camp where some men were sent for experiments. His daughter remained active as a physician and in the Resistance but she was not arrested. They never found out about her. M. Streisguth was already a sick man so I hardly can believe he survived. I was in my thirties; he was already a man in the sixties. I suppose he is dead now. I don't know what happened to the workers who were arrested.

After speaking to Robert, I took to the mountains and walked up fifteen kilometers from Clermont-Ferrand to Volvic. I left the store about 10:30 a.m. and I came into Volvic maybe about 3:00 in the afternoon. I went directly to the house. During this period Armand was home from the preventorium and he was going to school. In Volvic there were two regular schools, one for the lower grades and one for the higher grades, one at each end of town. Armand was in second or third grade. His teacher was the daughter of the blacksmith. In the house, I changed into a fatigue uniform I had received from the Belgian Red Cross. I kissed my wife and Eliane. Armand had not yet returned home from school. I told Chana only that I had to leave and go into the mountains by order of Duhin and I would stay in touch. I didn't mention the Maquis. Why should I terrorize her? Chana was frightened already, but there was nothing we could do but have courage. Duhin to us was like the holy grail because he always looked out for what was best for us, so Chana trusted him. The kids were too young to know. Before leaving, we did not feel like talking much. We held back tears but felt sadness in our hearts. We already had been fortunate to find each other a couple of times after being separated. Our good star was still shining, we hoped.

During this time, I was not very popular in the village. I was still considered a collaborator because Capitan Duhin would drive to see me, and on his car he had the flag with the three colors, the red, the white, and the blue, that told the inhabitants he was an official. And he had gasoline. Nobody had gasoline except a collaborator. Naturally we felt uncomfortable with that label, but I couldn't tell the truth because it was a time of war.

From Volvic it was easy to take to the *maquis*, the underbrush, and avoid the main road. You went by going around the café behind City Hall because from there you hit the mountain. I took that road and I went up into the mountains. As I was walking up, I would say about three-quarters of an hour, I heard somebody say, "Stop! We got you."

I knew that they would shoot first and ask questions later, and, being that I wasn't ready to die, I stood still and lifted my arms. As they came closer, they said, "Uh uh, we got the collaborator." They had got Bernard the Belge.

I said, "Don't pass comment. I have orders from"—and I gave them the name of the commandant of the Resistance whom Duhin had called on the telephone, Commandant Soleil Havop. That was his *nom de guerre*, his code name: "Fox." I thought maybe in this way I could keep their sentiments under control, because it would have been very easy for them to shoot me.

They tied my arms behind me and pushed the gun into my ribs, and we walked for a good hour and a half up to the plateau where the Resistance headquarters was. I was handed from one group to another. See, in that forest there were groups of watchmen, so one group would lead me up a ways, turn me over to another group of watchmen, and then go back to their right placement, and like this I came to a crown of trees at the top of the mountain. Underneath that crown of trees was an area roughly six hundred feet around. Hidden within that area were a huge abandoned storage barn and about twelve shacks. One was a pig sty, one was a cow barn, another one sheltered machinery, and in this area the guys from the Resistance lived.

About seventy men and women were milling around. Some were polishing weapons and some were preparing food. Some were just sitting around aimlessly discussing the situation, some preparing the few trucks that were in their possession. As I arrived the commanding officer heard the commotion. He stood at the door to his office, and he called, "Bernard." He made a friendly gesture toward me.

I said, "Yes, it's me, Bernard."

He said, "All right, fellows, I just had a call. Bernard is welcome. Bernard is one of ours."

We embraced and shook hands. He took me to his room and we had drinks together as I told him what happened in Clermont-Ferrand, the little I knew.

The Fox was a quiet man. He preferred more to listen than to talk, so I didn't ask him his thoughts. In fact, I never asked him his thoughts and he never offered them to me. But he had an open, friendly face that attracted me to him anyhow. He was a powerful man, intelligent, with a magnetic personality, and he was adored by the fighters, the men and the women. Often, he would go to meetings in other places in the mountains but I didn't know who he met with because I was not in his confidence. I don't know if he was Duhin's superior or Duhin was his, but I answered to The Fox until the end of the war.

When I was finished with my story, I said, "Now what?"

He said, "Now that you are part of the armed resistance, I will give you a handgun and a couple of hand grenades." He took out a handgun, gave it to me, and said, "Slip this in your belt." He also gave me the hand grenades to hang on my belt.

I had no idea what to do with those three pieces of machinery so he said, "Listen, the gun is to inspire fear. The grenades are one to throw and one to blow. If you have no alternative you throw one to kill some Nazis. The other one, in order to not fall into their hands, you just open it and blow yourself up."

So I listened. And I came to understand the phenomenon that was happening because it was a daily conversation. We heard so many horror stories of the Nazis that dying to us was nothing. When we heard of them removing legs, crushing testicles, inserting foreign objects into the body, and killing pregnant women by shooting them up the vagina, or taking men and hanging them by the arms and putting weights on their legs to stretch their bodies, it sounded like medieval times. We had a friend who was taken alive. They pulled his nails out. Do you realize in your mind what that means? Have you ever had a hang nail that you removed? They pulled his nails out and they tied his testicles with a wire and severed them from his body. The pain! Or of filing the teeth. That was their brutality.

So when you heard these stories, death was nothing. Once you're dead, you're dead. It's the suffering that's impossible, and many a fellow had suffered who never spoke. You knew in your heart that if you had to go through that test you were hoping you would not speak. We trained each other to be strong enough not to talk. For instance, we would let ants walk on our arms, without flinching, because we wanted to toughen up our will, the will of not moving, the will of not speaking. And it was hard.

Then The Fox said, "With the training I have given you, you must now go down to the city of Riom and one way or the other try to get your weapons." To do that, I thought, I would have to kill a Nazi.

At that time, the idea of killing was still very repulsive to me. I knew that in Volvic one of my neighbors, Dubois the farmer, had hidden, underneath straw in his stable where he kept his cattle, a Lebel, one of those old-fashioned rifles from the first world war. And he had two bottles with a hundred cartridges for that rifle. So I paid him a visit.

When I saw him, I think I was more frightened than he was, but I could not show any fear on my face. So, when I asked him gently for his rifle and bullets, he said to me, "I cannot give them."

I said, "Look, I have no alternative. You had better give them to me while we are good friends." I opened my jacket and he saw I had a gun and the grenades were hanging, and I was wearing my armband from the Maquis.

Upon reflection, he said, "Oh, all right," and he took me to the stable, where he dug up a well-greased rifle wrapped in oil and cloth. It was in perfect condition, and so he gave me that rifle of his and the bullets. I took it and I went back to the mountains without going to my house, because the less I was seen with my family during that period the better. Fortunately Chana did not talk too much because she had difficulty with the language and people did not question her much because we were refugees. So she did not have to explain my absences to the neighbors.

After I climbed back up the mountain, I came upon the commander, who said, "Are you familiar with shooting that gun?"

"Ah," I said, "it's no big deal. I shot once in awhile. And he said, "Go ahead."

So I put bullets in that gun, shot, and the recoil gave me such a slap in the face, I fell down and everyone started laughing. You know, when you hold a rifle you must press it into your shoulder. I had just let it lay.

That first night the fellows put me up and I started the life of the Resistance. We were very fortunate in that we were on top of a mountain that was worn down over the centuries. Trees had been planted in a crown and those trees made a tremendous curtain that prevented the Nazis from ever seeing what was happening underneath. Underneath were the shacks where we slept.

Inside the shacks we slept on bundles of straw. In the winter when the temperatures started dropping, we warmed our hands and body with sheep skins, so we had an odor of sheep around us but it didn't bother us, and we slept together to keep warm. There was nothing hygienic or fancy. We had no toilets, no showers. In the region all around us were springs that came down from the mountain, so when we were thirsty we would scoop up the water and drink it. Sometimes we had soapy water with the stinking odor of rotten eggs but it was wet. We didn't argue. We got used to it.

Those who were in action would go away. Those who stayed behind would not talk much of what went on. If you had something to do, the commanding officer would call you in, give you instructions, you would take two fellows, six fellows, whatever was necessary, and you would do whatever had to be done. Whether it was sabotage or bringing somebody or finding out something or blowing up some electrical towers, there was always the fear of being caught by collaborators or soldiers.

We were men and women. There was no difference, no inequality of sexes. The women in the Resistance were only those of intellectual caliber, who understood the political ramifications of living with men in the mountains. They were very elegant, well bred, of higher stature in life. But they never acted as if they were better than the rest of us. On the contrary, if they saw people with a little refinement, a little intelligence, they would seek friendship because it was here today, gone tomorrow, because many of us died.

The girls, those beautiful young ladies, knowing that we were destined any moment to die, very honestly and with pure beauty would say, "In case you have any desire for some solace, I'll be more than delighted to spend the night with you." And we had high respect for those girls. Never an insulting word or an obscenity. If you wanted something, very gently you would tell one of them. She would accept it or she would refuse you, and that was all. They knew that I was in love with my wife, that I was very attached to the children, so they held me with highest esteem. Nobody ever asked me to go have sex with them because they knew it wouldn't interest me.

I remember, of course, that many of the girls had to go through abortions because they got pregnant, so we had a doctor with us, and I would help him in his action. We barely had the means to sterilize his tools; we used alcohol. And we had no anesthesia, so we'd give the girl a rag in her teeth and she would hold the hands of some fellows. With a stick behind her legs I would pull up while the doctor would work to clean out her womb. It took ten, twenty seconds but those twenty seconds to her were like five years. It was horrible, but the strength of them biting on that rag. When it was finished we loved them like our own children, those girls. I was the same age as many of them but I was like a father to them. I understood the situation. And a few days later, those girls would be all right and none of them took sick or anything. They gave their bodies but they were also fighters. They threw grenades, they carried pistols, they did whatever they had to do. They dressed like the men, and to me this was extraordinary because I had never seen a woman wearing men's slacks, but they had to be able to move in the bushes.

And that's the way life was. When the war finished and we separated, it was like completely forgotten, for those who remained alive, of course. But many didn't make it because of the treachery, and because of fights with the Nazis. We had organized battles. One day, we saw a whole detachment of soldiers coming up the mountain by the road. From our Maquis, we saw them coming up so we organized our men, and at a single blow hand grenades were thrown and destroyed the whole battalion. But we paid dearly. Whenever we had an action, the Nazis took hostages in every village between where it happened and Riom.

Being a hostage was a sacrifice that the villagers had to make so that we would be able to fight again. They had no alternative because we didn't ask them. We did the damage and they paid the price. The Nazis sent up very strong forces against us. They sent a plane everyday at the same time to spy on us.

But we had no alternative either. The villagers were angry at us in one way; in another, they rejoiced that we destroyed their enemies. We couldn't do anything else. We couldn't stop fighting just because there would be victims. We were all victims of the war, and that war was a very bloody one.

For example, Oradour sur Glane was a village about sixty miles from Riom, and it was occupied by the Nazis. One day in 1944, another Maquis group had ambushed some Nazis forty kilometers from Riom and destroyed the whole contingent. In fury, the Nazis arrested everyone in the village of Oradour sur Glane, shackled them, pushed them into the church, surrounded the church, locked the doors, and threw flaming bombs in it. They burned all those people alive, and nobody was allowed to come and help. Only a few survivors who were hidden in the depth of the church were able to tell the story later on. Right after the war, chains were stretched around the church.

Nothing was touched, but cadavers were removed. They were national heroes, and a stone was set up saying that this is a monument created by the horror of the Nazi occupation. They lost six hundred people in Oradour sur Glane. I think it still exists.

I only found out after the war about the ghettoes, the exterminations, and Mengele and all those murders, but we had our share of suffering. We were the army of the shadow. We were here five minutes and then we were gone. We did our job and then we ran away because we were Franc Tireur—that means somebody who shoots without having an army in back of him. We were the Resistance, and that resistance was something that you had to have courage to do.

According to the Geneva Convention, if you were caught fighting without a uniform you were a terrorist and could be summarily shot. So we made armbands that said we were part of FFI and gave the name of a regiment. I was part of Le Corp-Franc de Riom. The armband bore the cross of Lorraine and Belgian emblems. The cross was a sign of the Resistance. On it were the letters FFI, which represented the internal forces of the Resistance. The Belgian emblems showed that I was a Belgian fighting in the French army. Although the Nazis killed us as terrorists, we claimed that we were soldiers without uniforms.

Within the Franc Tireur there were two factions. Many French people had very democratic ideas, which means they leaned more to the left, and they had joined the FTPF, the Franc Tireur et Partisan Francais. If I had been there under different circumstances I would have also been FTPF, but because I was an alien, and a Jew, I joined Le Corp-Franc de Riom, which was right of center. In 1944, these two sections were incorporated into the army of France, Franc Tireur et Partisan Francais, under Charles de Gaulle.

Le Corp-Franc de Riom was regimental; the FTPF had many factions. We would receive weapons from London and give them to FTPF, who did not have support from England. When we had to do an action, we would get orders tomorrow. The FTPF would get orders yesterday. The expeditions we led were limited, by orders received from higher command, to a specifically defined quadrant. The FTPF created damage wherever they could without looking to tomorrow. For instance, they would destroy a dam today if it would do damage to the enemy, even if the dam might be useful tomorrow when we were no longer at war.

In our whole Maquis were between forty and fifty men. When we needed, we could reunite a few hundred men from the Resistance in the mountains over Volvic. We tried to hit many spots with few men so that in case of a raid from the Nazis our losses would be minimized.

And so we lived in the Maquis. We went on expeditions. Also we had to forage for food, for ourselves and for our families. One day I went home and

Chana said to me, "You know, Bernard, I am very low on food and maybe the day after tomorrow we will have nothing. I said, "Don't worry." I took a big wheelbarrow that I had in the shack and I went to the home of a woman named Maria, a collaborator who was an old-time inhabitant of the village. Her family had been there for centuries. She had everything and she lived on a big property next to the City Hall of Volvic.

I went there with my wheelbarrow, rang the bell at the gate door, and went in. "Maria, a small little thing."

As I went in, she said to me, "Under what kind of an authority do you come in?" I opened my jacket and there were the two grenades and my revolver. I said, "I come in the name of the Resistance to take food for one of their families."

"What do you mean you're gonna take my food?" I said I had authority from the Resistance. I showed her my brassard, my armband which said I was Franc Tireur, and I said to her, "If you make noise I'll blow you up and I'll destroy your home with my grenades."

So she became terrorized. I looked around. I saw that she had laundry soap for washing, and I took a bunch of linen sheets. Then I said, "Is anything in the kitchen?" because I was thinking of the children and Chana.

In the kitchen, whatever was there I took with me. I took a bag of flour and I took some butter. I had a wheelbarrow I barely could *schlep* it was so full but I brought it home. I *schlepped* the wheelbarrow into the house so that later Armand could empty it from the side. They had to unload everything because I had no more time and I had to go back to the Maquis.

Often I went back past the church. In the basement of the church, being that in Volvic there was no sewer system, was a shack that was more than twenty-five feet long. Along the length of that shack were rows of huge steel drums supporting planks that you would sit on and do your needs, like in a latrine. Below the planks were barrels. A man would go into the fields and sit down and finish his business, grab a handful of leaves or grass, and wipe himself, but elderly people would go to the latrines to do their needs. For women and children we had hygienic pails that we kept in a little shack by the house. When the pail was practically full, we would go throw it into the barrels or in the fields.

In fact, after the war, when we came to Paris with Yvette the first time and we used paper to clean her, she started crying, "Where are my leaves?" She was so used to the leaves from the garden or a hunk of grass. Of course, that's all there was. Every week, when the barrels were full, they had an auction where you could buy the barrels of the fertilizer for your field, because human fertilizer is one of the richest.

One night coming down from the *maquis*, it was raining something fierce, with thunder and lightning. I sneaked into the house and kissed my wife and the children. After we had spoken and exchanged the news, she handed me the covered pail and said, "Before you go, would you please empty this?" because she recently had seen Gestapo with bayonets going into the latrine, maybe checking for guns.

I said, "It's okay. I'll take that pail." I went along the walls until I came to the church, went down, opened the door, and swung the pail. In the village was an old age home for alcoholics. They were always drunk, those people, and one was sitting on the plank. He received the contents of that whole pail and all I heard was a scream, "Waaah." I ran home. I was scared stiff. I said, "You know, Chanala, I must have drowned somebody with shit."

Meanwhile, as the days went by, new people came to us from the different Maquis. With some we had natural affinities. You would get friendly with a guy and he would get friendly with you. Not that you weren't friendly with another guy but you paired up with somebody, and I paired up with two guys.

Their names escape me, but those guys guided me, because actually I was far from being a fighter and they had come from Spain, where they had fought in the revolution against Franco. Often in the evening in our hovel they would reminisce about their past experiences.

I had never fought a guerrilla war. Guerrilla warfare implies doing damage and running. Don't get caught because you are an illegal soldier. Fortunately, whenever we fought we had the upper hand against the Nazis. We were only taken by them once, in July 1943 when we were crossing a meadow going to join an expedition with another group in Cantal. Cantal was another mountain region maybe eighty miles from where we were that was a strong nest of the French Fascistic guards of Marshal Petain. They were doing a lot of damage in the camps, so a group of nearly forty of us had received orders to go and quiet them down.

We did not have a plan, only an officer and a lot of courage to walk eighty miles through the forest and the mountains. When we could, we hitched rides from passing trucks, and we came to Cantal.

However, the Nazis had put heavy machine guns in the two corners of the field in preparation for us. As we were crossing the field, they began mowing us down with an attack of heavy fire from 150 feet away. We answered with grenades and rifle fire but we lost a lot of lives. I was fortunate to escape without a scratch, but only twelve others escaped with me.

Then we had to make a six-day walk in the mountains to get back to our Maquis. We had no provisions so we stopped at farm houses. We were told that some of the occupants were collaborators, so we waited for the night and then burned their shacks, and when they were arguing we would shoot them, take food that we needed, and run away. Like this, we came back to the mountains of Volvic after six days, dead tired, exhausted, very sad, and we weren't sent away on any expeditions for quite awhile.

We never found out how we were sold out, or even if it was found out, because, remember, there was a chain of command. I was only a plain soldier. I was not involved in commanding, being that I was a Belgian and being Belgian meant that I was not a hundred percent reliable to them.

And so the months and the weeks of battling went by. We attacked. Toward the end of 1941, Marshal Petain had created the Chantier de la Jeunesse, the youth groups, in order to remove the desire of the youth who wanted to join the Resistance. In Chantier de la Jeunesse, those young men would fix the roads, trim and cut the trees, and so forth. And they were given uniforms.

One day in the summer of 1944, about six weeks before the liberation of Riom, we raided a youth camp in Chattel Guylon, not too far from Volvic. Chattel Guylon was the residence of Pierre Laval. In normal times, it was a spa resort like Vichy or Saratoga. At the camp, they had recently received a shipment of beautiful leather jackets, plus blankets and tools and other furnishings for the winter ahead.

When we got to the camp, we found twelve men on watch on one side and twelve men on watch on the other side, and the camp was surrounded by barbed wire, so we started our raid with a trick. One fellow from the Maquis who was dressed like a farmer said, "I have a delivery of wine. I would like you to come and look at it." When the guy went out, somebody in the back put a bag over his head and muffled his cry. One after the other, we captured the guards and attached them to each other like sausages, but we didn't make any noise because if we had disturbed anybody we would have had an army of seven hundred young men on our hands.

Then we emptied the stores, not only of the uniforms but of whatever food they had, whatever they had received from the German army via Paris. Shoes and jackets and pants and underwear and mattresses. You name it, we took it. We took cases of food. We had four trucks with us, each with ten men and our weapons.

Everything we took we threw in our trucks and then we went back to the mountains. The men we left tied up but unharmed. They were young Frenchmen who were misled. We had nothing against them. The day after, again hostages were taken by the Nazis because everything was done under their supervision. I cannot remember how many they took but they always took a minimum of ten people, usually men of middle age.

Another time, when I was going down from the *maquis*, there was a parade of those young men in our village. They were singing songs that were very catchy and Eliane was walking in front of them, like a little mascot. She was maybe two and a half years old and two and a half feet tall, pretty blond, a little red beret, and she had a little stick on her shoulder imitating those guys who had shovels and brooms. They would sing: "I sing a song. In my cap a flower, on my lips a song. My heart is happy. This is all we young people need to go to the end of the world. You now see us go by under the stars and the sunshine. You think we are very courageous to march on the dusty roads, but you don't know the feeling of a flower in a cap." And Eliane would sing with them, and everybody would admire her. Pictures were taken of the children of the village gracefully accepting those young heroes of the nation. It was all the propaganda of Marshal Petain to see that the young didn't join the Resistance, because the danger was there. Patriotism was strong on the one hand, and on the other hand a lot of people believed that the French and the Germans would finally unify Europe as desired by Petain and Laval and all the other Reactionaries.

Politically we had little intellectual material at our disposal to counter Laval's propaganda because we had very few newspapers and the newspapers we did receive were full of Nazi propaganda and praise for Marshal Petain, and condemnation of the Allies for meddling in affairs where they didn't belong.

Once in awhile we heard a counter-message from London. The allies had a signal: "da da da dum. This is London." Then they would sing the national anthems of the foreign countries and give messages in code. For instance, if you heard, "My Uncle Joseph's collar was ripped twice and my wife's dress has been torn apart twice," you knew you could blow up a certain bridge, sabotage a dam, or tear up a tunnel. Those messages were sent to us via our commanders.

After I joined the Maquis, I never again heard from Capitan Duhin for the rest of the war, but I learned from a counter-message that he was wounded in a fight near the Swiss border and smuggled through Switzerland to England. The message said, "The father of Kalish is well arrived." "Kalish" in French jargon means "licorice." M. Duhin's cat's name was Kalish, and I knew that. So when I heard that Kalish had arrived in England I knew that Capitan Duhin was safe. But I am digressing.

My nephew David, the son of Chana's sister Topje, came to visit us in Volvic one day in 1943. He was maybe sixteen or seventeen, a typical, beautiful Jewish boy with black, curly hair and marvelous eyes. He was a gorgeous boy, and he had joined the Resistance because his father, Maurice, was a prisoner of war. He was carrying two American revolvers, six-shooters that were heavier than he was, and he was very tired. His hair was dyed red.

"David, what are you doing here?" "I am with the Resistance." And he put the guns on the table. "I belong to the Resistance in the Parisian region, but our work has brought us into your region. I took off a few days because I wasn't too far from Clermont-Ferrand and I wanted to see Tante Chana and the children, and I wanted to see you."

I said, "David, I too am part of the Resistance. I do acts of sabotage and we do harm to the Nazis, my group and I."

Well, I was really proud of him. He was very mature for his age. Also, we knew from correspondence with his mother that his father had been taken prisoner on the Maginot Line by the advancing armies of the Nazis. Because we knew David to be a brave young man, we had expected him to take part in our struggle, although I never asked him questions about his involvement. However, I took his two guns and hid them away amongst the rocks and stones in our tiny basement because you never knew when anybody would come. "When you leave," I said, "I have your weapons here."

Then I said to him, "What is the idea of your red hair?"

"Well," he said, "you know I really have black hair. But I looked so Jewish. Now I have red hair."

The following day David said to me, "What I would really like would be two tomatoes to take with me on the road," because he missed fruits and vegetables. Food supplies were low. We were eating what little we could find. We killed a pig in the fields and while he was still squeaking we removed the ham. Then we poured alcohol on it and flamed it and ate it while it was still raw because we were starved. Do you know that day in and day out we used to eat only cheese and drink only brandy? Your mouth becomes like a furnace, a stove, and your bowels don't work anymore.

So I gave David two tomatoes. Then we said our goodbyes, he left, and I went back up to the Maquis.

During the period when I worked at Streisguth's, many people in Volvic had thought I was a collaborator, but when the inhabitants found out I was with the Maquis, they got a new outlook about me. The Channeboux cheese merchants were good to my family. We received the highest respect from the villagers and they surrounded Chana and the children with care and goodwill. They shared with her more often than previously, so life became a little easier but I wasn't there so life wasn't very important anyway. The few times we could see our families we would sneak down for only a few hours. Because that's the way it was; it was one for all and all for one.

Yvette was born in Riom in 1943 in a hospital called Hotel Dieu, the House of God. In that House of God were alcoves made in the ninth century from lava. Inside those alcoves were mattresses on which the patients slept, very uncomfortably.

After Chanala gave birth, and while she was still at the hospital, she met a kind woman named Mme. Hoche. Mme. Hoche had numerous children and her husband was the head of food distribution for the collaborators of Vichy. Mme. Hoche had pity on us because we were Belgian refugees and the Belgians were very well received, with a lot of sympathy, because we had fought the first world war, we fought the second world war, and we were a small country, and not in the spirit of fighting.

When Yvette was born, Mme. Hoche asked my wife to accept the medal of the little virgin in gold. Chanala accepted but she explained that she could not take the little one to church there because she had to be baptized up in Volvic, and that lady believed her. Chana spent ten days in the hospital. In those ten days, Yvette was never bathed. She was washed with olive oil. Very primitive but evidently very sane because when Yvette came up to Volvic later on she flourished. She had the reddest cheeks in the world. She was the most gorgeous baby in the neighborhood, not because she's my Yvette but because she was. And she ate only mother's milk.

I was told about the birth of Yvette from Father Mattieu, the Catholic priest from Volvic who was with the Resistance, while I was in the Maquis. I was told also that I had to go to the hospital to bring them up but that there was no gasoline. Fortunately, when I told the farmers about our new baby they were compassionate and they gave me small medical bottles full of gasoline without barter.

I went to the hospital with a Parisian refugee who was kind enough to drive me in his car. Going there, we didn't use a drop of gasoline because it was all downhill and where it was flat we pushed the truck. But going up we had just enough gasoline to go back home.

At home, living next door to us were our landlords, very wealthy landowners. Jean Compaign was a guy who never knew what missing food was. He had large holdings up in the mountains, with farmers working for him. He had a fat belly and was typically Volvic. Mme. Compaign had given birth the same time as Chana.

My wife was breast-feeding Yvette, being that there was little food otherwise but Chanala always had enough milk, and Yvette was a beautiful baby. The lady next door had everything and her child looked pathetic, like an underfed baby. Yvette grew up marvelously, healthy, strong. The boy next door grew up with the help of doctors and the help of nurses and sickness. It wasn't something that we wished on him, but if you were a superstitious person you might think someone had cast an evil eye on that boy.

When the war finished and we were ready to leave, Mme. Compaign said to my wife, "I don't know by what miracle you made it, but your daughter, Yvette, looks like my child should have looked because we had everything and you had nothing." And Chana said, "Evidently love is more than anything else," because those people in Volvic had children like cattle. They had them in a drunken state. There was no love or affection. They didn't give the kind of care that you give to a child that is precious to you.

After awhile, Yvette grew up. Life in the village was going on and the children were part of it. The street on which we lived was very narrow, and just on the other side lived a M. Cotton. M. Cotton had a little tailor shop and he was also raising two pigs in the back of his own kitchen. From a pig they threw nothing away, so when the time came to kill it they kept the blood, the meat, the hooves, everything. Because the street was narrow, the pigs lived right in front of the house.

To kill a pig, M. Cotton would stick it right in the aorta and then empty its blood by pulling its hind legs. The blood would come out in spurts. Then he mixed it in a basin with vinegar and a little salt. After it was collected, the pig was opened. Everything was used, nothing was discarded, and the blood was boiled, along with apples and some cognac and spices. Then they added the derma to make a delicious bloodwurst called boudin.

The children saw these things happen. One day I saw the children playing in the house. Eliane was pretending to kill Yvette, who was squeaking like a pig. I said, "Children, what are you doing?" "Oh, we are playing 'Kill the pig.'" What could I do?

My children became used to a different life, a plain life. They knew that if you take a female rabbit to a male, she will have babies if the male touches her. They knew what a male goat does to a nanny goat. They knew all of that because it was natural. Everything was natural.

At that time we never thought we would survive so we made plans assuming Hitler would win the war. I said we go higher up into the mountains and we would really become Christians and make the children honest to god Christians. We'd save our lives. We believed Hitler would win everything. He would even win America. He already had plans for America. He would destroy all the Jews and enslave all the natives. He would take all the Aryans, the Swedish and the German, and make them the lords and masters of the country, and leave the Jews exclusively to be a curiosity in a museum. And he would annihilate two-thirds of the country.

Fortunately, I was never suspected of being a Jew because they had no image of what a Jew should be or what one might even look like. No one in the Resistance was ever known to be a Jew except for one other fellow, and he was an idiot who I stayed away from. I never even gave him a good morning or good night. He was slim and lively. Soon after he joined us, he decided he wanted to have a higher rank so he put an officer's belt across his chest and started to give us orders. We were not used to having any form of a commanding officer, much less a newcomer, and he was bragging that he was an ex-officer and Jewish. Quickly he learned to change his behavior after Commandant Fox spoke to him, but later he left us.

Other than him, my friends in the Maquis had never seen a Jew. They only heard of the Jew because of the legend of the Jew killing Christ. They knew the Jew to be a person with a pair of horns and a hooved foot, and the Jew as a money lender. All those, the typical stereotypes of the Jew, that was what they knew a Jew to be.

Of course, passing as a Christian wasn't easy because I had to remember. To help me remember, I took all the holy medals from all the saints I could find and I pinned them inside my jacket. Whenever I opened my jacket to take a handkerchief or made any movement, I would always show my medals, and that was protection against all the evil eyes. I was more Catholic than the pope.

In Volvic, where the people were Catholic, I was a Protestant. In Riom, where the people were Protestants, I was a Catholic. Then when someone in Volvic said, "How come you don't come to church on Sunday?" I would say, "It's not my church. I'm a Protestant. I go to Riom." In Riom, after I had become friends with Mme. Hoche and Robert Duhin and we were asked, "How come you don't come to Temple with us?" we would say, "We are Catholic. We go to church up in Volvic."

So with Yvette, too. "She's not a Christian?" "Ah, yes. We christened her upstairs." And upstairs we told them she was christened downstairs, that is, in the city.

I avoided anything having to do with Judaism. If I knew a synagogue was nearby I avoided it because my emotions got the best of me. I was a hidden Jew but the feelings were there.

With Eliane, however, it was not so easy. She was already getting to be a big girl, three, four years old. She wanted to be with all the other children, so on Sunday mornings there would be a commotion in the house because her friends would go to church and she wanted to go, too. We never could say, "You're Jewish. You don't go to church, but don't tell anyone," because that kind of secret she was too young to understand. So her mother would dress her, but we never could find her shoe or we never could find her stocking, and having no shoe or no stocking Eliane couldn't go to church. We always found it just when the church bell was ringing, so we'd dress her quickly and she would go and mingle with the children outside, but she never went inside the church.

One day when she was coming home, she said, "How come we always find my clothes when it's time to come home?" We said, "It's your fault." Of course we knew exactly where her clothes were. We hid them ourselves. But we felt it was important that she not go to church if it was at all possible. Later, we might have to be Christians because of the victory of Nazism, and we would go higher up in the mountains and lose ourselves. We would again do what the Spanish Jews had done. We would become Christians and we would keep our Jewishness in secret when it became absolutely necessary. But for the time being we would do one thing at a time. Period.

CHAPTER 19

LIKE BLOOD OUT OF THE AORTA OF A PIG

By the middle of 1944, the Allies had already had many successes. They took back El Alamein in October 1942, and won at Stalingrad four months later. In May 1943, the Axis Powers surrendered in North Africa, and four months later Italy surrendered. The Nazis had had many discomforts and tremendous losses and they were trying to concentrate their troops more and more. Then the Allies landed in Normandy on June 6, 1944.

At our camp, most of us had no idea of these victories. I didn't know of them until after the war when I was able to put my fingers on some history of what went on. We lived sheltered from all news except for the newspapers of Petain—which gave only positive news, like births and weddings—and occasional news bulletins from London.

I had no sense that we were moving toward victory. I was hoping, but I didn't know. We were just involved with trying to save our skins, with worrying and eating and trying to scrounge food and seeing that our families remained alive. I didn't make decisions; I just followed orders and tried to be anonymous. I tried just to be a grain of sand on that beach; that's all I wanted to be.

Then, one day in August or September, we were told by higher commanders from Paris that we had to go to Riom. I'm not sure of the exact date. You must remember, it was a time of extreme panic. We were afraid to speak to anyone and if we did we made sure we said nothing compromising. We had no calendars so we knew no sure dates.

We were on the top of the mountain in an early afternoon when the orders came. Some of the fellows and I were taking care of our weapons; others were napping. We were all waiting but we did not know what for. In the camp was an excellent Parisian cook and by a miracle he was preparing one of our rare cooked meals. We were tasting the aroma, so rare it was to have a good meal.

Suddenly, a motorcycle driver appeared with a message from the commander. The news spread like wild fire. In no time, we had orders to go to Riom to oppose a German resistance.

In preparing for our assignment, we became very wild, running around in just our shorts, turning over tables in the kitchen and throughout the camp. Nobody ate a thing. Then we jumped onto the platforms of the trucks that we had taken from the owners of the lava quarries. I was on the last truck with seventeen men.

The trucks that we used ran, like the buses that took me to Clermont-Ferrand, by means of *gazogène*. Instead of using gasoline, they were activated by charcoal. The flat truck on which I rode had difficulties starting so, because all the others had already left, we pushed it to a slope on the mountain, jumped on the flat bed of the truck, and then stood, eighteen men with weapons in hand, as the truck coasted downhill through the forest. Our adrenalin was pumping hard; we did not know to what adventure we were riding. We didn't know the war was almost over. We didn't know that we were now on our way to liberate Riom.

But when we came through the village of Volvic, we saw, hanging from the buildings, the flags of the Allies: Russians, French, English, American, Polish, Belgian. All those flags gave a beautiful spirit of alliance and fraternity and the streets were lined with all the villagers crying "Good luck" and waving and singing *"Vive la France"* and *"Vive la Resistance."* They were throwing flowers and bringing buckets of wine and cigarettes and food to us. We began to sing the Marselliaise.

Volvic was flat for about two miles and then we were back in the mountains. As we drove through Volvic, I saw Chana standing by the side of the street with Yvette in her arms. Armand was holding Eliane by the arm. Yvette didn't recognize me because she was too young, but Chana was crying and Armand and Eliane were hollering "Papa!" I was very upset; tears ran from my face. Friends around me went through the same emotions.

Then we were back in the mountains. We passed many villages until we arrived at last in Riom, where we were directed to divide and take positions on two sides of a wheat field.

Later on my wife told me, "Bernard, Mme. Compaign said to me, 'How dumb can your husband be? With three children, to be Resistance? Does he want to get killed?' And Armand said, 'My Papa didn't get killed, and he won't get killed. And we are Belgians. We are fighting.'"

Previously, Armand had received strict orders not to say that his father was in the Resistance. Eliane didn't know. If Eliane was missing me: "Where's my Papa?" "He's working in the mountains." That's all. But Armand knew because, when he was at home and I was in the mountains, he had responsibilities to take care of his sisters. When there was a minimum of food in the house he would bring in food; he was the provider of the house. He would go looking for food with a bag on his shoulders, and wherever he would go he said, "I am the son of the Belgian. When my dad comes home he will come and pay you." He never said where I was. He was very discreet. He implied that he did not know.

On that day when we liberated Riom, I was sitting on the road in Riom before we moved into the wheat field. I thought to myself: I need cheese, butter, meat for my family. I had in my possession cheese that I had taken from the home of a collaborator, and I was thinking, I wish Armand would come down from the mountains.

As I was thinking that, Armand says, "Papa!" I said, "Am I glad you're here!" The fellows couldn't believe he had come all the way down by himself, two, three hours walking. I said, "I have here all kinds of cheese." We spread a piece of burlap, folded the cheese in it, and he went home to his mother.

He never came home without something. He found lots of food for his sisters. Armand was a hard worker. He was eleven years old going on twenty-five, but circumstances made him grow up very fast. He is a man of nearly fifty-seven now but he is much more mature than his age. He is an exceptional person.

In Riom, we were directed to take positions in the wheat fields between Vichy and Riom on the Plain of Limoge. In that field, the French farmers had already cut the wheat and gathered it into bunches, but the bunches remained scattered in the field so the Nazis could not easily steal them. The ground was rich in clay that was used to make ceramics, so the farmers had dug a three-sided irrigation ditch to remove water from the ground. We took our position, sixteen or eighteen men, along two sides of the ditch, with half on each side. A couple men on each side had machine guns. I had a bag of grenades and a hundred bullets.

Our order was to not let any Germans go past us to reunite with their other forces. We didn't know what was on the other side, so we laid there on the stubs of straw with apprehension and fear, not knowing what would happen next. When dusk came a brilliant moon appeared. The fellows were drinking while we kept our positions.

Lying there with me was a twenty-year old fellow named Mort de Froid, which means "Die from cold." We lay there and in our hearts we were sad. We didn't know what was on the other side, and we were waiting for instructions.

By the light of the moon, I wrote a letter to Armand. "Dear Armand, Tonight I don't know what is going to be. In case I don't come back, please be the man of the family and take care of your sisters." I put it in my jacket.

Mort de Froid became drunk and said to me, "Bernard, my girlfriend said she is finished with me tonight. I want to die."

I said, "Mort de Froid, tonight I don't want to die. Move away from me." He moved away, fell into the ditch, and sobered up. I pulled him out and he laid with me on the grass. I spent the night nervously holding my finger on the grenade in front of me.

At four in the morning, along came a big truck, with Algerian, Senegalese, and African Maquis from another mountain, Cantal. Cantal was already liberated and they had received instructions from higher up to help us. The colonel said, "You simple idiots. Do you know what's on the other side of the field?" How did we know? We had been told to stay put and not let Germans go by.

He said to us, "There is a contingent of 3,500 troops from the German army over there, with heavy artillery that could in a second completely destroy you." And we were only sixteen or eighteen men. Like a spit in the ocean they could have destroyed us. It was with great relief that we left that place to those who came with heavy ammunition and material.

We found out later that the Germans wanted to surrender but they were waiting for the Americans because the Americans were obeying the Geneva Convention and we were not. I remember German prisoners having the best of foods while our children and wives had nothing. It was a big scandal. The Americans said, "We cannot help it. Under the Geneva Convention we have to feed the prisoners. Feeding your children is a local problem. Defend yourself." So we defended ourselves. Whenever the SS prisoners received food, we took it away and let them struggle, and we saw that our wives and children had food.

After we left that field, we reassembled and were sent to the *caserne* in Riom that the Nazis had vacated two days before. The *caserne* is what you call in English the barracks, where the soldiers stay. We thought the *caserne* was booby-trapped, so we checked for danger because we remembered how the Nazis had booby-trapped the train stations in Belgium after World War I.

In 1918, we lived about two miles from the train station that led to the slaughterhouse where they delivered the cattle, and about fifteen miles from the southern train station. A lot of merchandise the Germans couldn't take with them so when they left there was a free for all, but when a lot of the merchandise was opened it blew up. I remember seeing pieces of rail weighing a thousand kilos flying from the train station and piercing the street. On our street, hundreds of people were killed or maimed. Many children lost eyes and hands.

This time, in 1944, the Germans again didn't have a chance to take everything with them when they left. In our own enthusiasm—being that we were a free, willing army, with discipline freely accepted but never imposed—we ran through that *caserne* tossing bundles of whatever was there through the windows. As if by a miracle, carriages came to take away mattresses and leather coats and jackets and whatever they could put their hands on. With a fellow by the name of Kosicki who lived in the same street in Volvic with me, I went directly to the kitchen like our instincts told us.

Kosicki was my friend from three houses away on the street. He was about twenty years old, the oldest son of a large Polish family who had come to Volvic from Alsace, where they were miners. Kosicki was a serious young man. His family had wanted him to go to the youth camp, but he couldn't see himself there. Instead, he had recently joined the Resistance.

In the kitchen we found half a calf hanging in the refrigerator. Then we found a big bag of coffee. Real coffee! What we had been drinking was carbonized grain, called *toréaline*, with a few crushed coffee beans. I took hold of the meat and cut it in two. I slapped half of it on my body; Kosicki slapped some of it on his body. Then we attached the iron bands outside our pants below our ankles and we poured coffee down our pants legs so they ballooned like big columns, and like this we prepared to walk up the mountain to Volvic.

In the meantime, at the train station men found a long line of cars that were like big drums, 20,000-gallon drums, made from wood with iron circles around them. In the drums was wine made in Algeria. The Germans would fill the drums in Marseilles and send them to the wineries. That wine was so rich they mixed it with weaker wines to make vermouths and cooking wine. When the fellows discovered the wine, a group took buckets and with a machine gun blew little holes, and the wine ran like water into the buckets.

It took Kosicki and me only about an hour to go up the mountain to Volvic, even though it was five and three-quarters miles away, because we walked very fast. It was maybe about 4:30 p.m. when we took the little street not far from the church by our house. I had a very characteristic step. My shoes had heavy hobnails, and when I walked the earth trembled. As I came near the house, Armand heard my step, and he said to his mama, "This is Papa."

Mother said, "How could it be?" because I had been away a long time and was not expected home. Then there I was: "Bernard!"

They started kissing and hugging me and I said, "Look, I have no time. Do me a favor. Take a bed sheet and put it on the floor and don't ask questions."

So they took a bed sheet—we had pure linen bed sheets, like burlap, so thick it was—and they put it down. I opened my pants and started shaking my legs and that coffee started flying out. My wife was amazed. Pure coffee! Armand and Eliane and Yvette said, "Papa, what is that?" I said, "Don't ask," and I opened my jacket, took out half a veal. Then I took a rag, wiped my chest, buttoned my shirt and pants, kissed all three children at once, embraced Chana, and hurried back to the camp with Kosicki because we didn't want to be missed.

When we returned to the *caserne* we were told that our group was on the fourth floor. We didn't know that they had found two huge forty-liter barrels of rum. Eighty liters of rum they had, about a hundred quarts. The rum was what the French army gave out in the morning with coffee. You'd have a cup of coffee and a cup of rum. It would warm you for the whole day.

So the fellows upstairs on the fourth floor let themselves go. They were drunk. Carrying on. As we were going up the stairs we heard singing and dancing and shouting. And when we arrived on the fourth floor we saw a scene that you rarely see: fellows running around naked measuring the sizes of their penises. One fellow had put on a jacket backwards and another fellow standing behind him had put a pair of shoes on his hands and he had the shoes resting on the table and that was the size of the man. You know what I mean? The other guy, with arms sticking backwards through the sleeves, made it look so comical that we laughed hard and they saw us. Until then they didn't miss us because they were running around naked and having a great time being drunk.

Being Jewish, I was afraid to join in. First of all, going around naked, they would recognize I was Jewish immediately because none of them were circumcised. Secondly, I had to keep my head on my shoulders. I had a family, and I was not at home. I already was wondering, "When am I going back to Belgium? If all the groups have liberated their regions already and we are chasing the Nazi out of France, when can I go home?"

So I lay down on my cot. But as I lay down twelve guys came, six and six, and started throwing me in the air because I wouldn't participate in their libations. When you are with a bunch of crazy guys, you must do the same thing, so I took a glass and started making myself foolish. But I kept my head on my shoulders and my pants on my legs.

In that room was a beautiful lady. She was of the nobility. But she was a collaborator. Someone had shaved her head and smeared her with mercurochrome, and the stuff had run down her face. She looked pathetic and she was the object of abuse from everybody. I had no pity for her, but my heart was going out to her because she was still a human being. She was a collaborator and deserved to be punished. But they were abusing her something fierce, and I couldn't open my mouth because when people are drunk and you say something in disagreement with their actions you can get into trouble. So I looked away and I said nothing.

And every time someone found something he would throw it through the window into the yard from the fourth floor. One sight I will never forget. We were all very tired. One guy was drunk and naked so he lay down to rest and he fell asleep. Another drunk guy said he had to move his bowels. He looked for a toilet but couldn't find one, so he opened a door, squatted down, and did what he had to. On the floor was the first drunk guy. When that guy woke up, his body was covered with excrement. He didn't know how the hell that had happened, so he said, "How can that be? My pants are clean and I'm full of shit."

Another guy had to go. His toilet was the window and he peed on two guys messing and screwing around as homosexuals, but not because they were homosexuals. At that time there was not that much known about homosexuality and we didn't care. It was not recognized as a disease or a malfunction. It was just something that happened. That's forty-odd years ago. Things have changed. And we never made a remark or a disparaging word ever because whose business was it what you did? You understand? You want to stand on your head, it's your privilege.

Across from the *caserne* was a bordello. We had Moroccan soldiers with us who were so well endowed that the prostitutes were scared to see them coming in. But they couldn't refuse them. That was their business. The men would stand in line and everybody had his ten minutes and that's all. I was observing all of that and at 3 a.m. the commandant, who was very angry because of our behavior, called down the men and bawled them out. Then he said, "We're going on a raid. We are going to the Plain of Limoge to arrest the collaborators."

In the Plain of Limoge, we arrested farmers who had sold out Gypsies. You know, the Gypsies suffered a lot because of the Nazis. We had asked the farmers to follow the policy of the Russians and burn everything, but as collaborators they would sell material to the Nazis or to the French Marshal Petain. They even would sell out hidden people.

After we arrested those farmers, we kept on going. We were a string maybe three miles long of Resistance fighters now, not just our group but many groups together, at least 250 people. We walked in a line a rifle's length apart, going through the cities, woods, everywhere. Our C.O. ran back and forth. "Go, go, go!" We waded through water up to our navels. We surrounded one farm house and the farmer said, "I have explosives. I am going to blow everything up." He was answered, "Don't blow up anything. We'll blow you up or you come out alive." So he came out alive. We took him with us. What happened to him? He hanged himself in the cellar. No, he did not hang himself. He was hanged.

We hanged him because at that time we were far from being civilized. We had just come through the experience of finding the bodies of our friends, our comrades, and because we started finding those bodies we were in a rage. We were soldiers but they arrested us as terrorists, and it was brutal what they did to us. One friend, from Paris, had his chest opened, his eyelids cut off, and his lungs removed. They left his lungs outside his body until he died. His pregnant wife was a pharmacist. They introduced a machine gun into her vagina and let a row of bullets go. Nineteen bullets tore her apart and the fetus died also. We found her body later. The bodies were in the forest, disintegrating, so we found them by having sniffing dogs. I don't speak of what I heard. I saw these things. And I have tried to erase those memories, but I cannot.

After the liberation of Volvic, we began to find more remains of our assassinated companions, buried in the forest in hastily dug graves. By the legal counsel of Volvic, it was decided to rebury those bodies with military honors. The coffins rested at the City Hall of Volvic, covered in black and silver drapes, amongst fresh flowers. I was one of the honor guard. With six other men, I stood watch and saw the mourners come and cry with rage about the cruelty of the Nazis. We had no lead boxes to put those bodies in so we put them in wooden boxes. The juices were running out. Little mice were running around. We drank cognac, and every two hours changed the honor guard because it was too much for one person. Then four soldiers carried each coffin on their shoulders to the church for official religious funerals. The whole village of Volvic was in mourning. Officials from surrounding towns and villages came to pay tribute.

Look, by the time we liberated Riom we were animals. Earlier that day, as we were walking from the camp, we had encountered a group of collaborators in Chattel Guylon. We were on a walk of about four miles through the mountains and the farmland and the countryside and as we came to the outskirts of Chattel Guylon these collaborators came out with weapons, hid behind the trees, and started shooting at us.

To us this was no joke. We had received orders: "No unnecessary heroism. We don't need any more losses amongst our friends." So, we let them shoot and we waited patiently until we saw them clearly and then we shot them down. In that village I think we removed something like twelve collaborators who were the patriots of Marshal Petain: the mayor of the village and the chief of the Gendarmarie, all those people.

After that, we occupied all the important places of Chattel Guylon. Then our commanding officer assembled us and we went back to Riom. He left a few people in charge of the place. But, whereas in America a soldier is a soldier who obeys orders without questioning them, we were an army of Resistance fighters who accepted discipline willingly, but who did not have to accept an order blindly. We discussed it. We spoke about it. They would ask our advice because it was our lives being put at stake. We were going into the field. We were not an organized army. We were volunteers, and when you sent away four men, if those men came back it was a miracle, and often that miracle did not happen.

In Volvic, for instance, there was a father and three sons in the Resistance. The youngest one was twelve years old. One day they had a mission to steal gasoline from the Germans so they took a milk truck and drove it into Riom. In Riom, they were able to steal a truck full of gasoline but on the way back there was a battle. That young boy was manning a machine gun on top of the gasoline truck, and he was killed. The driver was able to escape. Another one who stood on the platform of the truck, he was killed. So from a family of four, they lost fifty percent. But they accomplished the mission. We never knew what hostages the enemy took. We never knew what was happening even in the next village.

So we made those raids and we brought in maybe two dozen collaborators. In the front of the *caserne* were the offices of the guard. Near those offices were the jails. We received strict orders to be good and careful with the prisoners and give them water and bread. But what do you do when a prisoner hangs himself? What do you do when a prisoner falls and knocks out his teeth? Or when he breaks his neck? That's what we said happened. Meanwhile, one after the other during the night, the Frenchmen would come and maim the collaborators until more orders came from above.

You see, we committed atrocities like they did to us, because there is no humanity when you are in war. When your pituitary glands work and you see red and you feel the anger of the torture they committed upon you, and then when you get your hands on somebody, you don't use reason. You let him have it. I'm telling you the truth. There was so much hatred then. You can't know how much we are capable of until you lose control. You don't kill knowing what you're doing. You kill because you lose control. It's anger that makes you kill.

Today, if you speak to somebody about killing a chicken, he looks at you like you're a barbarian. We are speaking of killing men. They were enemies. But they were men. I killed because it was me or him. Otherwise I don't know if I would have killed. So you take a piece of my land; you can give it back. So you take away part of my property; I will get another. But my life? That is something that when you take it I can't replace.

And that's the way it went. Injustices were committed. But we'll have to forgive those who did it because the life they had lived for months and years was so bitter, so filled with anger. We had songs and one song said: "There are people now asleep in bed/There are people now eating white bread/And there are people who raise their children in civility."

They sleep in bed while I slept on the cold ground. My children slept without a father. My wife was alone, not knowing the language....

I'm sorry I cry still when I sing it: "Do you hear the sound of the crow singing of death in the plain?" We felt the cry of the land that was killed, the cry of the working man, and the farmer. It's a warning to the enemy, of the price they will pay for our blood and our tears. "Come up from the mines; come down from the mountains, Comrade. Tomorrow they will taste our revenge." We would sing that song very softly at night, trying not to make too much noise in the forest. And it was very sad.

Right now I'm thinking of friends I lost, the fellow who worked at the airport, the twelve-year old child from Volvic who was shot down. His parents said he died for the cause.

I cannot talk. It's very hard on me.

It's very hard to talk about it.

And the song that came out: "Don't say that this is your last day because tomorrow a new star will come out, a star for the man who loves freedom." It's a Jewish song and also a French song. "Don't say this is the last time you will walk because the sky is dark and lead color. Tomorrow will come, the day for which we prayed. We will prove to the world that we are still there."

I sang these songs with my children when we came together. Often now we sing them because we cannot forget. Ah, we cannot forget. We tried to, but the memory is stronger than our ability to forget. The Germans. The collaborators.

Oo la la, the collaborators! What we did to them! We hanged them. We maimed them. And if we had orders not to touch them, we would tell the *comandante* they were so wild that they hurt themselves, and in hurting themselves they fractured their skulls. We took our revenge and I have no regrets. It was maybe inhuman, but when you are angry, anger colors your brain and you cannot be a pacifist even if you are a pacifist.

Was I involved in any of those atrocities? Unfortunately yes. But now I will tell you the truth. It's forty years after the war. In speaking publicly, I've never touched the subject of killings, of brutality. It was, and it is, hidden in my innermost self, and it is very hard. I have nightmares because of it. I had, for instance, a high fever one time and in my dream I was beating the *Boche*, the Germans, and Minnie said, "Bernard, what did you say?" I spoke in French in my nightmare. She understands it well but not enough to be able to make notes of what I'd said. I know that it plagues me. It hurts me. I wish I could come out with it, but it's so horrible that I don't know what to do to come out with it. And I would like to come out with it. It's part of life. The killing and everything else. Is it good to kill or good to be killed? What do you do? When you see a Nazi taking a gun, ready to shoot, don't you shoot first? And if you are not used to it, what do you do? Do you feel sorry for the one you're going to shoot? Do you let yourself get shot?

Or a guy is holding a depot of ammunition that you are supposed to blow up and you cannot do it because it's not in your stomach. So you ask somebody else to do it for you. Isn't it the same thing as if you had done it? It is. And that's what happened. I couldn't do it. I couldn't do it. And the fellow with me, I said to him, "You take the knife, and you plunge it into him. I can't." He said, "Bernard, your life is at stake." I said, "Maybe, but I can't." Later on I was able to.

And it is not pleasant when that blood spurts out onto you like blood out of the aorta of a pig and your hands are sticky and filthy and you like cannot wash them. The sleepless nights. The nightmares. The look in that man's face.

That first time was in 1942 in the mountains of Volvic. We were on the Plateau of Volvic, which was 3,000 meters above the ground level. Three thousand meters higher was what was called Cratere.

The Cratere was a majestic sight, as breathtaking as the Grand Canyon of Arizona. One day, a group of about ten German officers from a different area wanted to see for themselves what was meant by the *maquis*, the underbrush of Volvic, so they came in an open truck, one of those panzer-division cars with wheels like a tank that would go very fast. The officers were dressed in their full uniforms, and they were joking as they drove up the main road. From above we saw them coming up, so the commanding officer said to fifteen of us, "You go down. Take grenades and dismantle them." And that's what we did.

Some of the men took machine guns, others took grenades, I took grenades, and we snuck through the underbrush. Then we laid on our stomachs and waited as they approached us from below. When they were thirty feet away from us, we threw the grenades into the truck. I don't know who I killed. I was like an aviator of an airplane: You drop bombs, you destroy cities, but you don't see what you do. I preferred grenades over guns. It's much harder when you look your enemy in the eyes or you take him by treachery. I wasn't trained to be a commando. Therefore, it was hard, even in wartime, and what we did is not to be forgiven. You killed; you took lives. I did it in self-defense; that's my only excuse. And in self-defense you don't want to talk about it because it hurts. It is nothing to brag about.

After we dismantled everything, we ran down. Two of the German soldiers were still living. In order to quiet them down, two fellows were chosen to cut their mouths and their throats. We could not use bullets. I was one of the two, and I didn't know what to do. I took a German grenade, a potato masher it was called, and I hit one soldier in the skull and killed him. Then we emptied their pockets and took everything. For my share, I found a beautiful wallet and one fountain pen. The fellows took cameras and other leather work. We took all their clothes, everything, and threw the car off the road into the underbrush, where you could not see it. The car rolled down until it was stopped by trees. Then we camouflaged it and returned to the Maquis.

Four days later, the Nazis started looking. The village of Riom lost fifteen men as hostages. They were shot in the back of the church. But what could we do? It was war. We could not help them. Many men were shot for revenge by the Nazis.

With us in the Maquis was a girl who was the daughter of the minister of the reformed church in the southern part of France. She had been sodomized and raped by the Nazis, but she came out alive. When she spoke to us, we all felt ashamed for being live, human beings because never in your wildest imagination would you imagine what they did to her, and she came out alive to speak to us about it. Thinking of this, we had the strength to commit atrocities. Although two wrongs don't make one right, when it's war you don't test mathematical formulas of morality.

When I killed that second man I was thinking of that young girl, and I was also wondering, without knowing exactly, what was happening to my family. I always thought, because the Belgians were blood brothers with the Germans, maybe the Nazis would be milder with my people. I didn't know anything of the atrocities until I came back to Belgium. Now I regret so much having shown pity a lot of times when I didn't have to. My fury was greater. I could have been much more brutal. But it's done.

And yet it's still happening. Men are still killing men. When you kill another human being you feel inhuman. You feel that maybe tomorrow you'll die. Maybe you'll get killed. Maybe you don't have to show your face. But in the meantime you kill. That's all. You don't question too much. You have no time. Your belly is grumbling. You have to go. Some of the men made in their pants, lost their bowels. It's a frightening thing.

I presume I felt the same way as our youngsters felt when they came back from Vietnam, although in Vietnam the Vietnamese were not the aggressors. With us it was different. Those people had harmed us. Those people had burned us, destroyed our villages, taken our children and women.

And I think for the time being I will have to stop speaking of that and go back to my initial story. Maybe later I will say more. Maybe. I don't know. I'm confused, because this is what has been my nightmare since the war. You don't erase that. You cannot erase it. It was the war. I did what I had to do, and I snuffed out life. Sure it was me or him, but I did it. I had no alternative but that doesn't make me feel better. I never spoke of it, because there is nothing to speak of. There's nothing to be proud of. But when you remember that they pulled the nails from living human beings, and they squashed testicles and the scrotum, and they opened a man's chest and took out his lungs and let him die, and they shot into the vagina of a pregnant woman a whole series of bullets from a machine gun, you cannot put aside the memories.

Again, today you cannot blame the youth of Germany. They didn't do anything. But we are afraid, knowing the injustices of the world, that maybe twenty-five years from now there will be Germans who will look for revenge, because you go through history and you will see the Germans always look for fights. It's sad because they are an ingenious people. They have given so much to the world. But on the other hand they took a lot out of the world. Millions of people have been killed. It is very sad.

I'm speaking again about the second time, when a knife fell into that man's shoulder and then I took it out and it went into his belly while I held him and kept his mouth shut so that he couldn't scream. And then I had no water to wash off the blood. I am not a bloody person. I am not a warrior. I was then trying to save my life. Period.

That second time was near Riom, between Riom and Clermont-Ferrand. The Germans had made an ammunition plant and we had to destroy it. Six of us were chosen for that mission, so we left that night from Riom. It was the summer of 1944 and already after the liberation of Volvic and Chattel Guylon and much of our region. But that position was still held by the Nazis, and by French collaborators, so we were ordered to clean it up. The six of us left, we dirtied our faces with mud, and we didn't take any rifles, only sharp mountaineer knives. See, the Frenchmen with whom I was working on this raid were trained as knife wielders. To them, knives were for throwing. They could kill from thirty feet away. I went because I was a Belgian and they needed obligatory volunteers: "We are looking for volunteers. You and you and you."

The first or second time you kill you feel such a nausea coming over you that you throw your guts up. After you throw your guts up, you feel a rage coming over you and you can stab again and again and again and it doesn't bother you. But later on when you are calmed down, your mind makes you wonder who are you that you can take a life. Sure you defended yourself; it would have been you if not the other guy. That ammunition plant had to go because they were ready to blow up God knows what, Clermont-Ferrand and Riom. When our mission was finished all of us went back to the camp except two who remained to set the mines to blow up the depot. When it went up, the cities of Clermont-Ferrand and Riom shook and trembled. Our mission was accomplished; we never found anything but pieces of the cadavers. It was completely destroyed. But it is nothing to be proud of. Nothing. About twenty died from the explosion. No! Ach. Maybe twelve were killed.

Later on, our commanding officer, The Fox, said, "Whatever action was taken yesterday was an action that has saved lots of lives. You should be proud of what you did and your conscience should be at ease." He always tried to ease the pain. But I doubt if he was successful. I am speaking of forty-five, forty-eight years ago, and it is still something that is repugnant to speak of because it hurts. Wars are not something you speak of casually. And that's the reason I am certain that many veterans of Vietnam are sick today. They creep inside, as I did that day.

He was standing guard in front of the ammunition plant. His back was turned to me and he was listening for noises. I cut his throat. It was the only way. A very sharp knife. Afterwards, you drop it and you go away filthy. Never again did I do it. But for years I carried the heavy weight of it, even today as I speak.

Afterwards I was sick. I threw up. I felt despair. I had killed the son of a mother somewhere, the father of children. He was an enemy. Good. I would have been killed by him maybe. But nevertheless it was me. I was a Jew, Bernard. I killed him and I didn't want to. I had to. And no excuse, I'm not looking for a pardon. I am guilty and I carry that weight in my heart. I'm not a martyr.

That night. What did I do that night? I don't remember. Don't remember. Went back to our camp. What did I do? I don't remember....

It was a clear night, late summer....

The air was still....

The men mingled, quietly....

The Fox tried to ease our pain....

There was a woman who....

Oh, I remember now! There was a woman who was a collaborator, a beautiful woman, and I was sitting on my cot, and I was deep in thought, with a lot of sadness, about my misfortune and the war. She sat down next to me and she started kissing me out of pity and would you believe it I had a sexual encounter with her. I remember now! It was completely forgotten!

Never before had I done that. And never again. Never! I felt ashamed. Ah, I cheated on Chanala. *Ah, mon Dieu*, I had to relive all those years all over again to come out with it.

Ach, and she was a *collaborateur*, only lent to us to clean up the barracks. The next day, she was transferred to jail. She had her head shaved and colored with red dye, and I didn't know if I should pity her or condemn myself.

She was not the one I spoke of before. She was another one. But she was a normal woman with gorgeous long fingers and beautiful nails. You could see her hands were not the hands of a working woman. And she sympathized with me because she had heard we came back from a very hazardous mission. Evidently she must have done this with many other men, for cigarettes, for a glass of wine, but I was a trustworthy husband. I never cheated on Chanala, and here I fell into it.

I had no intentions of having anything to do with her. But my whole being was revolted against having killed and in that moment of revulsion when I hated myself, she came and sat down next to me and I was paralyzed. I was frustrated. I was numb. She took me in her arms and she started rubbing my body and it was war and one word led to another and I don't know how we made contact and there I was engaged in sexual activity. It was horrible, to be unfaithful on top of the killing. It was inhuman, because killing someone is a horrible thing. It shakes up your whole being. You throw up. You think, "What have I done?"

I never told Chana about that. Oh no, I was so ashamed. I had promised her never to cheat and here I was....

When I next saw her, we talked about the usual things: How glad I was to be back. Was everything all right? Were the children well? Was there enough food? Other than that, I was quiet because I felt very guilty, and she respected my silence.

She never even knew I killed anybody. I never spoke about it. Never told her in twenty-one years. Minnie tells me that occasionally, when I was very sick, I spoke from delirium and would come up with stories like that bloody one. But when I dreamed aloud, I cried in French and she didn't understand.

When I came to my senses I never would discuss it. Now I've come clean. I don't want to speak of it again. Once I finish speaking that will be all. I will never talk of it in public again.

There is nothing I haven't talked about.

That was the most serious part. That's my, how should I say it, something buried in me that I didn't want to touch. In speaking I have turned over my heart from right to left and upside down and it came out.

Now how do I feel?

How am I supposed to feel? Am I supposed to feel like I was a hero? Am I supposed to feel I was a murderer? Or am I supposed to feel better inside because I spoke? That's what I wonder.

I want to feel like a human being.

But human is not killing.

I'm exhausted, but I want to go on. I would like to finish my story.

I see the picture of the fellow I killed.

But there is nothing I want to say about it.

It's just that I am so tired.

Would you believe it, if I could I would get drunk but I cannot. I want now to finish my story. When it is finished, I'll say goodbye and go to join my ancestors.

CHAPTER 20

RETURN TO BELGIUM

A few days after the liberation of Riom, we received orders that the men from Volvic were to have a parade, mixed with groups from Cantal and other mountains.

Even though we were happy that the war was almost over, I don't know if many of us had the spirit for a parade. I didn't because I had reflected upon the war very deeply. It had cost us so much. Villages were destroyed. Families were separated. Many were killed. We had a lot of graves.

For the parade, we made a formation in the yard of our camp, with six or eight men abreast and flags unfurled. The sight of all those soldiers was immense. We were a few hundred altogether. We stood at attention. Some wore military uniforms. A lot of us wore Chantier de la Jeunesse costumes. Then we went first through Maloza.

In Maloza, people who had seen me coming down the mountain to work in the plant saw me on the platform and they wondered what the Belgian was doing there. I was not even French. Then they understood. They were told that when I worked in that plant I didn't work as a collaborator but as part of the Resistance. I know that because when I was in Riom people said to me, "You know, Belgian, we thought you were a collaborator working with the Nazis; we didn't know that you were in the Resistance."

I said, "You cannot speak. You cannot pass judgment." But people talk because we have a tongue, and the tongue has been made for talking. "But that's all right," I said. "There's no resentment. The main thing is, the end is good. I'm alive and I hope to remain alive."

From Maloza we went up to the next village, Riom, then higher up, to Chattel Guylon, and then back to the barracks. The whole walk took three hours, no more. The distance each way was ten kilometers, six miles, so the parade was twelve miles all the way around. My hobnail shoes were heavy on my legs as we walked along the asphalt roads, but we were now enthusiastic. The people greeted us with flowers, like they had when we liberated Riom. But we had been told after the liberation that we were going to be incorporated into the French army, so they couldn't come in and run with us and shake hands, and we couldn't run out and kiss them.

After the parade, I remained at the *caserne* for a few days. During this time, an important personality of the Resistance in liberated France, who was wounded near Clermont-Ferrand, was brought to a nearby castle to recuperate. We had orders to watch him so that nobody could come in and kill him. While he rested on the balcony of the castle, two other fellows and I were at the bottom of the castle, hidden underneath a step. We had machine guns and we had grenades and we were ready for everything. About four o'clock in the morning I was standing with one of the fellows, the third one was walking around, and we heard a noise. Quickly we cocked our guns, ready to shoot. We walked out slowly. It was pitch dark, and we heard the footsteps of like a half a dozen people. No sound, just footsteps. We didn't know what to do. Shoot? Was it foe? Was it friend? And us, one looking to the other for guidance. Then we heard "Moooo." It was two cows that had escaped from the farmhouse. Our scare was over. We chased them back into the farmhouse and resumed our guard.

In the morning, that news came to the ears of the fellow we were guarding, so we were brought to his bed. He said he was the minister of the Protestant church in the southern part of France, and he gave each of us a Bible from the Huguenot service. In it, he wrote in his own hand that he hoped the miserable life we had during the occupation of the Nazis would be only a memory and that our children would have a better life. He signed it, "Very fraternally in Christ, yours." Nobody knew I was Jewish, of course.

In the days immediately following the parade, the fellows became very disorderly because they didn't like discipline. We had been a free, willing army, without a lot of the saluting and fancy regulations, and now we were told that by the end of the week we would be a regular army. Those who were not French were given the privilege of being in the French army or getting an honorable discharge. With three children, and at my age, I didn't want to play soldier. I decided my job was done.

On my honorable discharge were the words: "Soldier Bernard Mednicki, of Belgian nationality, of free will and without selfishness, did help the French people liberate themselves from Hitler."

Meanwhile, the commanding officer, after seeing the behavior of some of the men and seeing that I was not a drinker, made me his confidant. The mail that we received from Clermont-Ferrand headquarters had to be picked up by train, so I received special permits in order to ride the train with the mail. I would go down, pick up the mail in Clermont-Ferrand, and bring it back. Remember, it was now the end of September, beginning of October 1944.

Coming out of the train station one day, I took a shortcut, a narrow little street. In front of the street I saw ten or twelve elderly men with *talisim*, Jewish prayer shawls, draped over their shoulders, and wearing *kepas*, skull caps, on their heads. In France they don't wear *kepas* like in America. Their *kepas* are made like a butcher's cap, round with a flat top. Seeing those men wearing the kepas, I was confused. What is today? What are they doing?

Now imagine I was wearing a black leather jacket. I had a rifle hanging from my shoulder, and a revolver, a small gun, on my hip. The war was not finished yet, although in our section it was. I stood in front of the men, wearing a bitter outlook, and I said to them, "What is that?"

Fearfully, the men replied, "We are Jewish people and today is Yom Kippur, our Day of Atonement. This is the reason we wear the prayer shawls."

As they said to me "Today is Yom Kippur," I remained numb for an instant, and then tears jumped from my eyes. This was a day I had ignored for four years, and now it was the holiest day of the Jewish year.

The men said, "Why are you crying?" I said to them, "It is now nearly five years since I was aware of any Judaism at all, and I am a Jew, too."

Well, this was a big thing for them. I was the first Jew they had seen from the Resistance, dressed in a uniform, with weapons.

They invited me to go to the synagogue, where I was received by the rabbi. I gave him my weapons, which he put in his closet, and I put on a *talis*. I was still in a daze. I couldn't understand what was happening to me. When I was given an *aliyah*, the honor of reciting the blessings over the Torah, the prayer just came out naturally. I didn't need the book. I was crying. It shook me up. Here I had just come out of the war pretending to not be Jewish and suddenly I'm back to being Jewish. Here I was ready to become Christian to save my life if Hitler won the war and now I'm reciting the blessings over the Torah.

When I finished, I was surrounded by the men who were present at the service. I remained with them for only about an hour because, after all, I was on a mission. I couldn't *kibbitz*.

You could see their pride in finding a Jew wearing the uniform of the FFI. They asked me so many questions that I was incoherent: Where are you from? What are you doing? How long were you there? Do you have a family? Maybe they knew already that there were concentration camps, but I didn't know yet. I felt confused but happy to have seen a synagogue with a congregation. My mind was directed to Brussels with hope.

After coming back to camp I told the C.O. that, being a Belgian and because my family was in Belgium, I would like to go back and see what had happened to them. He said very well.

I hadn't been back since I fled after the Nazis invaded. It would have been too dangerous because I was known there to be a Jew and a member of different democratic organizations; I fought the Belgian Nazis; I was on the blacklist. Now the war was almost over. Most of Belgium was free.

Before I could leave, I went to Vichy to see the Belgian consul. He was very proud to have a Belgian in the French Resistance and he gave me a beautiful letter of recommendation. In it, he wrote, in effect, that he was consul of Belgium in France, and he was very proud to give to young Bernard Mednicki, a Belgian citizen who had fought side by side with his French companions of the Resistance against the common enemy, a passport and a free train trip from Volvic to Brussels and back.

The morning that I left for Belgium, I arranged with the cheese merchant to see that Chana got whatever she needed while I was gone. Then I went back to Brussels for the first time in four years. I carried only a bag on my shoulders and in that bag I had no clothes, just a little bit of food, because there were no restaurants, no McDonald's, along the way.

Traveling that day was still very hazardous. Bridges were blown. We had to get off, take other trains. Many villages and cities were already liberated, and the Nazis were in disarray. The war was localized in Germany by now and the Allies were on the doorstep of Nazi land. A lot of soldiers were traveling, including many Americans on their way to Belgium. Refugees filled the remaining seats.

I finally arrived in Brussels in the evening after an all-day affair on the train. I didn't know where to turn, so I looked around and I found a delegation from the American Joint Distribution Committee in Brussels. We knew of the Joint Distribution Committee before the war; they helped the poor Jewish communities of the world that they could reach. Thank goodness we never needed their help because we always made a living. After the war, the Committee brought food and clothing and medical help to the first victims of the concentration camps as they came out from the camps. When I arrived in Brussels, I went to them to learn if they could tell me anything about my family.

The people there were pleased to see me. They spoke beautiful French. But, they regretted to say, they did not have information for me. However, they had heard that in different convents were different Jewish children, and they suggested I try there. The closest convent was near Louvain, which was not far from Brussels.

I took the train to Louvain. I was still wearing my uniform from the Maquis. I hadn't shaved for a few days and I had a red beard. In Louvain, somebody directed me to the convent. There, I was sent to the office of the Reverend Mother Superior, at the end of a long hall. At the other end of the hall was a group of children. I presented myself to the Reverend Mother Superior and I said, "I came to see if you have any Jewish children." She said, "Yes, we have Jewish children."

As we spoke, we walked from her office, and as we walked toward the children two screamed, "Uncle Bernard!"

I looked down the hall and saw two girls running toward me, my two nieces, Cecile and Annie, the children of my sister Sheva and her husband Adolph. When they reached me they started sobbing, "Our papa and our mama were taken from the house. When we came home from school they weren't there."

Cecile was ten years old. Annie was only two years older, but I could see that she was mothering Cecile in a loving, sheltering way. They both looked pale. They were wearing crosses on their chests.

A thousand questions came to my lips, but I didn't ask any of them. Instead, I said, "Don't cry, children. I'm here. Until your parents return I will take care of you. Now Tante Chana is in Volvic. When I bring her back here, you will stay with us until your parents come home."

"Oh, please, we would like to get out from here. They make us do things that we are not used to, pray to Jesus Christ and...."

I said, "Children, a little patience. Another few days."

In the meantime, after the war I had received from the Resistance a bundle of money, 12,000 francs, because we had cleaned out a few banks in Clermont-Ferrand. I was not a part of those robberies myself, but we believed that what's yours is mine and what's mine is yours. I took out a wad of money and said to the mother, "Reverend Mother, for your poor, just because you have committed such a charity by saving my sister's children, please accept."

She was thankful and she said, "But would you leave the children with us? We made Christians of them yesterday." I said, "Mother, once a Jew always a Jew. Besides, I'm alive. If I were not alive, there would be nobody to defend the children, and they would have stayed with you. I hope you understand. There is only one God for everybody. So you call him your way, I call him my way. We are still the same people."

I said goodbye but promised the children that I would come back to take them soon, and they became alive—because they had been sad. They were oppressed by all the changes in their lives. That religion poisoned their minds because a Jew, according to some Christians, had to pay for the crime he committed, the crime of killing Jesus Christ.

Three days later, thanks to the Joint Distribution Committee, the children were moved with sixty other children to an orphanage whose purpose was to collect Jewish children who had lost parents in the war. They remained there for one year and a half, until they came to America.

During my visit to Brussels, by some miracle I don't remember, I also found my sister Rebecca. We were, of course... "Excited" is not the word. There is no word for our coming together. Her husband, a M. Verheggen whose first name I don't remember, had been killed by a bomb. She had survived the war alone.

One day in late 1940, she came home and was told by a neighbor that the Gestapo had been there. She decided at that time to go into the countryside. There, she worked in a farm house as a servant until the farmer told her that, being from the city, she would do much better if she was working as a waitress. My sister didn't have a Jewish appearance. She had a look of neutrality. So she listened to that man and she went to the city and became a waitress. She rented a small furnished room, and nobody ever knew she was Jewish. She was born in Belgium so she was a Belgian. In Belgium, we never had to prove our identity until Hitler came. It was never written what your religion was.

She worked as a waitress for a few months, until she saw a lot of Nazis come into the place, and she couldn't take it, so she went back to the farmer. The farmer suggested that she go deeper into the forest, so she did, and found a little house there. She had made some money by being a waitress—and through black marketeering, of course—so she lived in the forest with what she had. She scrounged for two years. While she was there she took sick. Her sickness was a demineralization of her body because she had lived with what she had and it was not enough.

When I came back from Volvic, she was still not feeling well, but she said, "I'll be back. I'll be better tomorrow." Later, when we left for America, she didn't want to go with us. I said, "Rebecca, the papers are for you, too, as well as for me." She said, "I don't want to go. I want to wait until somebody comes back, because somebody will come back." And she waited, but nobody came back. Three years later, five vertebrae in her spine just disintegrated.

In the hospital, the doctors said to her, "We can put you in a cast and let nature take its course, but soon you will die, or we can try to operate." The operation meant they would remove the tibia bone from her leg. A team of eight doctors working on her took the heaviest leg bone, and they opened her up. They removed all the decomposed vertebrae, cut the tibia in two, and made a "V" on the end to connect it to the base of her cranium. From there, it ran to her pelvis. In there, they very gently put the spinal cord. But doing that, they injured her and she became paralyzed on her left side. In the beginning they thought she only had three months to live.

But I'm jumping ahead because that didn't happen until I was already in America.

While I was in Brussels, Rebecca explained to me that deportations had begun in August of 1942 and lasted until the following September. Father died when the Gestapo came into his house. He fought for his life and for the lives of his wife Sabina and their son, my half-brother Jacob. Father was not a passive person, but how do you resist when the Gestapo comes and brings every weapon in the world? Father was a black-bearded man. They hit him on the beard and broke his jaw. He was killed falling down the staircase. Then

Sabina and Jacob were taken to Malines, a concentration camp not far from Brussels.

My brother, Zulu, was caught with a group of Resistance fighters in Luxembourg and they hanged him there. That was all Rebecca knew about him.

Rosa was taken from her home and sent with her two children, Israel and Liliane, to Malines. When her husband Maurice Warman came home, the neighbors, who were Gentiles, told him, "Go away. The Gestapo was here and they're looking for you." This was all Rebecca knew. Later I learned from Maurice that he was hidden by his employer, a furniture polisher. After the war, he married a lady who had lost her husband and two sons. One was an apprentice of mine when I was working in the glove business. Maurice died in 1986.

My sister Sheva and her husband Adolph were taken from their home while the children were in school. They were never heard from again. When the children came home from school, neighbors hid them and sent them away to those safe places.

Charles, the brother of Cecile and Annie, was sent to a monastery on the French border, and he was just six years old. He remained with a group of boys who were cared for by a teacher who would travel from place to place with them because she didn't want the Germans to harm them. This is how he survived the war. After the war, he remained in an orphanage until he came to America with his sisters. But this I learned later. One day after I went back to Volvic and before I returned to Brussels with my family, the girls returned to the house where they had lived and rang the doorbell so they could speak to the people who lived there to find out about their parents. That same day, Charles also had come down from the monastery. They looked at each other and Cecile said, not having seen him for four years, "Are you not my brother Charles?" He said, "You're my sister Cecile?" And they fell into each other's arms. Since then, those children stick together like the fingers of a hand.

Besides Rebecca, I could only find my younger brother Maurice. Maurice had married a young Catholic woman named Louise, and he had converted to Catholicism. Of course, Catholicism was something that was against everything we believed, but it was a question of saving his life. Thanks to Louise, the Gestapo left them alone. Maurice was arrested but she was able to get him out of the concentration camp by proving that he was Catholic because he married her. When I spoke to him after the war, when I returned to Brussels with my family, he said to me, "So what's the difference, Bernard? I was not a practicing Jew anyway. I do not practice Catholicism. I save my life and I please my wife." After that, we never touched the subject of religion.

Maurice and Louise have a daughter, Monique, who had twin daughters. The girls know they have a Jewish grandfather. They know their cousins and everybody are Jewish. In fact, Monique is very resentful that we moved away from Belgium because we were the only Jewish family she had. Her mother's family are pure Belgian. I'm a Belgian because I was born in Belgium but she's a Belgian from a thousand years ago. Fifteen generations back, they had a priest in their family. In America we are all a bunch of newcomers, but if you're European you're a thousand, two thousand years old, and this to them is a big deal. So Louise's family don't claim Monique because her father was Jewish.

While I was in Brussels, I remained at Rebecca's apartment. During this period, I began to realize the extent of my despair. Practically all the people that I knew—friends, family, acquaintances—had died. After two weeks, I decided to return to Volvic so that I could bring my family back to Brussels. I also knew that I could not remain in Brussels because the streets were full of blood. But I was not yet thinking of America.

Returning to France, the trains were again filled. I rode to Paris. There, I could not go to see my sisters-in-law because curfew kept us inside the train station. I slept that night with thousands of people trying to sleep comfortably on large steps and in hallways. With me was a woman who had many children between the ages of five and ten. The children could not find a spot to rest, so I took the rucksack I was wearing and I made a nest-like sleeping cot for the two smallest children and I watched them sleep.

In the morning we took a train to Vichy; from Vichy to Clermont-Ferrand; from Clermont-Ferrand to Volvic. When I finally arrived in Volvic, I found everybody in good shape and very happy to see me. At that time, we decided to pack our belongings and get the necessary papers as soon as possible so we could go back home to Brussels to be with whomever remained of my family. It was then just three weeks before the Battle of the Bulge, 1944. It must have been around the end of November.

Before we left, I said goodbye to Father Mattieu, the old priest from our church who was with us in the Resistance and who had come to tell me when Yvette was born. I had met him a few months after we arrived in Volvic, because we stayed maybe six months in that house near the railroad and then moved near the church. That house was where the priest came to greet us and where we stayed until we left France.

When he came to the house that first time, Chana answered the door and she said, "Yes, Father, what can I do for you?"

He said, "I would like to speak to you. May I come in?"

I came down from the room on the first floor where Eliane was in her crib and he received us. We remained quiet. Chana said to me, "What do we do now?" I said, "Let me talk." She spoke those few words to me in Yiddish and he said, "What did you say?"

I said, "My wife wanted to greet you but French to her is a little difficult so she asked me to greet you in French. She greeted you in Flemish." He said, "That's very kind."

When we had first moved into Volvic and Father Mattieu learned that we were Belgians, he assumed that we were Catholics, too. So he asked when he met us why we didn't send the children to church. I told him that we were Huguenot Protestants because my ancestors came from Holland. You have no idea how much you have to remember when you lie. When you tell the truth it's easy; it comes alone. But to lie is hard. I told him that I was a Huguenot and we were married in Limbourg and my wife's name was Shana Laja. Shana Laja sounded very familiar there. Shana was a forest by that name that exists today, and we had a town Laja. She looked like they looked. You could not have confused her.

Father Mattieu was a short, stocky man, with blue eyes, smooth skin, and a high forehead. He was a patriot who had fought in the first world war, and he had a natural dislike for the *Boche*, but he was of a gentle nature. When he was in the Maquis with us up in the mountains he would bring us solace. He really was one of us but without weapons. To the Catholics in the Maquis he would bring confession, absolution. He would always say, "Whatever you do, God will forgive you. I forgive you." And when you are in danger, you use every drop of strength to pull yourself out.

The church in Volvic played a neutral role during the war. Many Nazi Catholics went to church. They would state their confessions, go through the devotions, and that's it. I don't recall seeing any manifestation of any extreme religiousness. Only elderly women went to church during the week, and on Sunday the young people would go, like in many faiths.

The Nazis left Father Mattieu alone out of sheer respect. Oh, yes, we also had an abbot who came from the seminary to help Father Mattieu. I don't know what city he was from, but he was beautiful and young. He wore a black uniform and he wore that big hat of the French priests. In Volvic we had a physician who was from the big city and he had twin daughters, beautiful, young girls about sixteen or seventeen. They went to church every Sunday, every holiday. They were good believers, and that young priest would go to their house to bring them confession. They didn't mingle with the people of Volvic, who were too coarse. Then one day in the fields he was found with both girls, screwing around with them. The following morning we heard that he was gone. He was never seen again in Volvic.

Because I was a Belgian and we were always the first ones to catch the brunt of any big heat, Father Mattieu had a lot of admiration for me. Believing that I was a Christian, he always respected me, even though I never went to his church. Before leaving Volvic, I went to visit him at his studio, a simply furnished room with a large crucifix and a picture of Jesus with a sad, mystical look on his face. My innermost thoughts were doubtful about the outcome of this meeting. For so many years, I had been hiding under the label of Protestant and here I was about to reveal my secret, so I did not come straight to the point.

First we had a long conversation. I told him that I was very happy he was in the Maquis, and I thanked him for the help he brought to my wife and children, not in providing food—he didn't provide food—but because he would visit them once in awhile when he came down from the Maquis to reassure the families.

Then I said, "Father, for four and a half years you have known me, and you have believed me to be a Christian. However, I don't want to leave Volvic with a lie. You deserve the truth."

He looked up very inquisitively, and I said, "Father, I'm Jewish. My wife and my children are Jewish."

At first he was incredulous. Then, with a big smile, he stood up from his chair and hugged me to his chest, and he said proudly to me, "Our Lord Jesus Christ was Jewish, too."

He is the only one in Volvic I told that I was Jewish. I don't know if he told anyone else. I had a lot of comments to make but I didn't make any because they weren't important at the time. He told his housekeeper to bring up a couple of bottles of wine from the mass.

That priest had a garden in which he grew the most beautiful fruits. During the war I would go there at two in the morning and take exactly what I needed for the children: peaches and grapes and apples and pears and tomatoes. And he would wonder who took only so much and no more. I remember filling our bags with peaches and the farmer coming with a gun and his dogs, and instead of running through the wire in the vineyard we tried to stand underneath the peach tree and slip under the wire. We squashed the peaches and juice ran down our legs. I arrived home with just enough fruit to put in the pot to make a compote. I took with discernment. I needed three peaches; I took three peaches. I needed a nice bunch of grapes; I took a nice bunch of grapes. And the priest never knew who did it.

So that evening I said, "Father, I plead guilty for I've been taking what didn't belong to me from your garden." "Ah," he said, "you were my thief. I was wondering who took exactly what he needed. How come?" I said, "Father, I only needed food for the children. I was not in business to sell it. I knew it was always there."

"Well," he said, "I am the servant of God, and I'm glad you did it." He came to the house one more time before we left. At that time, he blessed my family, and he brought some chocolate for the children and a couple of fresh eggs.

Also before we left, I went to Jean Compaign and told him that we were leaving. He wished us bon voyage. I gave him the keys and thanked him very much.

CHAPTER 21

NEVER BE AFRAID

And so we said our goodbyes to Volvic and then we took the bus to Clermont-Ferrand. In Clermont-Ferrand, we weren't too far from the train station so we walked over and took the train to Paris.

There again we didn't stop to see my sisters-in-law. We were mostly impatient to see what was happening in Brussels. We knew that we had no home but my sister had given me the use of her apartment, a beautiful, large fifth floor apartment on the high point of the city that she rented. Her husband had been killed and so she was living alone. She wasn't feeling well, but who was feeling well? We had just come out of the war, and it wasn't yet finished. There was still fighting in Eupen-Malmedy and Germany.

In Paris, we had to change trains, but the trains were all occupied by American soldiers, so we were refused space. Now, we didn't speak a word of English but I wanted to get on that train. How could I get onto a train for Americans without speaking English? It's a good thing I speak French. There is always somebody who speaks a little French. And the children were the best ambassadors. Men always love little girls and they were as cute as buttons. So I said to one American, "I have to go to Brussels, and this is my family." As the employee of the railroad looked away, he and another American said, "Come come come come come come," and they threw my luggage in the train, took the children, Eliane on the knee of one soldier, Yvette on the knee of another, and they squeezed together, and we had room. In the train, the children were adored. They received chocolates and chewing gum, and the guys kissed them, and they kissed the guys, I received cigarettes, and like this we rode to Brussels.

Again, however, it was a very hazardous trip. Trains were held back; bridges were blown up. Instead of making the trip from Clermont-Ferrand through Paris in six hours, that trip took two days and a night. The children slept on baggage. I carried a large bag in which I was allowed to bring so much oil, and so much brandy, and so much flour from Volvic to Brussels. I always had food on me, so the children weren't hungry.

Finally we arrived at the southern station in Brussels. As we left the station an employee said, "What are you doing here? This is an American train."

I said, "We have tickets. We have passports. We are now in Belgium. Don't ask me how. Here I am."

But on the way to my sister's apartment and in the following days, we started looking for people coming back, and we found very few people that we knew. In the thirteen months of deportations, some 35,000 Jews had been deported or sent to prison. The losses were tremendous. Nearly 30,000 died, almost half the Belgian Jewish population before the war. On my first trip back to Brussels, when I went there by myself, I was involved only with my nephew, my nieces, my sister and brother, and myself. Now, with my family, I saw that there was no longer a Jewish grocery store, no Jewish baker, no kosher butcher, no Jewish life.

In the meantime, the Germans were sending V-1 bombs from Holland trying to destroy England. When they flew you heard the "Ch Ch Ch Ch Ch Ch Ch" and knew there was no danger. Once the sound stopped, then came the danger. The English said they had perfected a system to catch and destroy them in the air, but how many could they not catch? One day, after we had been in Brussels for four weeks, a V-1 fell short, landed in the back of our home, and blew up, taking away part of our roof.

"Bernard," Chana said, "we went through nearly five years with the Gestapo, with all the deviltry, and now we're going to get killed stupidly by a German bomb? Let's go back to Paris."

I was working again in the glove business, making a lot of money, but I had no ambition to remain in Brussels. In Belgium after the war, you could not open up a business unless you were a Belgian. Even if you were a genius from China, you could not open up a business, but an idiot from Belgium could start a business by signing his name on the right papers. Ninety percent of the few Jews left in Belgium were not from Belgium. They were Jews from Poland or Rumania. So right away I had propositions to go into business with all kinds of Jews who had made a mint working for the Nazis, making fur jackets for them to wear when they were attacking Russia.

How did these people wash themselves clean? By paying to the United Jewish Appeal mountains of money that they had made from the Nazis. So I had propositions from people I never before knew: a million francs, two million francs. I was horrified. And the Jewish community I had known was completely gone. The streets were full of blood.

I said to Chana, "You know what? You're right. Let's go tonight." "But we cannot cross the border. We have no passport," she said. "Doesn't matter. You come."

That afternoon, I took a trolley with the whole family to Tournai. Because of transferring from village to village, that trip took eight hours. I wore a big backpack in which I carried Yvette. In whatever room remained, I poured tobacco because tobacco was unregulated in Belgium, where in France it was a government monopoly, so there was always a customer for loose shredded Belgian tobacco. It was almost as good as money.

Tournai is a Belgian town on the French border near Lille. From Tournai you have to cross a half mile of fields to come into France. Once you are in Lille you can take a train to Paris but the problem for us was in crossing the border in the first place. I had received a visa to cross from France to Belgium the first time, but I had no visa to go from Belgium to France. Once we arrived in France we would be okay because I had never cancelled our identity cards that said we were Belgians living in France.

In Tournai, we went to a little café to ask for help. That café was also a place where you could spend the night. I said to the man, "I would like a room," and he said, "Okay." That evening, as the family was preparing to go to sleep, I went down to him and said, "Listen, I need someone to smuggle me to the border tomorrow or tonight. You got somebody?"

"It'll cost you five hundred francs," he said. Five hundred francs was a lot of money. I said, "Okay." "3:30 in the morning," he said. "I'll have somebody come for you."

At 3:30 in the morning, as we were bundling up the kids to leave Tournai, the sky over Eupen-Malmedy was covered with clouds and it was cold and snowy. The Battle of the Bulge had begun a few days before. The Americans couldn't take off, and the Nazis were advancing thanks to the fog. Then, suddenly, the fog was dispelled and the sky lifted, like by a miracle, and the Americans were able to send out five squadrons of planes, twenty-five in a squadron, to bomb the Nazis. We were two hundred kilometers away from Eupen-Malmedy in Tournai, but with 125 airplanes dropping bombs, there was a ruckus that made the ground at the hotel tremble.

We waited until the noise stopped. Then we crossed a frozen, muddy field that led over the border and into the city of Lille. The whole trip took two hours. Eliane was holding Armand and Armand was holding his mother, and they all carried bundles. Yvette was shaking in my bag. I was afraid there would be French police because we had no permits with which to cross the border, but once we arrived in Lille we were safe. We walked to the trolley car and took it to Paris, where my sister-in-law, Topje, was waiting for us.

Topje always waited because she knew that we would come. She waited instinctively every day at the station for trains coming from the border. The war was going on in Eupen-Malmedy and Germany, and the Russians were squashing the Nazis from one side, but the war was finished in France.

Topje was the oldest of Chana's six sisters and two brothers. She was the mother of David, my nephew, who visited me in Volvic, and she was the wife of Maurice, a French soldier who was then still a prisoner of war after almost five years.

Topje still lived in the same court where she had lived with David and Maurice before the war but now she lived with her sister, Brandel. Because Topje was the wife of a French soldier, she had been allowed to live openly as a Jew, although she didn't brag about her good fortune. She was sad and worried, not knowing the fate of Maurice.

Because Brandel was a refugee, she lived there with Topje illegally. In the evenings, Topje would walk the streets of Paris and pick the garbage cans of the German army, and she would bring home garbage and cook it to feed Brandel. Brandel remained hidden during the days in the side of the bathroom that was no more than maybe four feet by four feet. She would only go out at night to get some fresh air and stretch and to eat the food Topje brought for her. After the war, her liver solidified and her skin turned yellow. It took her two years to get well. Then, after another sickness, she was always under medical care.

Before the war, Maurice had been a cobbler. In fact, while he was a prisoner of war, he survived because he made shoes for the Nazis. Next door to where he and Topje lived, he had a shoe shop the size of a very small room. In it was a room that had one bed and a miniature stove. That room had not been papered for maybe thirty years. Bedbugs were crawling all over. There was no coal, no wood, nothing, and we lived in that room. That's all she could get for us, but it was near her, so whatever she had we split, and we ate. I looked for a job and I found one in a pocketbook factory on Place de Republique where they made exquisite pocketbooks.

One day I received a letter from a cousin Herman, who was in General Patton's army. He was from Philadelphia and he was the son of my father's sister, Baila Nathanson. He had asked someone to write the letter in French for me. In that letter he wrote that he would be coming to Paris in a few days and he hoped to meet me. He also said that I would be getting another letter before he came.

One afternoon four months later, my wife came running to the pocketbook factory with Topje. She was all excited. "Bernard, we have the letter! Your cousin, Herman, will be at the Hotel St. George near the Champs-Élysées about 4:00 this afternoon, and you can meet him there."

I had never seen that cousin. I had never even spoken to any of them. But I was very excited, so my employer gave me time off. I left the factory and took the subway over to the Champs-Élysées. The ride was long, seventeen miles, but I arrived at the Hotel St. George before 4 o'clock. I went to the desk and I said, "Excuse me, would you be able to page a soldier from Philadelphia by the name of Herman Nathanson?" The man says, "Fine." On the loudspeaker he screams and howls. Nobody hears it. "I'm sorry," he said.

"But there must be a few hundred thousand American soldiers visiting Paris now. Come back later."

Oh! My heart just fell into my shoes. I was so somber and sad as I walked out to the street. The Champs-Élysées was full of American soldiers. They were gay and very happy and smoking and talking, but their language was very irritating to my nerves. I couldn't understand a word of English. And they were flicking half-cigarettes away. Where we French and Belgian people would smoke a cigarette until you couldn't put a pin in it and five butts would make an extra cigarette, the Americans had so much tobacco they could afford to throw it away.

I walked around and looked every soldier in the face. No luck. I walked some more. By dusk, I was getting sadder by the second. I was walking behind the Arc de Triomphe. Soldiers were everywhere. How could I recognize somebody I had never met and who didn't know me either?

As I walked I saw three soldiers walking arm in arm with their little bayonets at their sides. They were talking and smiling and as I looked the one in the middle began to look familiar. My heart started beating. I went to him and the three soldiers stopped. In Yiddish I said, "Are you Herman?"

He stopped. Then he said in Yiddish, "You are Bernard."

I said, "Yes." And we flew into each other's arms. We were so happy! Then he said in Yiddish, "How did you know I am Herman?"

I said, "You know what? You look like Cecile, my niece. She has a round face like you. She has the same rich lips. You look like Cecile."

Well, what can I tell you? It was like opening the gates of Heaven. He asked me questions. I didn't know what to answer. "Where is your father? Where is your brother?" Then he explained that his mother was my father's sister; and that my Uncle Boris, my father's brother, the one who had left Belgium when I was four years old, had passed away only a few months before.

We started talking and he saw me reach into my pocket to take out a butt. "Bernard," he said, "what kind of shit are you smoking?" He opened a pack of cigarettes and gave me one. It must have been a Camel or a Lucky Strike. The aroma! He gave me the whole package. It was like eating fresh fruit, so I chewed the cigarette. I didn't want to smoke it—so good it was. I was sick like a horse. I threw up my guts. But to smoke, it was heavenly.

We went to his hotel room and we were talking and crying and talking and crying. He proved he was my blood cousin by remembering the story that his mother had told him of the pogrom in Kishinev and by telling me about the hard times that his parents had in America. What he told me about Kishinev was the exact story my father had told me. He said his father had passed away, and he had many brothers and sisters.

He took me to his room. In his room, he gave me cigarettes and he said, "Wait a minute." He went into the hallway and he screamed something in a savage language that I couldn't understand. It was English, of course.

In seconds, soldiers were running down the hallway of the hotel to his room with packages. In a few minutes the room was full of packages: dried bananas, dried prunes, soap, powdered milk, cigarettes, tobacco. You name it and I had it. Chewing gum, candy for the children, chocolate. To us these were luxuries that we couldn't obtain. Then he said, "Let me wash up." I said, "Fine."

He removed his shirt and I saw he was like a gorilla, with a fur that I had never seen in my life. I wondered, "Is he for real? Is he a descendant of Tarzan?" Then he took his upper and lower teeth out of his mouth, brushed them, and put them back in his mouth. I was completely out of my mind. I said to him in Yiddish, "Are you going to show me that you can unscrew other parts of your anatomy?"

"No," he said. "In America, when you suffer from your teeth, you get them pulled out and you get false teeth, and you never have problems."

"And being hairy," he said, "my father is hairy."

In the meantime, we had a room full of stuff. I don't know how a Jeep handled the weight. Maybe six guys helped him carry the stuff outside. Then he threw a tarpaulin over it so you couldn't see what it was. I told him where we lived, and I drove with him and two friends to Rue Du Poteau, number 60.

The commotion in the street was unbelievable as we came into the court. People surrounded the three fellows because they were Americans and the Americans had been our saviors. We knocked on the door and we went in. Eliane and Armand had been sent away to a place sixty kilometers from Paris by the Belgium Red Cross, who were providing them with food and clothing because I had no room and we were having a hard time taking care of them. They remained away for ten weeks, but Yvette was still with us, so Herman saw Yvette. She was an adorable child, three years old. My cousin gave her a fresh, unpeeled banana. She bit into it without unpeeling it and spit it out and said "Keh keh." She never ate a banana before.

Then he sat down and we started drinking. My sister-in-law said to him, "Would you like a home-cooked meal?" "Oh," he said, "would I like!"

There is a Jewish dish called *bobolach* and *kliskelech*, which means beans and pasta. "What I would like to get," he said, "is a plate of beans and pasta." In peace time, the pasta is homemade. But this was just after the war. We had nothing. My poor sister-in-law went out and bought on the black market a pound of flour to make noodles, she paid top price for two eggs, and we made him that dish of pasta and beans.

Those three fellows sat and ate and they enjoyed that meal like it could have been the finest of French cooked dinners. We were speaking and talking, and my cousin said to me, "Look, Europe is not the place for you. There isn't much left. We want you to come to America. We have a large family there."

We were a family of five. To come to America with a family of five you needed an affidavit of a million dollars. He told me his brother-in-law, who was in a huge appliance business in Bridgeton, New Jersey, had made an affidavit for my family but he didn't know how long it would take to arrive. After awhile, he went back to his hotel room.

That night, Chana and I talked about all the beautiful bundles he had brought us: the dried bananas, the dried prunes, chocolates, cigarettes, tobacco. And we talked about America.

America? Would we be going to a country of idiots and cowboys, gangsters, liars, bluffers? America had a poor reputation. They were our saviors but that was beside the point. They saved us for the future to save themselves, because they knew that Hitler had a plan for America. Jews would have been destroyed, blacks would have been enslaved, and all of America's raw material would have been sent to Germany. Their farms would have produced food for Europe. The Germans would have enslaved anyone who wasn't an Aryan.

So we had mixed feelings. We wanted to come to family in America. We didn't care if they lived on top of the mountain. On the other hand, we were very fearful. At the turn of the century America had not been a country of beautiful immigrants; it was all swindlers or people who stole money from widows. Its reputation was horrible.

But Paris was not our home, and we could not raise our children in Belgium.

Chana said to me, "I hope that our going to America is a lucky decision because I'm very afraid. The Americans are known for bluffing. I hope Herman keeps his promise." I said, "You know, I hope he does, too."

Meanwhile, I had an address in Belgium where my Capitan Duhin had once lived. I wrote a letter to him one day not knowing if anybody would be there, and I received an answer from his estranged wife telling me he lived now in Bouque Maison, which is near Amien about 150 kilometers from Paris. When I received that letter, I went to the post office to try to get a telegram to him because there was no telephone in the house. In the telegram I said, "The last news I heard about you was when you were wounded in Switzerland. If you are living at this address, would you please send me a card and at least I will know that you are alive."

A few days later, I got a letter: "I'll be in Paris. Wait for me." He asked me to rendezvous in the Northern Station. I went there. I was impatient, on pins and needles. Suddenly, here he comes, dressed in uniform like a French officer, a captain in the army. And we embraced.

"Bernard," he said, "how marvelous it is we are both alive." He told me that he was wounded in a fight when a bullet hit him while he was leading an expedition near the Swiss border in 1943. After he was wounded, they smuggled him over into Switzerland and took him to a hospital. From there they took him away to England, and a month later I heard that "the father of Kalish is all right." He finished the war with the army of General deGaulle.

Capitan Duhin had an old mother, Mme. Duhin. When I first told him I was Jewish, he had said to me, "I think it would be a wise idea if you take my mother in with you for a few months. You will find a room for her to sleep."

I said, "Why?" She hated Jews with a passion. You know what that means? If she could bite you in two she would. "You want me to take in an anti-Semite?"

"Bernard," he said, "It would be good protection for you, because having my mother, who is a simple patriot and a Petain-ist, that would be a cover. Besides, she is such an anti-Semite that if she stays with you even Hitler will believe that you are not Jewish."

When he told me that, I heard it was a request, and a request was very important. I wanted to stay in Robert Duhin's good graces, so I said okay.

Capitan Duhin's mother was a little thin lady, very prim and very official. She was a school teacher, and the children had to address her as Mme. Duhin. She would teach Armand and Eliane calculus, and she would tell Chana, "Isn't that beautiful? You brave Belgian people. All those Jews." And we had to sit still for four months. We suffered because of her.

When I met him this time, he said, "You know, Mother died." I offered him my condolences. He said, "Isn't that odd? I worked for one cause and she was for the other cause."

Then I took him to see Chana and the children.

After a while, winter passed and we remained good friends. I would do little things for him, like errands. He sent me to Brussels one day because he needed money and I told him I was able to borrow it. I had money of my own there, but I didn't tell him it was my own. I borrowed it, and I lent it to him. He paid me back, and I was like his alter ego and his right arm.

He lived with his girlfriend in Montargis, which was a very old part of France. She had met my family, and she was in love with my children. Her father was a retired principal and her mother was a teacher. They were very respectable.

One day, he said to me, "I would like you to go to Montargis with an envelope." I was a little bit afraid, because he was involved in all kinds of intrigues and I wasn't sure that he didn't belong to the French CIA, and I was afraid to put my finger into something that could get me hurt. I said to him, "To my regret, I cannot go to Montargis with an envelope because I have to go to...." "I'll pay you," he said, "for a week."

He did everything to encourage me to go, until finally I came out and said, "Is this anything harm can come from? I'm a stranger in France. I'm not a French man; I'm a Belgian."

He said, "No." He was sending back to that girl all his love letters and he wanted me to deliver them to her. He wanted to separate from her and he wanted to make sure he had given everything back to her.

So I went to Montargis and memories from our days with the Resistance returned to both of us. She was one of Duhin's many lovers when they lived in Chamaillere, but she was a special one. They had fought together in the Resistance and she had been a heroine. We spoke of food because food was always a topic of conversation. I had by this time talked to Herman about America, but to her I didn't speak of America. I didn't want to raise my hopes until I had the affidavits. I was Jewish again, but I had no way of raising a flag. But we did talk about the future. The future then was day by day. I spent two days there, and then I came back.

At Passover, we had nothing to celebrate with. So M. Duhin said, "Don't worry. I'll bring everything for Passover." Now, he was a Catholic. He brought me a wooden crate filled with fish, meat, and a big ham. I said, "You know we Jews don't eat ham." "All right," he said, "but cook the ham because I'll come to your Seder." I said, "Why should I cook the ham for you to eat at my Seder? You take the ham back."

So he took the ham back and brought us two chickens, and we had abundant food. And he brought plenty of wine. He was a big drinker. He drank constantly. He would have a glass of scotch before breakfast and he would smoke cigarettes without stopping. While I was preparing the Seder he was drinking and he became slightly inebriated and started whistling. There I was preparing to lead the Seder, Maurice wasn't there, this one was sick, the family in Belgium was not there, the V-1s were shooting over, and he's whistling. I said to him, "Jewish people do not whistle in the house." He said to me, "Bernard, I'm not Jewish." I said, "I know, but you are in a Jewish home." He said, "Okay."

We had the Seder at Topje's. It was very sad. My brother-in-law, Maurice, was still a prisoner of war. My nephew, David, was now walking with much difficulty. In a battle between the Nazis and his group of Resistance fighters, when they fell down near a ravine, he hit his spine, and since that day he has been dying from the bottom up. But his brain is so alive. He was under the doctor's care but they had been ordered by the state to minimize the extent of his injuries because had the state been found responsible for his health they might have had to pay him. Later he became paralyzed and he received all kinds of awards from the French government, but he never received a pension of any kind, and he never regained his health. He went to Bulgaria, Russia, Rumania, Turkey. Everybody said that somebody else could help him but nobody could. David was at the Seder, and my wife and my three children, and Robert Duhin, and my sisters-in-law, Topje and Brandel. Feiga had not yet returned. Another sister, Ida, had not yet returned. But Sheva and Assne we knew already had died in Poland, along with their brothers, Meyer and Moisheleh.

I don't have to tell you how sad it was. Lot of tears, lot of memories. We were naming the names of all those who couldn't make it, of those who had died. We already knew that in France and Belgium and Poland many Jews had been killed. The size and the dimension of the catastrophe were tremendous, but who could realize that six million had died? We didn't know numbers. We only knew many had died.

We started reminiscing about the days when there was a family, the days when there was peace. We couldn't sing like you usually do at the Seder because our hearts weren't in it. Usually a Seder should be something of joy, but it was full of sadness. Instead of the traditional four questions, I substituted other questions. I asked, "How come this year we are so few when once we were so many?" And there was no answer to my question. Then I said with sarcasm, "Here is another question," and again I had no answer: "Why did we have this cataclysm upon our people? Why? Because of an alienated, hysterical, insane person like Hitler who didn't even have the courage to take his punishment but committed suicide instead." We were hoping that he committed suicide.

Then I thanked my good star for having a good friend like Capitan Duhin who thought enough of us to bring food at a time when food was so rare. Capitan Duhin said, "Do you know how hard it is to be a Jew? You're following traditions thousands of years old." I said, "This is our life. Don't you follow in your Catholic faith the same thing?" He said that I was right.

The Seder finished quite early. Capitan Duhin left us. We remained. My girls had been interested but they exhibited no expression of knowledge of what was happening. I don't think they understood that this had anything to do with Judaism because Yvette was four and Eliane was seven and no explanation was given. Remember, when I asked questions at the time, they weren't the typical Jewish four questions.

But Armand was very impressed. He couldn't believe that I remembered because I had said no more Judaism. He said very little. He was always the silent type. Today he doesn't speak a word of Yiddish.

A few months went by. The children were well. The Germans left Eupen-Malmedy and returned to Germany.

In Paris that winter, we stood in line for hours to get food. I would carry Yvette on my shoulders. To keep warm, she buried her feet in my bosom, and I put a blanket over her head. Like this, I would stand in line to get two kilos of frozen potatoes, sweet from the frost. Another day in another line, I might get two pounds of apples and the apples were frozen.

From Marseilles in the southern part of France the fishermen, through the government, sent in a shipment of octopus. We had never eaten octopus before, so when I brought one home I didn't know what to do with it. It was a big black one—black with the ink—so we used Clorox to remove the paint. Then we boiled the pieces. The meat stunk, so we used lots of garlic. We ate it by holding our noses.

We didn't have any heat in the house and Eliane got an inflammation of the ear. With a prescription from the doctor, we were able to obtain a fifty-kilo bag of coal from City Hall. We made it last a week.

In January or February 1946, I heard that the government had cut up big, old trees fifteen miles out of Paris, about three miles past the end of the subway. These hunks of wood were five feet tall, so I said to my nephew David, "You know what? If you want to, we will leave about midnight, we'll take the subway, and we'll go see what's what."

And we did that. We saw the wood, so I said to him, "How much wood can you *schlep*? I tell you what, you stand on this corner and guard the wood."

While he stood on the corner, I picked up one piece of wood at a time—each piece was about my weight—and brought it back to where he stood. I made five trips. We *schlepped* that wood down into the subway and arrived there at 4:00 in the morning. We were allowed to take it in the train then, and like this we came to where we lived in Monmartre.

I didn't have an ax or a saw, so with a screwdriver and a shoemaker's hammer I split the trees. The fire I made stunk up the house because the wood was soaking wet. The smoke was terrible; we had no fire.

But, going to the woods we had gone along the River Seine, where we had seen barges bringing coal to a hospital. I figured by going into the water I could reach the barge and take some coal, because the barge was low in the river. So that's what we did. David stood on the bank while I slipped into the water. It was bitter cold. I was knocking my teeth together, but I was able to get us a whole bag of coal. We came home and we had warmth in the house.

After this, spring came and Chana said, "Let's go home. Maybe somebody will come. Here we are, alone, and we are not home, and the bedbugs are eating us up. It's terrible."

I said, "All right," and we took the train, again with difficulties, into Brussels to my sister's apartment. I started inquiring but I found nothing. Nobody came back.

Again, I had many business offers. I would get all the money. You name it and I could get it. But it was not in my mind to remain in Belgium. I had no one left. I had no friends, no family, nothing. The streets to me were soaked in blood, and the collaborators weren't being punished. I found a job in my trade and made very good money, but I was angry and upset.

Then one day that summer, I received a package from America containing milk powder, soap powder, and chocolate. Hallelujah! But they had packed it like it would be going from Philadelphia to New Jersey, very lightly. We couldn't use anything in the package because everything was cracked and broken and mixed together: the milk powder and the soap powder and the chocolate. But that was of no importance. We managed.

During this period also, I secured, from the organization called the Jewish Victims of the War, the documents that proved my family had been destroyed by the Nazis. From these documents, I learned from where they were taken in Belgium and the dates they were taken, and that's all. The documents didn't tell me where they were sent or where in Germany they were killed.

Later, of course, I found out. In Belgium a monument was built in memory of those who were taken away. That monument was inside a garden with iron doors, and the walls were marble stone engraved with the names and the places where they were taken from. We saw my father's name and my brother's name, and those of everybody else: uncles, aunts, cousins, their children, friends and neighbors. It was a sad enumeration of names on a black marble wall in a Jewish section of Brussels now empty of Jews. Unfortunately. Altogether about seventy members of my family were annihilated. Only one cousin survived in hiding. He now makes his home in Israel.

By this time, we had decided we were going to America, but first we had to run around to get all the documents necessary. The American consul gave us a lot of difficulty. Even though the Belgian quota was open and Chana was married to me, she had been born in Warsaw, so according to the Americans she belonged to the Polish quota, and the Polish quota was full for the next ten years because they had accepted so many displaced people. I was finally able to prove to them that we had three children: two born in Belgium and one born in France. French and Belgian immigration were both open. "The mother of those children you're gonna keep because of some formality?"

Finally, in September or October, our affidavit came from Washington. Chana was okay. We only had six months to get to America and then the visa would be invalid. Right away we were offered two, three million francs for our papers. I said, "You cannot fake papers."

Instead, we began to pack whatever *schmatas*, whatever rags, we had, because Chana said, "Bernard, we know what we have but we don't know what we are going to get. We are moving to America, a country of people who are different." And, in fact, she was right. We took everything we had. We had sixty-three bundles with us—no suitcases.

At that time, my sister-in-law, Feiga, came back from the hospital where she had been sent to recuperate after she was released from the concentration camp. Feiga was a woman who never weighed less than 160 pounds, but during the war she had been subjected to Mengele's experiments and she now weighed maybe 105 pounds. During the war, she had lost her husband, Louis, and her son, Henry, but two other children, David and Regina, had survived. She was remarried to a fellow named Joseph whose wife and children had been destroyed in Ravensbrück, a women's camp. He had survived Mauthausen. They met coming back to Belgium and got married in Belgium. Later, they opened a tailor shop and were successful. They had a little child by the name of Alex.

I also learned that my future brother-in-law, Leon from Lithuania, was safe but that he lost his first wife and their children in the concentration camp. He was saved because he was strong and knew how to use his hands with machinery. He worked for the Nazis in the concentration camp making benches. He married Brandel in 1950 in Belgium. When they came to America in 1951, he worked in a hat factory making ladies' hats.

When we got our papers, we wanted to leave immediately. However, we could not take the ship in Antwerp because the port of Antwerp was strictly a military port occupied by the American reserve forces. Piles and piles of everything filled the port: ammunition and food and whatever the American army needed. The only way for us to go was through Sweden by train. To get the necessary papers took four months. We left in February 1947.

In Brussels our decision to leave was a big affair: One of the natives of the Jewish people was leaving the country. We were so few. We were happy to be alive but very sad because everyone was missing someone. Of course, they could understand my decision to leave: I had three children and I had to take care of myself. Emotionally I was drained, and I was looking forward to seeing my family in America. So the Jewish community made a large farewell party for us, but they were sad to see us leave.

Over 150 people met us at the train station. At that time the community had a lot of stamps to buy food so the food was there. Knowing we had four days of traveling to get to Gothenburg and there was no restaurant service on the trains then, one person brought us a third of a salami, one brought eight grapefruits, another brought us eight oranges, somebody gave us a loaf of bread. They brought enough food to enable us to reach America, because we didn't know if we would have enough food on the ship. It was all unknown.

Before I left Belgium, a man in Antwerp had called me to say he wanted to see me concerning my trip to America. I didn't know that man from Adam but I went to see him. "Look, I am dealing with your cousin, Benjamin Shapiro in Bridgeton, New Jersey," he said. "Mr. Shapiro has asked me to give you $5,000 so you can buy your tickets and some food and have money in your pocket."

Benjamin Shapiro's wife was my first cousin, and he had put up the affidavit for a million dollars. Five thousand dollars was a lot of Belgian money. So with that I bought our tickets and our berths, and we crossed the city of Hamburg. It was all destroyed. Children stood along the train tracks asking for food and my children looked at me. "Papa, can I throw them some food?"

I said, "Go ahead." Children cannot be guilty. They threw down grapefruits, pieces of salami, bread, and finally we came into Denmark. From Denmark, we took a boat to Norway. From there, we took a train into Sweden. Sweden was bitter cold with the snow and the people were dressed gorgeously. There was no war in neutral Sweden, so those people had not suffered. After spending a day in the city of Gothenburg, which is a very well-known city on the Strait of Skagerrak, we boarded the ship, *Gripsholm*.

The *Gripsholm* was an international exchange ship for prisoners of war and for diplomats. If the Germans wanted to exchange some eminent person he would be sent on the *Gripsholm*, and the same with the Americans if they sent somebody. For luggage, we had only the sixty-three little bundles of items we had received from the Red Cross, things I had collected since leaving the Maquis, a little underwear. We were immigrants in the full sense of the word. I figured I'd go to America, make a living, and get everything I needed.

Tickets for the ship were very expensive, although I cannot remember the prices—it was forty odd years ago. I still have the tickets from the baggage, from the hotel room. I have the menu from the restaurant in which we ate. It was written in English and in Swedish, and I spoke neither of the languages. When it came time to order food, I didn't know what to order, so I put my hand on the menu and by sign language I ordered five. The waiter brought five herring, five steaks, five potatoes, five pitchers of milk, five loaves of bread, five of everything.

The first day on the ship was a pleasure. Everybody on board ate because we were still at the dock. The second day was so cold that the ship became icebound and we were unable to escape the Skagerrak to go into the North Sea. During the night, powerful icebreaking ships worked in the Strait to make a passage for our ship to sail to the unfrozen North Sea. The tearing and splitting and cracking of heavy sheets of ice kept us awake all night. Through the porthole we watched the ships at work.

In the morning at breakfast my wife said, "Oh, Bernard, I hope the whole trip is like this." It was the last meal she took for the whole trip. After that, as soon as she saw food, she turned sick. She was in her berth throwing up all twelve days of the passage. A nurse from the ship stayed with her those twelve days. I was in charge of the three children. Armand already was fourteen. Eliane was eight, and Yvette was four or five. My poor baby.

The third day we hit the ocean and the ship started to fly all over the place. In the dining room, the chairs were stuck to the floor. The plates were set on wet tablecloths so they wouldn't slide.

My children turned green and they could not eat because the food went back and forth and up and down with the ship's movement. Seeing this, I figured it was going to be very dangerous. The children had to be made to eat. So I became very strict and I said, "Everybody's going to swallow their food, and everybody's going to eat. If one of you throws up, I'll shoot you." I became very brutal to the children. All during the passage of the ship, my poor children had to swallow everything that was brought to the table because had they not eaten they would have been so sick it would have been pathetic.

By a miracle nothing bothered me, so I ate three solid meals a day, and in between I had three more meals because whatever we didn't eat during the meals I would put in a napkin and take to the cabin and eat during the day. I was in love with food, of course. The waiter was in Heaven. He was so thrilled to see the way I took my food.

We were the only table with five people all related. Sometimes somebody had a child with him, but it was only a ship of immigrants, displaced persons, leftovers from the war. Altogether there must have been eight or nine hundred people. Everybody had lost family, but we were a complete family. I was a regular immigrant. I had affidavit and papers. The captain of the ship came to our table to congratulate us for having saved our lives. Some congratulation! But nevertheless he was very kind to us.

Between meals, I would sit in the cabin near Chana while they fed her sugar water intravenously. We did not speak of dreams and ambitions: "What are you gonna do in America?" "I'm gonna conquer the world." No, no, no, none of that, because we didn't believe in that anymore. We had just come through Hell. Finally we arrived at the port of New York.

When you arrive from the ocean and you see from far away little lights circling in the darkness and those little lights are moving like night flies and when you don't know what it is, the effect is mysterious. My children stood with me in the enclosed deck and admired the beauty but we didn't know what it was. Was it the lamps along the dock, or was it automobiles, or was it some special effect? We slept well that night because the ship did not move. We were in the harbor but not at the dock.

About 7 o'clock in the morning, they pulled us in and by 8 o'clock we were off the ship. As we were leaving the ship they checked our documents. A young fellow, an employee of the customs agent, looked at me, he looked at my children, and with a smile he said, "*Landsman?*" I thought he was looking at my mother's maiden name, Lanzman. I said, "No, no, Mednicki." I didn't know that in America *landsman* meant he was a Jewish fellow, too. So he looked at me thinking maybe I was nuts. No *landsman?*

We left the ship and were told our luggage would be at cordon "M." I found all my food and luggage laying there in bundles attached with rope and electric wire. I counted my sixty-three bundles; they were all there. I was a little ashamed because I didn't have a suitcase. Everybody came with nice suitcases and I had nothing, *goornisht*.

A customs agent came over, looked at my bundles, looked at me, and asked, "That's yours?" in English. I understood what he said. I said, "Yes, this is mine" in French. The guy looked around right and left and he started putting stamps on everything. Then he ran away.

Before coming to America the man from Antwerp had said to me, "I would like you to do an errand for me." "What can I do?"

"I have a little bag for you to take with you to give to somebody. You will get $10,000." I said, "I want to know what it is."

The man opened a little velvet box and it was diamonds. I was torn between making $10,000 and taking a chance in a new country with my children and my wife. After speaking to my wife she said, "Look, we are coming to a new country. We don't want to start with the left foot. Why take a chance that all our lives we will look behind us to see if anybody is calling us? We'll get rich a little later."

I said, "Fine." And I said no to the fellow.

After that customs agent didn't touch my luggage, oy, was I sorry! Why didn't I take that $10,000? But in the long run I felt good. I didn't do anything illegal. I'm not afraid of having done anything bad.

That day I landed in America with my family was March 11, 1947. On that day, I completed the journey that my parents began at the turn of the century when they fled the pogroms in Kishinev. My parents survived the pogroms because they resisted. I survived the Nazis and hunger because I resisted. We weren't cowards. We did our share to resist. The Warsaw Ghetto has created a story that you will hear for a thousand years, but it was only the best known of many. We leave them all as a legacy to you because we are proud of you. Never be afraid.

EPILOGUE (1996)

Minnie died in March 1991. Bernard called me a few days after to tell me. It was important to him that I knew. He knew I would want to know also.

Of course he was right. I loved Bernard, as I had since I had met him five years before at Millersville University, where we had both come to speak about Jewish resistance against the Nazis. And I loved Minnie also, as I had since I met her that summer when I passed through Philadelphia with my wife Emily and my son David on a vacation trip to New York.

She greeted me warmly and kissed me graciously that first time. She had heard a lot about me from Bernard—all good I'm sure because that's how Bernard described people. Though recovered from a stroke she had suffered in 1974, Minnie was still a physically frail woman. Nevertheless, she was strong spoken, radiant behind her smile, and unexpectedly funny. During our brief visit, Minnie often would play Bernard's "straight man," setting him up to launch into stories of their adventures together or his experiences during the war—not that Bernard needed someone else to launch him. At other times, she bantered with Bernard. Then, while Bernard was elaborating upon an anecdote or reinterpreting her memory to fit his story line, she would whisper to me, in an aside, the truth behind Bernard's exaggeration.

Emily, David, and I spent that evening enjoying their hospitality. Bernard delighted three-year old David with funny stories and Jewish songs. Emily felt right at home. The next morning at breakfast, Bernard honored me by asking me to write his story.

I had wanted to tell Bernard's story from the day I met him in Millersville, from the moment in fact that I realized he was a veteran of the Jewish anti-Nazi Resistance and not just someone's grandfather. To me, he was living proof that the humiliating "lambs to the slaughter" charge against my heritage was a lie. Feminists recount tales of lost feminist heroines from the 1800s and early 1900s to expose their lost herstory. Blacks laud successful blacks from years past who have contributed to mainstream America's greater success. For Jews, our suppressed history is of those who fought back, who didn't go like lambs to the slaughter. Bernard is one of those Jews, and I loved him for his strength.

I accepted Bernard's offer immediately, but for logistical reasons—Emily finishing school in East Lansing, Michigan; us moving to Ann Arbor, finding work, and getting settled—we were unable to begin our first concentrated round of interviews for this book until May 1988, when Bernard and Minnie finally came to Ann Arbor to stay with us for two weeks.

I ended Bernard's story with his arrival in America in 1947 because at this point his unique experience merges with "the typical immigrant experience."

In the early years of Bernard's adventure as an immigrant, his desire to return to Belgium, where he could have earned a healthy living in any number of business partnerships due to his good fortune at having been born in Belgium, competed with his dream of a better life for his children in America. In 1952, the Mednickis became United States citizens. Bernard struggled to learn the language and the culture so that he could raise his children and also his two nieces and his nephew, who came to live with him one and a half years after his own arrival. Thanks to his having learned a skill in his youth, as his father had advised, he was in time able to find a good job in an orthopedic shop, where he remained until his retirement twenty-four years later.

Meanwhile, he pushed Armand and Charles to excel in school so that they could get into college. Today Charles is a surgeon and Armand is an artist who has expressed his childhood experiences through works of ceramic pottery. Eliane lives and works in New Jersey, Yvette in Arizona, and nieces Cecile and Annie in New York. Bernard's children have made him a proud grandfather eleven times over.

In 1964, Chana died from pemphigus vulgaris, a rare skin disease, after a three-year illness. That period after her death was one of great sorrow and difficulty for Bernard.

"It's very hard when you lose a mate on whose advice you have counted all your life. Suddenly you have no one to decide but yourself. After Chana Laja passed away, I remained alone. I wanted to commit suicide, but I was too strong for that. I was afraid to hang myself. With a knife you make a mess around you; a gun makes a lot of noise. So I decided to drink myself to death. I drank, became sick, threw up like a pig, took a shower, and went back to work. Like this, I *schlepped* around for five months, and then I turned blind. Thanks to Charles, my nephew, I was operated on."

By the time Chana died, Bernard had already met and become friends with Minnie, who was in fact Bernard's second cousin once removed—Minnie's grandmother and Bernard's father were first cousins. Minnie's husband, Ben, was a dear friend of Bernard's until he died in 1961. The marriage between Bernard and Minnie was encouraged by their respective children, who had already been friends for many years. Minnie had one daughter and two sons.

"I married Minnie in 1965, nine months after Chana Laja passed away. I wanted to wait longer, but the children said, 'What's the use of waiting? You're not going to bring mother back.' It was coincidental that we were already related, but it was written in the stars that we should be together. We wanted to get married in the rabbi's study but the children insisted we get married at home and have a big party. So we invited a rabbi to come to Minnie's home in New York. Her older son, and my nephew, Simon, and my son, Armand, were witnesses. The following week 150 people came to offer their congratulations. Her father wanted us to take a honeymoon but we were a little too old for that fantasy. You take a honeymoon when you are timid and just married and have never kissed and held your bride."

After the wedding, Bernard moved in with Minnie because he could no longer stand to live in the house where Chana Laja had died. Later, they moved back to Philadelphia. Minnie and Bernard became devoted companions, and yet they continued to hold places of honor in their shared memories for Ben and Chana.

"Minnie was a sweet person. She was called 'Minnie the Good One.' In Yiddish, 'Minnola da Gitta.' We were very happy, very compatible. I didn't demand much, she didn't require much, and we joined our two miseries and made a happy life. Our children were tickled pink because they didn't have to worry about neglecting us. They called us often and would come down when they could. They knew Minnie and I would make a good life together because she had had a good life with her family and I had had a good life with mine. And so it was. She was very generous. She is a product of her parents, who came from the same pogrom as my parents. We did not forget our first mates because the memories of yesterday are part of our life. There's nothing to hide."

Throughout this entire period of adjustment and change in America right up until they came to Ann Arbor, a subtheme ran through Bernard's life story. Like the concentration camp survivors who vowed to get out alive to tell their stories "so that the world would not forget," Bernard also was compelled to tell his story.

More clearly, he was compelled to "deal" with his past. Telling the story wasn't his first method of dealing. He chose first to suppress it.

"Once three days after I arrived in Philadelphia, I told the story to the members of my family. They wanted to know why we were taken without resisting. I explained to them that when a street is mobilized by heavy artillery on both sides and groups come in and take your wives and children, and they tell you you will join them later, and later they send you away somewhere else and you have nothing to fight with against their immense strength, you cannot easily fight. Those who fought were killed. I told them 'I am going to tell you the story once because it's a very depressing and heartbreaking story.' At that time I spoke only Yiddish with them. I sat down and I spoke, a day, a night, another day. Neighbors would bring food and drinks for the table. Everybody was glued to my lips. Chanala would just correct me; she'd never speak because Chanala was very unhappy. When I finished speaking, after maybe forty-eight or sixty hours, I was exhausted. After that, I never spoke for the next thirty years because it broke my heart to think of what I went through."

In fact, during that period Bernard did speak—often, but never publicly. With his sister, Rebecca, who remained in Belgium after the war, and with Minnie, he would share experiences and recall significant anniversaries.

"The memories worked on me day in and day out. Sometimes in letters to my sister, I would write a line about the Maquis. I would speak to Minnola and answer her questions. We would sit evenings listening to music. She would be doing embroidering, and I would be sitting and I would explain to her, 'This time that year I was in the mountains and I was dreaming of my family.' A lot of memories went through my mind. That's the way it was.

"Minnie was like a breath of air to a person who was unable to breathe anymore. Minnie brought life back to me with her kindness and her understanding. When she would see me thinking and she would see a cloud on my forehead, she would come to me and she would hold me and she would speak to me softly."

In 1967, a chance meeting with Philip Rosen on his way to a demonstration in Washington, DC, led to Bernard's first public speaking engagement. Dr. Rosen is director of the Holocaust Awareness Museum at Gratz College in Philadelphia.

"In the paper was an announcement about a demonstration in Washington, DC, for the liberation of Jerusalem and there were buses going. I said to Minnie, 'I'm going to Washington because we need a homeland.' I didn't say the Palestinians didn't need a homeland, just that the Jews did need a homeland. On the bus were a photographer, a lot of survivors of the Holocaust, and a fellow, Dr. Philip Rosen. We started speaking, one thing leading to another, and he said 'I am teaching a course to teachers about the Holocaust. I almost always have survivors but I never have one who fought the war, who was in the Resistance. Would you please talk for us?' He made me a financial reward, I went to talk, he found my talking to his liking, and I became his talker. Whenever he had meetings I spoke.

"At that first meeting, I didn't go into great detail because I only spoke for forty minutes and then took twenty minutes of questions. I only told them what I felt was necessary to show them that you don't need courage; you must just have the wits to do it. Courage comes later. Fear we all have. Nevertheless, after I came home, I felt very annoyed that I had opened myself up and divulged secrets. The rest of the day I did not speak because I had woken up memories from the Maquis."

In Bernard's story, he tells of memories that he expressed through nightmares but that Minnie couldn't decipher because she didn't understand French. Those memories were exacerbated by Bernard's public speaking.

"Minnie was tremendously influential in soothing my conscience by saying, 'Bernard, if you keep it inside many young Jewish children will not know there were Jewish fighters and they will think we were all a bunch of sheep.' But, she said, if I would speak to congregations of young children, I could show them that we have not lost the spirit of defending ourselves. We are not combative people, we are not a warmonger people, we love peace. According to the Bible, we are a nation of shepherds and farmers. We want peace. We like a song, we like a psalm, we like a poem, and that was my pleasure, to read poetry to Minnie at night and to sing songs to her.

"After I began talking with Dr. Rosen and after I had been sick with the flu or a high fever for a few days, I woke up one morning and my heart was very heavy. Tears choked me but I could not cry because I didn't want to aggravate Minnie. Minnie said, 'Bernard, you were speaking. Maybe you should look for help.'

"At that time there was an ad in the *Exponent* for those who needed some psychiatric relief, those who had inside themselves a piece of the past, so I went. The doctor was a very kind soul, but in order to be helped I had to tell her everything. That means I could not show her my finger and say my heart was aching. After two sessions, I figured if I told her everything she would have material to be a better doctor later, but in the meantime I would be her guinea pig. So I thanked her, I paid her, and I came home. That night, I sat in front of the mirror and said, 'Bernard, now you speak to me. You tell me what's bothering you.' I spoke to me and I answered to me and I put away the idea that I was a lunatic speaking to a mirror and spoke to my alter ego, and I was able to repress the desire to go see a psychiatrist. If you speak to yourself with honesty, you don't need to talk to someone who knows nothing about you."

After this cathartic self-discovery, Bernard began speaking publicly more and more, not just to Dr. Rosen's classes but to senior citizens groups, to grade school children, to college audiences. Even as his health deteriorated due to advancing age and he was forced to cut back on appearances, he made sure that he was available for Dr. Rosen whenever the occasion demanded.

I remember meeting Bernard and Minnie at the Detroit airport that afternoon in May 1988. Bernard was the first one to leave the airplane. When I caught sight of him, he was being pushed in a wheelchair into the waiting room by a stewardess. Minnie followed closely behind. Bernard could walk without a wheelchair but he used it to conserve his energy for the longer walk to my car. He insisted he didn't need help, but he didn't refuse it either. He had slowed down tremendously in the two years since we last saw each other in Philadelphia. In addition, Bernard had only three weeks before left the hospital, where he had gone after the left side of his mouth lost its muscular strength. In the hospital, he learned that he had contacted a case of Bell's palsy, an inflammation of the nerves.

Fortunately, Bell's palsy is a temporary condition, but while he was in Ann Arbor, he was unable to open that side of his mouth without help from his own hand. Still, he spoke once each at Eastern Michigan University and the University of Michigan, thrilled a class of young boys and girls at the Jewish Community Center day school, appeared as a special radio guest of Ted Heusel on radio station WAAM-AM, and was videotaped telling his story to Rabbi Charles Rosenzveig of the West Bloomfield Hills Holocaust Memorial Center. Bernard introduced more than one of his talks by referring to his new, temporary affliction: "It is said a dishonest man speaks out of both sides of his mouth. You know I am an honest man because I only speak out of one side of my mouth."

It was this commitment of Bernard's to telling his story, and the passion with which he told it, encompassing a full range of hand movements and emotions, from sadness to humor, that I first fell in love with, but only in Ann Arbor did I become fully aware of at least one hidden reason for his compulsion.

I learned that he was telling his story not only so the world would know, as was the stated motivation of so many Holocaust survivors, but to make peace with actions he had taken under stress that he couldn't control but that he also couldn't excuse. *Never Be Afraid* is not a blood and guts story. Bernard killed but he never glorifies his actions. He preferred a hand grenade to a gun, he would tell me often, because with the former he never had to look in the eyes of his victim. Only twice did he kill a man with his hands. The trauma of that second time and the events that followed are what he ultimately repressed from his memory. Three days later, he saw Chana again but didn't tell her. The war ended, they settled in America, she died in 1964. He never told her. At some point along the way, he forgot. In retelling his story through the years, I believe he was trying to unblock the memories to free himself from his own pain, but his efforts were blocked by the standard format of his presentation, forty minutes of the same oft-repeated anecdotes and twenty minutes of surface questions and answers.

Only by first allowing Bernard to tell his whole story without constraints of the clock and then probing deeper into areas of his story that were literarily incomplete or still surface, including his experiences in the Maquis, was I able to help Bernard break through those blocked memories midway through our eleventh of twelve ninety-minute interview sessions. Bernard had begun to slow down by this time anyhow, even in his enthusiasm to tell his story, from sheer force of stress and—despite the fact that in Ann Arbor he was taking a sleeping pill every night instead of his regular three per week—lack of sleep. Still, he had patiently answered all my questions and even allowed me to repeat one session when that day's tape was found to be defective. By the end of that eleventh interview session, Bernard had become impatient for the first time. The next morning, I ate breakfast alone for the first time as he finally was able to sleep soundly, and for more than his usual four hours, without having taken a sleeping pill the night before.

In Chapter 19, "Like Blood out of the Aorta of a Pig," I've tried to retain the feel of his struggling to open his memory and unleash those painful secrets that had haunted him since that time, so that the reader can actually experience his pain along with him, as I did that day. That one chapter's outline is less chronological than the traditional biographical chapter and more like one might feel getting pulled into the funnel of a cyclone.

Bernard's story is a story of survival, but it also is a love story. Bernard loved his children and he loved Chana. Then he loved Minnie. "It was an ideal twenty-six years I shared with her," he said over the phone when he called to tell me about Minnie. "And before her I had thirty-two good years with my first wife. I was lucky."

In the summer of 1994, after suffering a stroke, Bernard moved into a nursing home in Cherry Hill, New Jersey, near where Eliane lives with her family. Bernard joined his ancestors and his two beloved wives on January 2, 1995. He was buried in King David Cemetery in Bensalem, Pennsylvania, next to Chana.

APPENDIX

by Philip Rosen

As someone who frequently speaks about the Holocaust, I am often asked the question, particularly by young people, "Why didn't the Jews fight back?" Of course the Jews did fight back when they could, as partisans, as ghetto fighters, even in the death camps. They paid a heavy price, for the ruthless genociders killed their families and murdered hundreds for attacks on Germans. Also native populations had many anti-Semites who not only refused to aid the Jews, but who turned them in to the Nazi occupiers. When I came across Bernard Mednicki at a rally in Washington, I discovered a dimension of fighting back by Jews not usually mentioned—Jews who anonymously joined national Resistance forces and fought the Nazis and their allies.

Bernard Mednicki first came to my attention when the editor of the *Jewish Exponent*, a Philadelphia-based Anglo-Jewish newspaper, called me and told me about him some time after I wrote an article in that paper about Jewish resistance. On the way to and from the 1976 rally in Washington on behalf of Israel, Bernard told me his story. At the time, I was teaching teachers in the Philadelphia school system about the Holocaust and I asked Bernard if he would address them. He was more than happy to, for by that time he realized the importance of bearing witness. Bernard's Santa Claus appearance, Belgian accent, wit, and charm mesmerized the teachers. They began to invite him to their classrooms to tell his adventures to children. Bernard and I became fast friends, close and personal as Europeans tend to be when they embrace someone.

In the spring of 1977, I wrote up his story for the *Jewish Exponent*, for the editor and I believed his tale of bravery deserved a wider audience. The next year, about Passover time, I wrote another article based on Bernard's narrative. Both were warmly welcomed by teachers who used the articles for background in their own classes to teach about the Holocaust. Bernard continued to speak to schoolchildren with even more passion. This book is an expanded version of Bernard's wartime experiences. An even larger audience may now read of a Jew in the French Resistance. However, Bernard represents thousands of Jews who resisted but were unidentified as Jews. Indeed, it is believed that as many as twenty-five percent of the members of the Maquis, the French underground force, were Jewish.

I took Bernard to the Holocaust conference in Millersville, Pennsylvania, where he met and shared a podium with Ken Wachsberger. As Ken writes in his introduction, he was so impressed with Bernard that he wanted to develop a whole book on the resistance fighter. I am grateful that he has carried out this project and honored that I have been invited to offer some words for the sake of background.

The Mednicki narrative can be better understood by knowing something of the chronology and events occurring in both France and Belgium during World War II. What follows is a brief history of the war, the Resistance, particularly in France, and the fate of the Jews. Allusions are made to Bernard's narrative.

In April 1940, Bernard had his last Seder in freedom until April 1945. The Seder ceremony was the most dramatic event in Bernard's Jewish pantheon. In May 1940, the German blitzkrieg hit Belgium, Luxembourg, and northern France. By the end of the month, a badly mauled British and French army barely escaped by sea from Dunkirk. Belgium surrendered and hundreds of thousands of Belgians and Frenchmen, largely refugees, Bernard and his family among them, poured into southern France to escape the Nazi onslaught. By June, six weeks after the blitzkrieg, the Battle of France was over. Marshal Henri Petain, World War I hero of Verdum, commander of the victorious French army in that war, became premier and sued for peace. Brigadier General Charles deGaulle, late undersecretary of state for war, fled to Britain to continue the fight.

The armistice terms were harsh, but not as harsh as the one inflicted by Hitler upon Poland in 1939, for that one wiped out Poland's national existence and provided for complete military occupation of the whole country. The French armistice created an Occupied Zone made up of three-fifths of France, the whole northern part including Paris, and the entire strip of land bordering the Atlantic coast. The German army was stationed there, but not inside the Free or Unoccupied Zone located in central and southern France. While Italy had declared war on France in the last days of the Battle of France, she gained virtually no territory in the southeastern regions.

The new collaborationist government permitted under the armistice was officially titled L'Etat Francaise, but it became popularly known as Vichy after the city in south-central France where Marshal Petain and his government officiated. In theory, Vichy was to have sovereignty over all of France, in both the Free Zone and the Occupied Zone. But with the presence of German troops in the latter zone, Vichy sovereignty was greatly diminished. Hitler did not want to destroy France, for that nation still had some trump military cards—a huge, powerful fleet and vast overseas colonies with soldiers, particularly in North and Central Africa. The *führer* did not want the French fleet to join the Allies (Britain and defeated governments in exile), nor did he want the soldiers in the overseas colonies to join General deGaulle and his Free French carrying on the war from London. The Vichy government was recognized by the major nations, including the United States, which sent Admiral Leahy to Vichy as ambassador.

The French soon realized they had to pay a high price for the armistice. In November, the provinces of Alsace-Lorraine were annexed to Germany. The French army was reduced to 100,000 men. The collaborationist regime had to pay for the cost of German occupation, twenty million *reichsmarks* per day, which added up to three billion dollars by July 31, 1941. The occupiers took seventy-five percent of French copper. In 1942, when Bernard was working in a radio transmitter factory, he was told by the Resistance to wrap rolls of copper wire around his waist and take them past the guards to a nearby dentist. Using his great personal charm, he had befriended the guards, who never bothered to examine him. Stealing copper was resistance.

The occupiers took twenty-five percent of French coal and eighty percent of their petroleum. The Third Reich just appropriated many French products on "credit," claiming that Germany would pay back the value of them after the war. By July 1944, this stealing amounted to over $8.2 billion. Those who opposed the armistice sought to "steal" goods from the Germans and use the funds to finance resistance activities, as it was explained to Bernard. Germany also did not release French prisoners of war; over 1.5 million were kept in prison camps as leverage for Nazi demands on Vichy and to keep the regime militarily weak.

On June 22, 1941, Germany attacked the Soviet Union without warning. Hitler placed three million of Germany's healthiest manhood on the front lines. In December 1941, the *führer* expanded the war by declaring war on the United States, honoring a pact he had with Japan. The expansion of the war greatly taxed Germany's labor force. The Nazis demanded that Vichy recruit Frenchmen for labor service inside the Reich. The Germans did not trust Frenchmen working on their own soil, believing that only under direct German supervision and in completely German surroundings would the French work efficiently. Vichy established compulsory labor service for men between eighteen and thirty-five (they later extended this to sixty) and unmarried women between twenty and thirty-five. Exceptions were made for those working in essential industries.

By this time in Bernard's story, he had already concealed his Jewish identity and was living instead as a Gentile. Now, not yet ready to leave his family and certainly not wanting to go to Germany, where his circumcision would give away his Jewish identity (circumcision was rare among Gentiles in those times), he resorted to another rouse to get an exemption and prevent capture. By dressing up as an executive, he walked into the recruiting hall as a figure of importance who obviously had received the draft notice by mistake. Here, a timid young secretary is fooled. "Can you make pocketbooks?" she asks. Bernard bluffs again. He never made pocketbooks, but his view is, "I never say I cannot. I believe I can do anything until proven otherwise." Bernard is exempted from service, for the pocketbook firm makes this item for German women in the armed forces.

These forced labor decrees caused great French resentment against Vichy. But other events were to turn Frenchmen even more. November 1942 was a crucial month for both Vichy and Germany. The British and Americans landed in North Africa, and Admiral Darlan, head of all Vichy armed forces in Africa, surrendered to the Americans after only brief fighting. The Germans, using the excuse that the Allies would follow through their African invasion with an attack on southern France, violated the armistice terms and occupied the Free Zone. As the German forces moved into Toulon, the mighty French fleet was scuttled. Hitler wanted France to declare war on the Allies. Franklin Roosevelt, the American president, guaranteed Marshal Petain that the American landings would not dismantle the African French empire. Pierre Laval, head of government, and Marshal Petain, head of state, could get no such guarantee on the integrity of the empire from Adolf Hitler, so Vichy's reply to the Allied invasion was merely to break off diplomatic relations. During the German occupation of the Free Zone, Italian forces moved into eight departments along the Riviera on France's southeastern border.

The year 1943 saw the defeat of German armies in Russia, North Africa, and Sicily, and the surrender of Italy. To most Frenchmen, a German defeat seemed assured and with it the end of the Vichy collaborationist regime. DeGaulle's Free French swelled with the general's control over the overseas French empire and fresh troops from Africa. Resistance inside France expanded.

In June 1944, the Allies invaded Normandy, France. By July, British and American troops effected their own blitzkrieg in France. In August, the Allies landed on the southern French coast with eleven divisions, seven of them French. By the closing days of August, deGaulle was in a liberated Paris as head of government. By early September, the Germans were out of France and large parts of Belgium, including Brussels, Bernard Mednicki's hometown. Petain, Laval, and some Vichy diehards formed a rump government in Signaingin Castle in Germany. With the flight of collaborationist leaders, pro-Vichy support in France collapsed. Vichy's hope rose when Hitler gambled his last-card offensive in the Ardenne, Belgium, known as the Battle of the Bulge.

The Allied counteroffensive routed the Germans, and a badly defeated German armed forces surrendered unconditionally on May 8-9, 1945.

THE FRENCH RESISTANCE

With the fall of France in June 1940, and the assumption of power of the grandfatherly Henri Petain, many Frenchmen sought to bide their time and make do as well as possible. The French upper and middle classes welcomed the right-wing, ultra-conservative government of Vichy because they knew it would dismantle the socialistic previous regime. The pro-Vichyites saw themselves as protecting life and property and accommodating just enough to prevent Germany from "Polandizing" France—that is, wiping out her sovereignty and ruling with military force. Some collaborators were truly pro-German, but most were patriotic Frenchmen who saw German victory as inevitable and wanted France to have a place in Europe's new order.

As early as June 23, 1940, General Charles deGaulle broadcast from London that France had lost a battle, but not the war. He called for French resistance, not collaboration with the Nazi occupiers. He had very few followers. However, in late summer, Chad, French Equatorial Africa, the Cameroons, and French Oceania joined the "Free French Movement," as deGaulle's party was called. Inside France itself, resistance was sporadic, administered by uncoordinated cells, small groups which published underground newspapers, leaflets, and other handouts. They set up safe houses for Allied airmen shot down, and found ways for them to escape to England to fight again.

As time went on, it became apparent that Germany was despoiling France, bleeding her of her natural resources and manufactured goods, and Vichy was doing the dirty work to aid the conqueror. The large and extraordinarily well-organized French communist party, being used to clandestine activity, refrained from resistance as long as the Soviet Union honored its 1939 non-aggression, friendship pact with Nazi Germany. After the German invasion of the USSR in June 1941, what the communists called an "imperialist war" became a "people's war." The party formed a resistance wing entitled Franc Tireur et Partisans (FTP). This military arm attacked and assassinated German soldiers. Hatred of the *Boche*, the Germans, increased greatly as the Germans shot ten innocent Frenchmen for each German soldier assassinated. The Family Hostage law enabled German authorities to murder all the family members of a known partisan. Despite these threats, resistance increased with each German military defeat.

More than any other factor, it was *le service du travail obligatoire*, the forced labor inside Germany, that led to the Maquis. The first Maquis bands (the word *maquis* comes from the scrubby underbrush of Corsica, hideout places of outlaws and rebels) were young Frenchmen who just did not want to work outside their homes in Germany. On November 29, when the French armistice army of 100,000 was dissolved, seasoned officers joined the Maquis, providing it with military and aggressive leadership. In 1943, the Germans increased their demands for forced labor. Marshal Petain, eager to arrest the flow of young men to Germany, and wanting instead to encourage loyalty to the Vichy regime, set up the Chantiers de la Juinesse (workshops of youth). Members had to be twenty years old and willing to serve in an eight-month program that included camping, hard exercise, forestry, and other agricultural pursuits, as well as military drill. The Juinesse camps fell prey to Maquis bands who stole from them food, clothing, and other supplies. In the narrative, Bernard relates about a Juinesse raid and finds what other commentators have said about the young men—they couldn't care less about Petain's right-wing ideology, and they were hostile to the German occupiers.

As early as July 1940, Winston Churchill, the wartime prime minister, created the British Special Operation Executive (SOE). Its purpose included the tying down of the German army with a large occupation force and sabotaging the Nazi war machine. SOE contained British and foreign personnel from governments in exile (such as France), and sent agents to Europe to establish contact with the Resistance. SOE supported Resistance groups by air with vital arms, supplies, and information. Bernard aided in the distribution of such supplies while a member of the underground in Riom, before he hid out in the Maquis.

Against the Resistance were the armed services of the Vichy regime and those of the occupiers. Bernard met up with the German SS security services, which included Flemish, French, and other volunteers. Often they were called Gestapo. Another "Gestapo" group, the Geheime Feldpolizei, were secret military police, former members of the German criminal police. They served in army uniforms or in civilian clothes to carry out their anti-espionage and anti-sabotage tasks. Bernard had brushes with them. While the Vichy French police laid low against the resistants, collaborationist diehards joined the Milice Francaise (French Militia). Its permanent force numbered 5,000 and its part-time back-up forces numbered 8,000. It is interesting to note that resistants and collaborators were about equal as the war dragged on. Once the invasion of Normandy was on and Allied victory was assured, the Resistance swelled. The Milice sought to destroy the Resistance. According to Bernard, his Maquis just dodged them to avoid bloody confrontations between French and French.

General deGaulle and his Free French increased in power and prestige after the capitulation of the North African colonial empire. Free French armies were recruited from Algeria and Morocco. He had access to the British Broadcasting Company (BBC), which often publicized his name. The fact that deGaulle was connected to the SOE, and received and distributed arms and supplies to the Resistance, enhanced his prestige. In the beginning of 1943, Jean Moulin, a superb Free Frenchman with authority from deGaulle, organized the diverse Resistance into the Mouvements Unis de la Resistance. The council of this organization included representatives from many elements—trade unions, political parties, aristocrats, ex-army officers, and escapees. It even had links with the vibrant and numerous communists, who grudgingly acknowledged deGaulle's supremacy. Yet, the party's FTP stood separate.

With the Allied invasion of France approaching, orders went out from the council to derail trains, blow up bridges, and sabotage communications, particularly electric power supplies. Bernard was heavily occupied with destroying electric power transmitters and towers.

After the Normandy landings in June 1944, the Resistance was grouped under the title Forces Francaises del'Interieur (FFI). This did not include the communists, whom the Allies feared would take it over at war's end. Bernard belonged to a band called Maquis Volvic. Volvic was a town in a volcanic area of southern France whose craters and dome were long extinct. This town was located in the French department (loosely like the American state, administrative unit) called Puy de Dome. The department was in a region called Auvergne, a very hilly and mountainous area with thick underbrush, ideal for resistance activity. The cities of Clermont-Ferrand and Riom were in Puy de Dome, while Vichy, the seat of government for Petain, was only forty miles to the north. The sites of Bernard's narrative, particularly Clermont-Ferrand, were the most active center of resistance in all Vichy France. Close to the time of liberation, in the summer of 1944, Puy de Dome had 10,000 resistants. It became an area of pitched battles. The open battles with German soldiers and SS ended tragically for the Maquis. More successful were the guerrilla operations, the picking off of isolated German units, and the disruption of railroads. Arrayed against the Resistance was an expanded Milice, which went on a rampage of assassinations and arrests and summary executions. Bernard was in constant mortal danger.

Allied armies swept across France in August and full liberation came in early September. The Resistance settled many scores with the Vichyites and a short reign of terror ensued. However, in general, a new Republican government took power smoothly. Members of the FFI were requested to become part of the regular French army fighting in the field with the Americans and British, and many did, seeing action inside Germany.

FRENCH JEWRY

The military defeat of France in June 1940 was an unexpected catastrophe for the country and particularly for the Jews. Those Jews who had volunteered by the thousands to fight for the French army were singled out by both Vichy and the Germans and placed in forced labor battalions in metropolitan France and in the wastes of colonial French North Africa. A hard labor group of 1,500 Jews worked on a railroad in the Sahara Desert.

Almost 20,000 Jews were expelled from Alsace-Lorraine. They were permitted to take only one suitcase apiece and a small sum of money. Trucks unloaded them in a deserted area in the Unoccupied Zone. Many made their way to the Clermont-Ferrand environs where a rabbinic district was formed. No wonder Bernard saw so many Alsatian Jews and was able to participate in a secret Passover service with them. Bernard had concealed his own and his family's Jewish identities but his heart ached for some identification with his people. He was fearful that his son, whose name Bernard had changed from Avram to the less Jewish-sounding Armand when they assumed Christian identities, would truly lose his Jewish identity. When the opportunity arose to participate in a Seder with Armand, even though it could have been a trick by the Gestapo that would have meant certain death to participants, Bernard took a chance. "I wanted Armand to know he was Jewish. I did not want him lost to the Jewish people," Bernard later reflected.

Over 35,000 Belgian Jews found refuge in France. With the division of the country into Free and Occupied Zones, Jewry was also cut in two. Estimates placed 180,000 in the Occupied Zone and 250,000 in the Unoccupied Zone. There were no means of communication between the two. "No Jews or Negroes allowed in the Occupied Zone," was an official sign at the demarcation line.

There were laws that applied to the northern area but not to the Free Zone, even after the German invasion south in November 1942. They included no change in residence, a curfew from 8 p.m. to 6 a.m., wearing a yellow star with the word "Jew" in front and back for every Jew six years of age or older, and the forced registration of Jews. Bernard's deliberate failure to comply proved to be a move with great foresight, for Jews on the official lists of French police often ended up in concentration camps.

Other laws applied to Jews all over France. Jews were excluded from jobs in civil service, banking, real estate, and the media. A *numerus clausus*, a percentage of Jews set at three percent enrollment, was instituted at all schools and colleges. A General Commissariat for Jewish Affairs was established, one that proposed and carried out anti-Jewish measures. It soon "aryanized" Jewish businesses, which meant Jews were dispossessed from their properties, non-Jewish administrators were appointed to oversee the businesses, but for efficiency's sake the former owners were allowed to work and run their former businesses. Jews without French citizenship could be interned in special camps or forced to live in designated areas. All Jews had to have the word "*Juif*" on their identification and ration cards.

Jews were subject to raids by French police. When Vichy leader Pierre Laval was commanded to turn over all Jews to the Nazis, he negotiated to arrest for deportation just the foreign Jews residing in France. He also insisted that Vichy French police, not Nazi authorities, be responsible for catching Jews. He did this to keep the Germans aware of Vichy's sovereignty. The most infamous raids were made by the French police near Paris, July 16-17, 1942, when 12,884 were arrested. Many were imprisoned in the Vel d'Hiv, a large sports center that had been transformed into a reception area. Over 4,000 children were interned under very poor living conditions. The arrest of children under sixteen by the Vichy police was one of the most repugnant examples of collaboration by Frenchmen, for the Nazis only asked for the detention of those over sixteen. Police chief René Bousquet appealed to the German authorities in Berlin to include the children. Foreign Jews, whole families, had been placed in special internment camps since 1940. The most well known included Drancy, outside Paris, and Gurs at the foot of the Pyrenees. Most of the deported children came from these camps and they died at Auschwitz.

When the German armed forces occupied the Free Zone in 1942, all the anti-Jewish practices in the north, such as wearing the yellow star, were not applied to the southern area. The Nazis allowed Vichy some amount of sovereignty in the form of protection for France's longstanding Jewish citizens. Nevertheless, there were numerous Gestapo raids and arrests. Jews, often those from French internment camps, were often chosen as hostages to die for acts committed by partisans.

At the same time as Germany occupied southern France, the Italian army, Germany's Axis partner, advanced and occupied eight departments of southeastern France. The Italians practiced a liberal and humane policy toward the Jews until September 1943. With the fall of Benito Mussolini, dictator of fascist Italy, and the surrender of that country to the Allies, German forces moved into Italian-held southern France where 30,000 Jews had found refuge. The Nazis, not under Vichy restrictions, and not having to respect Italy, which was now friendly to the Allies, rounded up 25,000 Jews, including 6,500 from Nice, and deported them to death camps.

While precise numbers cannot be ascertained because of the confusion of war, it seems that 180,000 French Jews survived, about seventy-five percent of those present in the nation in 1940. Over 77,000 met their deaths in concentration camps and 3,000 died from conditions of internment in detention camps. Of the murdered Jews, two-thirds were not French citizens. Because of unique circumstances, quite a number of Jews in France, both foreign and natives, did what Bernard did—disguised themselves, hid out, and often joined the underground Resistance forces.

JEWISH RESISTANCE

The Jews of France played an outstanding role in resistance movements of all shades. According to some estimates, twenty-five percent of *maquisards* were Jewish. The overwhelming majority of Jews fought not as Jews but as patriotic Frenchmen. However, there were strictly Jewish Resistance movements. Zionist youth became the nucleus of the Armee Juive. The Jewish Boy Scouts played a major role in hiding Jewish children. As they matured, they moved on to the Armee Juive. Their numbers are difficult to ascertain; an early account placed them at 2,000. Hundreds of Jews died in face-to-face battles with the genocidists. Hundreds were executed as resistants.

The Jews of the city of Algiers played a major role in making the landing of American forces in North Africa a relatively bloodless one. It is a story left out of most history books. A Gaullist group of 377 Frenchmen, 297 of them Jews, captured strategic positions in Algiers on November 7-8, 1942. Led by the Aboulker clan, they arrested Admiral Darlan and General Juin and arranged for Robert Murphy, the American consul general and personal aide to President Roosevelt, to negotiate with the two supreme Vichy commanders in North Africa. The results were a general surrender of Vichy French troops and a peaceful Allied landing. A short time later, when General Charles deGaulle took over in North Africa, the Aboulkers and hundreds of other Algerian Jews, and the Jews from the Foreign Legion doing forced labor in the Sahara, joined the Free French to fight the Germans.

While some French people did denounce Jews to the Germans, the behavior of the French population, particularly in the countryside, was favorable to Jews. Catholic churches, schools, convents, and monasteries offered refuge to Jewish children. Bernard's nephew and nieces were saved by such institutions. While the Catholic church as a religious body did not disapprove of the anti-Jewish measures of the Vichy regime, it stopped short of approving deportation, which it knew meant death. The Vatican was well informed of the nature of the camps and the true meaning of the Final Solution. Deportations were strongly condemned from the pulpit.

The Protestant churches, numerically smaller, were more actively opposed to the persecution of the Jews and they became centers for rescue. The most famous example, the rescue of 5,000 Jews by the villagers of le Chambon, is told in the book *Lest Innocent Blood Be Shed* (Philip Paul Hallie, Harper & Row, 1979).

From 1943 on, the Maquis had control of the countryside. There were 3,000 Jews in Puy de Dome, sixty-five percent from Alsace. Most received false identification cards, which enabled them to avoid police regulation. By 1943, with German defeat mounting and resistance climbing, the French police abandoned Jew-catching. In the cities, where the German military forces were strong and the Gestapo was active, Jews were in greater danger. The Gestapo itself made Jew-catching raids and anti-Resistance roundups such as the one against the faculty and students of the University of Strasbourg (which had moved to Clermont-Ferrand in 1940 after the armistice) in November 1943.

Bernard was wise to make his quarters for himself and his family in Volvic, a village at the foot of a volcano, flush against the thick underbrush, or *maquis*. Later, when the German Gestapo raided the orthopedic shop where he was working, Bernard showed his ability to be an imposter for survival. With the Gestapo were members of the Belgium political police, the Rexists, homegrown Nazis under the leadership of Leon Degrelle. Being familiar with Degrelle's ideas, Bernard pretended to be a follower and was able to convince the Rexists to leave him alone in the shop while they arrested the others and took them to Gestapo headquarters. When they drove away, Bernard escaped, rushed back to Volvic, and joined the local Maquis.

The last Germans left Puy de Dome on August 27, 1944. The transition from Maquis to Fighting Free French and legitimate provisional government was for the most part smooth. The Germans made an orderly retreat and fought on, not surrendering until May 1945. For Bernard, though, August meant the war was over. He left Volvic in the early fall and returned to Belgium to discover what the Nazi subjugators had brought.

Before the war, 90,000 Jews lived in Belgium, most of them concentrated in Antwerp (55,000) and Brussels (30,000). About 35,000 fled the country, mainly to France. Of those who remained, 40,000 perished, representing forty-four percent of pre-war Belgian Jewry. Among the victims were Bernard's parents and most of his family. A sister who fought in the Resistance became very sick. (Bernard visited her every year in Belgium until she died in 1992.) A brother died fighting. Bernard did not want to stay on the bloodstained soil of Europe. Like so many survivors, he took his wife and three children and made his way to the United States.

Bernard Mednicki's story should be told for its own worth. It also represents a genre that reveals those Jews who, in the face of overwhelming odds, found a way of cheating Hitler and fighting back against their would-be murderers.

FINAL WORD TO READERS

Thank you for purchasing and reading *Never Be Afraid: A Belgian Jew in the French Resistance*. If you found this book enjoyable, please be kind enough to review it on your blog, through your social media networks, or at your favorite retailer so that other readers can find it. Then again, if you didn't enjoy it, go ahead and review it as well. (I just hope there are fewer of you than the former.) It is also available as an ebook from smashwords.com and amazon.com.

OTHER BOOKS BY KEN WACHSBERGER

Your Partner Has Breast Cancer: 21 Ways to Keep Sane as a Support Person on Your Journey from Victim to Survivor is Ken's first ebook. Also available in print.

Next ebook: *Beercans on the Side of the Road: The Story of Henry the Hitchhiker*, considered a cult classic when it was first released in print in 1987. Coming soon as an ebook but it may be purchased now at www.azenphonypress.com.

Also available from www.azenphonypress.com:
Transforming Lives: A Socially Responsible Guide to the Magic of Writing and Researching
The Ballad of Ken and Emily: or, Tales from the Counterculture
The Last Selection: A Child's Journey through the Holocaust (co-authors Goldie Szachter Kalib and Sylvan Kalib)
Facts On File Banned Books Series (edited)

Available from www.voicesfromtheunderground.com:

Voices from the Underground Series (compiled and edited):
Insider Histories of the Vietnam Era Underground Press, Part 1
My Odyssey through the Underground Press (by Michael "Mica" Kindman)
Insider Histories of the Vietnam Era Underground Press, Part 2
Stop the Presses! I Want to Get Off!: A Brief History of the Prisoners' Digest International (by Joseph W. Grant)

Coming soon: *Puns for the Job Searcher*. Still in the works but getting closer to reality. Ken explains: "I'd be moving faster on it but I've got too many penned up emotions."

www.ingramcontent.com/pod-product-compliance
Lightning Source LLC
Chambersburg PA
CBHW050629300426
44112CB00012B/1726